16187

H. L. MENCKEN AND THE
AMERICAN MERCURY ADVENTURE

H. L. MENCKEN

AND THE

AMERICAN MERCURY

ADVENTURE

M. K. SINGLETON

DUKE UNIVERSITY PRESS   *Durham*   N. C.   *1962*

Library of Congress Catalogue Card number 62-10053

Cambridge University Press, London N.W. 1, England

*This book was published with
the assistance of income from the*
P. HUBER HANES FUND

*Printed in the United States of America
by the Seeman Printery, Inc., Durham, N. C.*

PREFACE

There is a superabundance of material for a documented account of H. L. Mencken's editorship of the *American Mercury,* and this fortunate state of affairs is partly the result of efforts by H. L. Mencken himself. His diligence in assembling and prefacing, during the late thirties and early forties, scores of beautifully bound documents, puts interested researchers in Baltimore's Enoch Pratt Free Library greatly in his debt. I am grateful to Mr. Richard Hart, Head of the Literature and Language Division of the Enoch Pratt Free Library, for arranging my visits to the H. L. Mencken Collection. Mr. Hart's assistant, Betty Adler, has my thanks for unearthing Menckeniana which I might otherwise have overlooked, including Mrs. Rosalind Lohrfinck's "Notes for an H. L. Mencken Bibliography," a useful 1957 compilation which includes a listing of the many pseudonyms under which Mencken wrote during his early years of journalism. Other valuable sources in the Enoch Pratt Mencken Collection are "Clinical Notes . . . The American Mercury, 1924-25," "The American Mercury Miscellanea, 1923-1933," "Editorials . . . The American Mercury," 3 vols., "Book Reviews . . . American Mercury," 5 vols., "Letters to Philip Goodman, 1918-1933," 3 vols., "Publisher's Royalty Statements: H. L. Mencken: 1916-1941," "the 'Hatrack' Case, 1926-1927; The American Mercury vs. The New England Watch and Ward Society, The Postmaster-General of the United States, *et al.*," 8 vols.

I wish to thank Mr. Robert W. Hill, Keeper of Manuscripts in the New York Public Library, for allowing me to

examine the unrestricted portions of the H. L. Mencken Collection in that library. Dr. Julian P. Boyd, former Librarian of the Princeton University Library, deserves the gratitude of all students of Mencken's career for his collection of thousands of Mencken letters and transcripts made before Mencken's death. This selection from a vast correspondence includes a good deal of material which would otherwise not presently be accessible. The present Librarian of the Princeton University Library, Dr. William S. Dix, has my thanks for securing permission from Mr. August Mencken for my examination of this collection; and Mr. Alexander P. Clark, Curator of Manuscripts in the Princeton Library, helped me to find information, made photostats of letters, and performed other services.

Dr. Benjamin E. Powell, Librarian of the Duke University Library, made several intercessions in behalf of this study, and Dr. Mattie Russell, Curator of Manuscripts in the Duke University Library, found some Mencken letters of relevance, especially in the Louise Pound Collection. Mrs. George Jean Nathan thoughtfully made available material pertinent to my history from her George Jean Nathan Studio Library, Riverdale-on-the-Hudson, New York. I am also indebted to Sir Herbert Read, Mr. Charles Angoff, Mr. James Mallahan Cain, Mr. Edmund Wilson, and others for encouraging and informative letters about the *American Mercury*. Mr. Alfred Knopf's many letters concerning the monthly and his detailed criticism of the financial story of the magazine deserve my thanks: Mr. Knopf showed great patience with my mistakes, correcting scores of them without despairing of the project. I appreciate the permission of Alfred A. Knopf, Inc., to quote from published and copyrighted works of H. L. Mencken.

Because this work is closely based on my 1960 Duke University doctoral dissertation, "A History of the *American Mercury* under the Editorship of Henry Mencken, 1924-1933," I am vastly indebted to my director, Dr. Clarence Gohdes, and to Dr. Lionel Stevenson, Dr. John Alden, Dr.

Arlin Turner, and Dr. Charles Sanders, all of Duke University. I am also grateful to the Duke University Graduate Committee on Publications, which awarded to my dissertation a $1,000 grant to facilitate publication. Other academic aid and encouragement came from Dr. Frederick J. Hoffman and Dr. Carl Bode, who kindly permitted me to read portions of this study to their University of Wisconsin students; and my own students were likewise imposed on, especially those who undertook useful research projects on H. L. Mencken and George Jean Nathan: Marshall Mintz, Janet Minar, Hy Chase, Janet Meloy, Elaine Bay, Edward Perdew, and Thomas Kelly were all workers in the vineyard. Mrs. Betty Grasmick spent tedious hours arranging a complete author index to the *American Mercury* for the years of Mencken's editorship, a piece of drudgery which made my work easier. I also thank the Department of English in the University of Wisconsin; the Department has permitted me to establish what I believe to be the first university course primarily devoted to H. L. Mencken studies. The willingness of the Wisconsin English Department to staff such a specialized course during a time of limited budgets and increased enrollments is evidence of the rebirth of interest in H. L. Mencken, an interest which no doubt will be further deepened when Mr. Alfred A. Knopf's plan to publish Mr. Guy Forgue's edition of Mencken letters is fulfilled.

I wish to acknowledge the help of Mr. August Mencken, who granted permission to visit the several H. L. Mencken collections which made possible a documented account of the *American Mercury*. Nevertheless, despite his original sympathetic interest in and help with my research, it should be made quite clear that Mr. August Mencken, after reading my manuscript and corresponding with me for many months about my history, disagrees fervently with portions of the ninth chapter of my study.

Madison, Wisconsin   M. K. SINGLETON
August 27, 1961.

CONTENTS

1. INTRODUCTION 3

2. THE BACKGROUND OF THE *MERCURY*
BEFORE 1923 10

> A LITERARY PARTNERSHIP, 10—THE *SMART SET* AP-
> PRENTICESHIP, 11—MENCKEN'S JUDGMENTS OF
> MAGAZINES, 22

3. THE ORIGINS OF THE *MERCURY* IN 1923 28

> ALFRED KNOPF'S DESIRE FOR A MAGAZINE, 28—MENCK-
> EN'S SEARCH FOR CONTRIBUTORS, 31—THE FIRST
> NUMBER OF THE *MERCURY*, 39—THE GREENWICH
> VILLAGE RESPONSE, 49—THE PUBLIC APPROVES, 52

4. MENCKEN AS EDITOR 55

> EDITORIAL CONSOLIDATION, 55—THE IRON EDITOR, 61
> —THE CIRCULATION, 1924-1925, 64—POLITICS: THE
> COOLIDGE ERA, 65—RELIGION: THE ANTI-PURITAN, 70—
> LITERATURE: FICTION, 73—LITERATURE: POETRY
> AND DRAMA, 78—"THE LIBRARY," 81—"CLINICAL
> NOTES" AND EDITORIALS, 88—"AMERICANA," 96

5. NATHAN AS CONTRIBUTING EDITOR 111

> "CLINICAL NOTES," 111—"THE THEATRE" AS HUMOR,
> 117—AMERICAN PLAYWRIGHTS, 122—FOREIGN PLAY-
> WRIGHTS, 126—NATHAN AS CONSERVATIVE, 127—
> OTHER CRITICS, 131—NATHAN'S IMPORTANCE TO
> THE *MERCURY*, 133

6. OTHER CONTRIBUTORS   134

    NEWSPAPER REPORTERS, 134—LEARNED CONTRIBUTORS
    AND WRITINGS ON EDUCATIONAL MATTERS, 138
    —CONTRIBUTORS OF BELLES-LETTRES, 142
    —MISCELLANEOUS CONTRIBUTORS, 146

7. THE ACCEPTANCE OF THE *MERCURY* 1924-1928   156

    THE READERS, 156—A FINANCIAL SUCCESS, 164—THE
    "HATRACK" CONTROVERSY, 167—THE *MERCURY* AS
    AN INFLUENCE ON OTHER MAGAZINES, 181—THE
    YEARS OF ACCLAIM, 188

8. CRITICS OF THE *MERCURY* BEFORE 1930   195

    CRITICISMS FROM THE RIGHT, 195—BARBS FROM THE
    LEFT, 202—OTHER CRITICS, 206

9. CRISIS AND DEFEAT   215

    THE *MERCURY* DECLINE, 215—THE DEPRESSION STRIKES,
    217—ATTACKS BY CRITICS INTENSIFY, 223—MENCKEN'S
    RESIGNATION, 228—THE BITTER DREGS, 234—THE
    LATER *MERCURY*, 238

10. CONCLUSIONS   242

    THE *MERCURY* ACCOMPLISHMENT, 242—THE *MERCURY*
    DEFEAT, 245

SELECTED BIBLIOGRAPHY   247

INDEX   261

INSERTS

THE *AMERICAN MERCURY*   *frontispiece*
RANDALL THOMPSON'S SETTING OF
    "AMERICANA"   *facing page 6*

H. L. MENCKEN AND THE
AMERICAN MERCURY ADVENTURE

INTRODUCTION

Oₙₑ of the ironies of twentieth-century magazine publishing in America has been the decline of the original *American Mercury* to its present condition. There is no resemblance between Henry Louis Mencken's magazine and the current *American Mercury,* nor is this history intended to trace in detail the erratic downward course of the monthly after Mencken's departure from the staff. Instead, this is a study of its first and most significant decade, with considerable attention to criticism of both the magazine and its editor.

After a brief introduction to the *American Mercury,* the second chapter is a survey of the background of the *Mercury*'s editors as editors of the *Smart Set.* There follows an historical account of the *Mercury* from its establishment in 1923 by Mencken, George Jean Nathan, and Alfred Knopf to Mencken's resignation from the editorship in 1933. A short sketch of the continuation of the periodical under various editors after Mencken and a chapter of conclusions close the book.

Any study of thirty volumes of a lively magazine will find some of the contents sadly dated, and certainly much of the *Mercury* was perishable, even with such contributors as Carl Sandburg, Vachel Lindsay, William Faulkner, Sinclair Lewis, Carl Van Doren, and, of course, George Jean Nathan and H. L. Mencken. Nevertheless, the *Mercury* has a lasting importance which is not strictly literary; it was "a national institution"[1] transcending the limitations and prejudices of its editorial staff. One sweeping comment, by James Playsted Wood, was that the *Mercury* "permanently affected American fiction and American literary criticism. It changed the attitude toward the conventions and affected the tastes of an entire generation." Mr. Wood concludes: "*The American Mercury* was one of the loudest voices whose noise combined to make the Roaring Twenties roar."[2] Arthur M. Schlesinger gives a fair example of how sober historians view the periodical as a cultural phenomenon. Writing of the twenties, Schlesinger observes that magazines, when compared with the radio or the movies, "wielded slight influence. . . . The principal exception was the *American Mercury*. . . . To the delight of sophisticates, Mencken alike bludgeoned reformers, professors, 'Bible-belt Fundamentalists' and 'booboisie.' "[3] Frederick Lewis Allen, in his history of the twenties, gives a more elaborate statement of the mission of the *Mercury* during its heyday:

The green cover of the *Mercury* and its format were as sedate as the marble-trimmed façade of Mencken's house in Baltimore, but its contents were explosive. . . . The magazine lustily championed writers such as Dreiser, Cabell, Sherwood Anderson, Willa Cather, and Sinclair Lewis, who defied the polite traditions represented by the American Academy of Arts and Letters; it poured critical acid upon sentimentality and evasion and academic pomposity in books and in life; it lambasted Babbitts, Rotarians, Methodists, and reformers, ridiculed both the religion of Coolidge Prosperity and what Mencken called the 'bilge of idealism,' and looked upon the American scene in general with raucous and profane laughter.[4]

Although Allen's description must be modified in several

---

[1] Mark Sullivan, *Our Times: The United States 1900-1925.* Vol. VI: *The Twenties* (New York, 1937), p. 413. Hereinafter cited as Sullivan, *Our Times.*
[2] *Magazines in the United States: Their Social and Economic Influence* (2nd ed.; New York, [1956]), p. 196.
[3] *The Rise of Modern America* (New York, 1951), p. 390.
[4] *Only Yesterday* (New York, [1957]), pp. 163-164.

particulars, it is expressive of the special role of the *Mercury* during the twenties.[5]

Certainly the vogue of the *Mercury* was, for a time, considerable for a quality monthly intended for educated readers. A mere statement of its circulation is not sufficient to explain its impact on the American scene, but the peak of over 77,000 purchasers which it averaged for every month in 1927, a circulation surpassing that of *Scribner's* and more than half that of either *Harper's* or the *Atlantic* during the same year, is not negligible.[6] The *Saturday Evening Post* and several other magazines might tower over all the serious monthlies in numbers of readers, but the editors of the latter class of periodicals could console themselves that their readers were more sophisticated. The *Mercury* staff prided themselves, during the twenties, on the quality of the readers of their magazine, admitting freely that their publication made "no appeal to the hill-billies who eat salt pork and sleep in their homespuns," but was intended for the "urbane and washed,"[7] a statement reminiscent of the early *New Yorker*'s serene warning, "Not for the old lady from Dubuque."[8]

The readers of the *Mercury* were of various kinds. Many read it because it published essays, fiction, poetry, and criticism that they found intellectually refreshing. By 1926 there was a captive audience of college students who were confronted with textbooks based on selections from the turbulent and frank monthly. There were students who flaunted the Paris-green magazine as a sign of intellectual independence—a kind of mental hipflask. It was waved be-

[5] Allen elsewhere consistently ranks the *Mercury* with the quality monthlies, but only when referring to a "brief period of iconoclastic brilliance under Henry Mencken in the twenties . . ." ("The American Magazine Grows Up," *Atlantic Monthly*, CLXXXVI [Nov., 1950], 80).

[6] Ayer's *American Newspaper Annual and Directory*, 1928. Audit Bureau of Circulations statements. Hereinafter cited as Ayer's *Directory*.

[7] [Earle Bachman, *et al.*], *Three Years 1924-1927: The Story of a New Idea and Its Successful Adaptation* (New York, [1927]), p. 29. Hereinafter cited as *Three Years*.

[8] Dale Kramer, *Ross and the New Yorker* (Garden City, N. Y., 1951), p. 62.

fore conservative lecturers, and students protested its occasional suppression from college libraries. When they had copies, they eagerly read how foolish were the majority of their countrymen. Others besides collegians displayed the *Mercury* as "the badge of intellectual nonconformity,"[9] and its exhibition in all parts of the country gave entrance into an order of select readers. Better educated followers of the *Mercury* could hymn Randall Thompson's "Sequence of Five Choruses: Texts from the American Mercury," while less genteel readers played jazz inspired by the same magazine. The frequency of allusion to the monthly in sermons, autobiographies, and more ephemeral writings gives ample support to the cultural historians' references to the frantic contemporary celebration and denunciation directed toward it.

One of the chief symptoms of the vitality and variety of the *Mercury* has been the continued controversy which it has elicited. Not only did the *Mercury* mean many different things to its period, but the story of the magazine is still being debated with warmth. Norman Thomas, Harold Laski, Michael Gold, and Upton Sinclair found the magazine a conservative, even reactionary, publication under Mencken. The animadversions of the radicals are balanced by the comments of patriots who were equally clear that the monthly was a Moscow sheet. If Americans found a variety of political theories in its contents, there was less doubt about the theological position of its editor: Mencken's outspoken materialism drew the condemnation of the religious press. The alarming news was spread that "Mercurianity is the name of a new religion, the Bible of which is a green-covered monthly magazine."[10] Nor was the target limited to the middle classes, as some writers have claimed.[11]

---

[9] Allen, "The American Magazine Grows Up," p. 80.

[10] Sullivan, *Our Times,* p. 413.

[11] Kramer, in *Ross and the New Yorker,* p. 120, inaccurately claims that the *Mercury* was content to fire "volleys into the calm ranks of the Babbitts," whereas the *New Yorker* would attack the "self-conscious revolters themselves" without assistance.

The *Mercury* criticized the avant-garde, both exiles and Greenwich Villagers, with such force that they were soon sneering at its philistinism.

The literary controversies set off by the review are indeed numerous. One hears charges from proletarian quarters that the *Mercury* exploited talented amateurs such as James Stevens and Louis Adamic, whom it discovered. Some critics conclude that the *Mercury* was never more than the magazine of an Algonquin Hotel coterie. Norman Cousins, Alfred Kazin, and Charles Angoff have expressed opinions, favorable or otherwise, that need to be sifted. The accumulation of charges by one influential critic alone, Malcolm Cowley, is surprising; one finds that Cowley has waged a continuous war against the *Mercury*.

Statements about the influence of Mencken's monthly on other periodicals are frequent but confused. No one has seriously examined claims that the *Mercury* forced considerable changes in such important magazines as the *Atlantic, Harper's,* and *Scribner's* and that it was directly imitated by periodicals ranging from the *New Yorker* to *McNaught's Monthly, Panorama,* and *Plain-Talk*. Nor has anyone traced the curious relationship of the *American Spectator* to the *Mercury*. Carl R. Dolmetsch's recent "History of the *Smart Set* Magazine, 1914-1923," a helpful account of the co-editorship of Mencken and Nathan immediately before their launching of the *Mercury,* is not wholly satisfactory.[12]

Most of the controversies are sparked by differences about the worth of H. L. Mencken. His editorship of the *Mercury* spanned the period of his greatest acclaim and was directly related to the swift drop in his reputation during the early thirties. He spent ten years editing and writing

[12] Unpublished doctoral dissertation, University of Chicago, 1957. Hereinafter cited as Dolmetsch, "History of the *Smart Set*." It is necessary to supplement Dolmetsch's history with Burton Rascoe's " 'Smart Set' History," printed in *The Smart Set Anthology of World Famous Authors,* ed. Burton Rascoe and Groff Conklin (New York, [1934]), pp. xiii-xliv.

for his monthly, a sustained effort probably surpassed by him only in his arduous work on *The American Language* and its revisions. This latter has come to be regarded by many literary historians as the mainstay of his once large reputation—certainly a sad end for a prolific writer called by Walter Lippman in 1926 "the most powerful personal influence on this whole generation of educated people."[13]

There has been, it is true, a recent revival of interest in Mencken, a revival partly inaugurated by the publication in the *New Yorker* of his mellow and well-written memoirs[14] and reinforced by the reprinting of some of his better writings. This new interest has also been stimulated by a recognition that there are resemblances between the decade following World War II and the 1920's.[15] If his many contributions to and conduct of the *Mercury* do not augment his disputed importance in American letters, then the burden of his reputation must continue to be borne by *The American Language* and perhaps some of the early *Prejudices*. Certainly his editorship was unique. His humane and imaginative editing wrung respectable writing from writers who could be found only by pursuing a deliberate policy of "discovery." With painstaking advice, Mencken helped to mature the writing talent of James Stevens, George Milburn, James T. Farrell, and many journalists, Negroes, isolated Midwestern women, and even convicts. Mencken's aim to outrage the most cherished beliefs of the majority of his fellow citizens was as rare in an editor of a quality monthly as was his policy of discovery. He was praised by other editors for the technical excellence of his editing and by writers for his prompt and courteous handling of manuscripts. These aspects of his editing achieved results that should perhaps continue to interest people.

[13] "H. L. Mencken," *Saturday Review of Literature,* III (Dec. 11, 1926), 414.
[14] Published in book form as *Happy Days* (New York, 1940), *Newspaper Days* (New York, 1941), and *Heathen Days* (New York, 1943).
[15] James T. Farrell, "Introduction," *Prejudices: A Selection,* ed. James T. Farrell (New York, 1958), p. v.

It should not be assumed that Mencken, for all his patience in assembling tomes of clippings, *Mercury* memoranda, and other such items now housed in the Enoch Pratt Library, wrote freely about his association with his periodical. In fact, after 1933 he was strangely silent about his *Mercury* experiences. Whether because of his quarrels with Nathan, Dreiser, his good friend Philip Goodman, and others, or because of his inability to change the magazine with the times, there is little later reference by Mencken to this major episode in his life. His explanations of his departure from the editorship, as found in letters to old friends, are plaintive and reflect a troubled spirit. As early as 1934 his editorial suggestions are directed, not to the new editor of the *Mercury,* but to the staff of the *New Yorker.* In the three volumes of his autobiography there is a remarkable absence of reference to his editorship, and his single statement to the reading public about his association with the *Mercury,* with the exception of an evasive parting editorial, is a pathetic epilogue to the ten years spent with his monthly.[16] This relative silence, combined with the release of *Mercury* documents to the Enoch Pratt Library, means that a complete account remains to be written by someone other than the editor. Such an account, because of the hullaballoo that surrounds Mencken, should be an arrangement of the sources so that they will speak for themselves whenever possible.

[16] "Memoirs of an Editor," *Vanity Fair,* XLI (Feb., 1934), 16, 54. Hereinafter cited as Mencken, "Memoirs."

THE BACKGROUND OF THE *MERCURY* BEFORE 1923

A LITERARY PARTNERSHIP

EVEN before the twenties, Mencken had become known in literary circles for his part in promoting a rebellion in American literature. His sturdy championing of Theodore Dreiser, James Branch Cabell, and Sinclair Lewis in blunt, forceful book reviews for the *Smart Set* and in his *Prejudices* had earned him the regard of many. In addition to his services as critic, he was recognized for his *American Language,* first published in the spring of 1919. To citizens of Baltimore, he was a native son whose newspaper writings were often iconoclastic. Students of the drama might have consulted his handbook *George Bernard Shaw: His Plays,* which appeared in 1905. Laymen interested in philosophy might have read his exposition, *The Philosophy of Friedrich Nietzsche,* published in 1908.

Among several less consequential books by Mencken, *The American Credo,* written with the help of G. J. Nathan, gave in 1920 hint of an increasing fascination with the ridiculous side of the American mentality. *The American Credo* was but one of several books written in collaboration with Nathan, and these works, together with their association on the *Smart Set,* had made the two men literary partners. Nathan, a native of Indiana and a graduate of Cornell, had traveled in Europe with Mencken, but his cosmopolitanism far outshone that of his Baltimore colleague. Nathan found metropolitan life to his taste, and by 1905 he was on the staff of the New York *Herald* as dramatic critic. On the *Herald* his carefully cultivated urbanity and his withering attacks on the paltry state of the American theater of the day made him distinguishable from other newspaper critics of the stage. He was partly responsible for the acceptance by the more knowing theatergoers in New York of several modern European playwrights, including Ibsen, Shaw, Hauptmann, and Strindberg. He encouraged the early efforts of Eugene O'Neill, but damned most other American playwrights, producers, and actors in reviews that showed discrimination but little tenderness.[1] He soon began the publication of books on the theater that were to total more than thirty before his death.

THE *SMART SET* APPRENTICESHIP

THE work of Mencken and Nathan on the *Smart Set* has never been examined in the light of their later editorial philosophy and practice. In fact, no wholly satisfactory account of the *Smart Set* has been written, and this lack makes it imperative for an historian of the *Mercury* to survey briefly the earlier magazine. The most extensive history of the *Smart Set* states that "the *American Mercury* was in no sense a successor to the earlier *Smart Set*,"[2] a very misleading conclusion.[3]

The experiences of Mencken and Nathan on the *Smart Set* were to influence their later editorial work in many ways. It will be shown that the *Mercury* idea was born, not

---

[1] Even Nathan's personal friendship with Eugene O'Neill, as will be seen, did not always prevent him from ridiculing the dramatist.

[2] Dolmetsch, "History of the *Smart Set*," p. 142.

[3] For a list of rather trivial mistakes in Dolmetsch, "History of the *Smart Set*," see my "History of the *American Mercury* under the Editorship of Henry Mencken, 1924 to 1933" (unpublished doctoral dissertation, Duke University, 1960), p. 14 n. 3.

in 1923, but over ten years earlier, and that it was gradually shaped by the suggestions and editorial experiments of such writers as Theodore Dreiser, Ezra Pound, H. G. Wells, Ford Madox Ford, and Willard Huntington Wright.[4] In addition, Mencken's many comments from as early as 1910 about English and American magazines show the development of his concern for their shortcomings. It has apparently not been recognized that the first number of the *Mercury* contained material previously printed in the *Smart Set*.[5]

Mencken first began work on the *Smart Set* as a writer of book reviews, his first notable position on the staff of a magazine.[6] The monthly had been launched on March 10, 1900, by Colonel William D'Alton Mann, a Civil War cavalry hero, inventor, and publisher.[7] Colonel Mann had in 1891 purchased the periodical entitled *Town Topics,* a magazine chiefly devoted to accounts of the *haut monde* in New York City.[8] It was popularly believed that Mann collected scandalous information about people of consequence, confronted them with a threat to print thinly fictionalized reports of their misdeeds, and then showed himself willing to "listen to reason."[9] The *Town Topics* monthly published enough fiction to make a quarterly

[4] Wright later became better known as "S. S. Van Dine," the author of mystery stories. Ford, who had his surname changed from "Hueffer" during World War I, will be referred to as "Ford" at all times in this study.

[5] Except for the correction of a misprint, and some changes in punctuation, the poem "For a Moment the Wind Died" of 1916 in "Four Poems," *Smart Set,* XLIX (May, 1916), 277, is the same "For a Moment the Wind Died" that appeared in the "Four Poems" in the *American Mercury,* I (Jan., 1924), 9. Hereinafter the *Smart Set* will be cited as *SS*.

[6] His first contribution was "The Good, the Bad, and the Best Sellers," *SS,* XXVI (Nov., 1908), 155-159.

[7] Robert R. Rowe, "Mann of Town Topics," *American Mercury,* VIII (July, 1926), 272-274.

[8] Frank L. Mott, *A History of American Magazines,* vol. IV: *1885-1905* (Cambridge, Mass., 1957), p. 753. Hereinafter cited as Mott, *Magazines, 1885-1905.*

[9] Mann's reputation as a blackmailer, long considered to have been well-deserved, has been further illuminated by Mott (*Magazines, 1885-1905,* p. 754). The furore about Mann was greatest in 1905, when Norman Hapgood, editor of the crusading *Collier's Weekly,* undertook to expose the Colonel's machinations. Mann was foolish enough to bring suit against Hapgood for libel—the only result being that Mann himself was nearly sent to jail for perjury (Rowe, "Mann of Town Topics," *American Mercury,* VIII, 273-274).

anthology feasible, and *Tales from Town Topics* was issued from 1891 to 1908. It was the success of this quarterly which suggested the *Smart Set* to Mann. The early *Smart Set* has been regarded lightly, partly because much of its contents was concerned with the upper classes as chronicled by "fashionable women with a literary bent,"[10] and partly because people came to associate it with the dubious *Town Topics*. Despite the undeservedly bad reputation which clung to the *Smart Set* "like the odors of a broken phial,"[11] it was very early, under the successive editorships of Arthur Grissom, Marvin Dana, and Charles Hanson Towne, publishing work by O. Henry, Clyde Fitch, David Belasco, James Branch Cabell, Frank Norris, Jack London, Henry Seidel Canby, Brander Matthews, and Edgar Saltus.[12] Although it is true that such contributors were outnumbered by lesser writers, any periodical that printed writings by Anatole France without bothering to translate them deserves more attention than it has received.

On February 20, 1911,[13] Colonel Mann sold the *Smart Set* to John Adams Thayer, who took an interest in the magazine somewhat unusual for a publisher. He regularly discussed the problems of the magazine in an essay closing each issue. As a self-styled "autocrat of the contents table" he tried to purge his magazine of its bad reputation, and he worried about the flippant title and worse subtitle: "A Magazine of Cleverness."[14] Thayer permitted Mencken to begin some experiments with the monthly, and "Owen

[10] William Manchester, *Disturber of the Peace: The Life of H. L. Mencken* (New York, [1951]), p. 40. Hereinafter cited as Manchester, *Mencken*.

[11] Isaac Goldberg, *The Man Mencken: A Biographical and Critical Survey* (New York, 1925), p. 193.

[12] Work by Saltus was printed in the first numbers of the *Smart Set* and for a number of years thereafter. Later Saltus became a friend of the editors (Charles H. Towne, *So Far So Good* [New York, 1945], pp. 115-116).

[13] J. A. Thayer, "Something Personal," *SS*, XXXIII (April, 1911), 176.

[14] Thayer requested, and received, suggestions about the title, but the only change made was the substitution of the subtitle "Its Prime Purpose is to Provide Lively Entertainment for Minds That Are Not Primitive" for the traditional "A Magazine of Cleverness." The new subtitle was first used in the December, 1911, issue. The publisher's melancholy about the title continued for years after 1911.

Hatteras," Mencken's and Nathan's pen name, was born in April, 1912.[15] Most important, Thayer began addressing his "Something Personal by the Publisher" toward writers more than readers, and the policy of "discovering" worthy new authors was announced.[16] Such matters as the color and style of magazine covers, advertising, and critical acclaim were threshed out before the eyes of the readers—and Mencken.[17]

As Thayer occupied himself with improving the *Smart Set,* Mencken began to dream of a new review that would be Nietzschean in philosophy and national in scope. His preference as editor was the young Willard Huntington Wright, then a writer for the Los Angeles *Times*. Wright had acclaimed Mencken's book on Nietzsche with fervor, and Mencken, as early as May, 1910, was promising his readers that they would hear more of Wright.[18] The literary inspiration for the projected new review was two-fold. First, Mencken had been greatly impressed by H. G. Wells's *The New Machiavelli,* which was published in book form in 1911. Mencken's admiration for the novel was in part caused by the hero's apostasy from Fabian socialism,[19] and in part by the hero's creation of a "Blue Weekly," a periodical meant for enlightened Tories: "We marked our claim upon Toryism even in the colour of our wrapper, and spoke of

[15] "Pertinent and Impertinent," *SS,* XXXVI (April, 1912), 157-159.
[16] "We scour the field for what is new . . . it is immaterial to us whether the author is a leader of society . . . or a deckhand on one of Uncle Sam's submarines. We are the city of refuge of the gifted but unrecognized beginner, the one publication that prides itself on its search for the unknown genius; and to find him we are ready to examine . . . any contributions . . . from any quarter whatsoever. So send us your offerings . . ." (*SS,* XXXVII [May, 1912], 160). Thayer's interest in discovery, as seen in several years' commentary, might well have influenced Mencken's later concern for discovering new authors.
[17] An inveterate experimenter, Thayer would shift the advertising policies or the style of the cover, then gauge the effect on his readers by their letters.
[18] "In Praise of a Poet," *SS,* XXXI (May, 1910), 154. By the fall of 1911, Mencken introduced Wright to Norman Boyer, who was then editor of the *Smart Set,* and by December Wright was an assistant editor (Rascoe, " 'Smart Set' History," *The Smart Set Anthology of World Famous Authors,* pp. xxi-xxii).
[19] H. L. Mencken, "The Meredith of Tomorrow," *SS,* XXXIII (April, 1911), 162.

ourselves collectively as the Blue Weeklies."[20] Mencken's admiration for the novel was remarkable,[21] and was shared by Nathan.[22] The second literary influence was Ford Madox Ford's *English Review,* which had been established in 1908 when other magazines refused to publish a poem by Thomas Hardy.[23] Wright and Mencken admired the *English Review*.[24] They probably sensed its editor's toryism,[25] and they read with interest the series of Nietzsche letters published in it.[26] Wright, Nathan, and Mencken approached Thayer and asked him to support a weekly magazine concerned with the American scene and chiefly satirical in approach. Nathan, recalling Wells's "Blue Weekly," suggested "Blue Review" as the title.[27] Thayer, however, refused support, and the scheme remained unfulfilled, but the "Blue Review" can be considered an early formulation of the "Mercury" idea.[28]

Instead of founding a new review, Thayer accepted Mencken's suggestion that Wright be elevated to the editorship of the *Smart Set,* and in 1913 Wright began his first and only year as editor. Thayer gave him funds enough to

[20] H. G. Wells, *The New Machiavelli* (London, [1911]), p. 391.

[21] His praise of the novel was repeated in the following essays: "Synge and Others," *SS*, XXXVIII (Oct., 1912), 150; "Again the Busy Fictioneers," *SS*, XXXIX (Jan., 1913), 153; "Roosevelt, Bulwer-Lytton and Anthony Comstock," *SS*, XLII (April, 1914), 152; "The Plague of Books," *SS*, LII (June, 1917), 139; and "The Late Mr. Wells," *SS*, LVII (Dec., 1918), 139-140.

[22] "The New Machiavelli," *SS*, LXVI (Nov., 1921), 35. Wells himself thought little of the novel: "that queer, confused novel *The New Machiavelli,* one of my worst and one of my most revealing . . ." (*Experiment in Autobiography* [New York, 1934], p. 661).

[23] Ford Madox Ford, "Communications," *Transatlantic Review,* I (Jan., 1924), 93-94.

[24] For instance, in Mencken's "A Counterblast to Buncombe," *SS*, XL (Aug., 1913), 156, the *English Review* was praised for printing in its June and July numbers for 1913 "Correspondence of Friedrich Nietzsche with Georg Brandes," a total of twenty-two letters.

[25] Ford Madox Ford, *Ancient Lights . . . Being the Memories of a Young Man* (London, 1911), p. 121. The actual founder of the *English Review* was also a Tory (Ford, "Communications," *Transatlantic Review,* I, 93).

[26] Wright's own book on Nietzsche appeared in 1914.

[27] Edgar Kemler, *The Irreverent Mr. Mencken* (Boston, 1950), p. 51. Hereinafter cited as Kemler, *Mr. Mencken.*

[28] The title "Blue Review" was strongly favored by Mencken and Nathan in 1923 as the title for the *Mercury.*

encourage contributors, and signed a contract promising not
to interfere with his new editor during the experimental
year.[29] But when faced with his editor's extravagance and
a drop in circulation, Thayer was not faithful to his promise.
Wright's achievement, nevertheless, drew attention. Ezra
Pound, watching from England, observed that "Wright . . .
took [Ford's] first year and a half of *The English Review*
as his model."[30] Ford was a contributor to the *Smart Set*
during Wright's brief reign, as were a number of other
Western European writers, including William Butler Yeats,
Frank Wedekind, Arthur Schnitzler, August Strindberg,
D. H. Lawrence, George Moore, W. L. George, Joseph
Conrad, and Gabriele D'Annunzio. Among American writers published in Wright's monthly were Ezra Pound, James
Huneker, Harriet Monroe, Floyd Dell, Robinson Jeffers,
Theodore Dreiser, and Sara Teasdale. "Owen Hatteras" was
formally introduced to the readers, who were also treated to
an imprudent sequence of Wright's editorials that may have
delighted struggling writers but which must have helped to
lower the circulation.[31] Thayer, chastened by the loss of
thousands of subscribers, forced Wright's resignation.[32] The
Smart Set, under the short and colorless editorship of Mark
Lee Luther, then did its best to atone for Wright's spirited

[29] Rascoe, " 'Smart Set' History," *The Smart Set Anthology,* p. xix.

[30] Pound to Harriet Monroe, Nov. 9, 1914. Printed in *The Letters of Ezra Pound: 1907-1941,* ed. D. D. Paige (New York, [1950]), p. 46.

[31] "We find it difficult to get hold of stories, or poems . . . that we find sufficiently meritorious to publish. . . . For the past month not a dozen stories of high order have been submitted to this office. . . . In this issue . . . are four stories which have been turned down by practically every magazine of any importance of America. We are not ashamed to accept stories with a past. . . . A great number of manuscripts submitted . . . are rejected because of the timid and puritanical policies of those magazines. The editor of this magazine is after the best stories which are being written today, and is willing to publish them, no matter what their themes" ("A Word to Authors," *SS,* XXXIX [April, 1913], 159). "This month we have placed what we think a very re-markable short story—'Daughters of Joy'—at the beginning of the maga-zine. . . . If a sex story is worth telling, it should present the facts truthfully and employ the language which the telling demands" ("Something Personal," *SS,* XL [May, 1913], 159).

[32] Wright's downfall was hastened by his ordering of a dummy issue of the "even more outspoken anti-Puritan *Blue Review,*" which he had printed at Thayer's expense. Thayer refused to pay (Kemler, *Mr. Mencken,* p. 58).

rebellion against commonplace periodical fiction, drama, and poetry.[33]

Mencken and Nathan, who had somehow managed to keep aloof from Wright's experimental course, became co-editors in October, 1914.[34] Thayer forced them to continue abject apologies to the readers for Wright's efforts, and they were sharply limited in the money they could pay for contributions.[35] Despite appeals, the readers did not return, and Thayer, in financial difficulties, had to yield control of the monthly to Eugene F. Crowe, a paper magnate, who assigned Eltinge F. Warner to conduct the business affairs of his new acquisition.[36]

During the nine years from 1914 to 1923, the co-editors strove to keep the *Smart Set* solvent, yet they also tried to print the best material they could purchase. Their first results were not impressive. They were obliged themselves to write large portions of the contents under pseudonyms.[37]

[33] On March 18, 1914, Mencken wrote to Dreiser: "God knows, this country needs that weekly I once planned. . . . Even the *Smart Set* is now as righteous as a decrepit and converted madame." The complaint is printed in *Letters of Theodore Dreiser: A Selection*, ed. Robert H. Elias, *et al.* (3 vols.; Philadelphia, [1959]), I, 162. Hereinafter cited as *Letters of Theodore Dreiser*.

[34] The editors immediately promised their readers that the *Smart Set* had no "other 'policy' in the world than to give its readers a moderately intelligent and awfully good time" ("The November Number of Smart Set," *SS*, XLIV [Oct., 1914], 37).

[35] The slogan that accompanied the December, 1914, number was "Nothing to 'improve' your mind, but plenty to tickle you." The traditional rates of payment for prose (one cent a word) and poetry (twenty-five cents a line) were re-imposed (Dolmetsch, "History of the *Smart Set*," p. 37).

[36] Rascoe, " 'Smart Set' History," *The Smart Set Anthology*, p. xxxi.

[37] Neither of the *Smart Set* historians has realized the degree to which Mencken, during the first months of his editorship, used pseudonyms. In the Nov., 1914, number, "Ah, Che la Morte!," by "Raoul Della Torre"; "Clubs," by "W. L. D. Bell"; "The Rewards of Science," by "R. B. McLoughlin"; "Thoughts on Mortality," by "William Fink"; "The Old Trails," by "Harriet Morgan"; "The Ballade of Cockaigne," by "Herbert Winslow Archer"; "Song," by "Janet Jefferson"; "Veneration," by "Marie de Verdi"; "The Blind Goddess," by "George Weems Peregoy"; "Epithalamium," by "Francis Clegg Thompson"; and, of course, many of the contributions of "Owen Hatteras," were by Mencken. In the December, 1914, issue, a poem written in German ("An Ode to Munich"), by "Pierre D'Aubigny"; "Mr. John Smith," by "Irving S. Watson"; "Death: A Discussion," by "Robert W. Woodruff"; "After All, What's the Use," by "J. D. Gilray"; and again "Owen Hatteras" were by Mencken. (I am indebted to Mrs. Rosalind C. Lohrfinck's "Notes for a Henry L. Mencken Bibliography," H. L. Mencken Collection, Enoch Pratt Free Library [hereinafter cited as E.P.M.C.], for a knowledge of the editor's pseudonyms.)

During World War I, they were hampered by their refusal to endorse the conflict; and the paper which Crowe provided, despite his connections with the paper industry, was of a very poor quality.[38] The monthly was, after all, a newsstand magazine, and its flippant title was hardly redeemed by supporting captions, such as "A Magazine of Cleverness," "The Only American Magazine with an European Air," "alla moderna," "The Magazine of Fifth Avenue," "Angels could do no more," and "We don't buy names; we make them." Its cover, during most of its years under Mencken and Nathan, was graced by two winged hearts fluttering from ribbons held by a suave-looking devil. The editors were forced to ask their colleagues on better financed and more staid periodicals to send them rejected manuscripts. Some of the writers who appeared in the monthly chose to disguise themselves with pseudonyms.

Despite these drawbacks, the editors did surprisingly well with a journal that, unlike the "little magazines," had to be frankly commercial.[39] From 1914, they "published authors who had no haven elsewhere."[40] By the end of World War I and until about 1922, they edited "an important magazine of modern letters,"[41] and they set themselves to explaining away the "curious misconception of *The Smart Set* [which seemed] to persist in certain quarters." An editorial in the February, 1922, issue is of more importance as a revelation of the literary enthusiasms of the editors than as a true estimate of what had been accomplished. It was admitted that the periodical had been at one time abandoned "in considerable part to the fluffy and

---

[38] The coarse paper was the occasion for an office joke: " 'If our readers desert, we can sell the magazine for tooth picks' " (Dolmetsch, "History of the *Smart Set*," pp. 57-58).

[39] Frederick J. Hoffman, *et al.*, *The Little Magazine: A History and Bibliography* (2nd ed.; Princeton, N. J., 1947), p. 9. Hereinafter cited as Hoffman, *The Little Magazine*.

[40] John K. Hutchens, "A Note on the Nineteen Twenties," *The American Twenties: A Literary Panorama,* ed. John K. Hutchens (New York, [1952]), p. 13.

[41] Hoffman, *The Little Magazine*, p. 380.

inconsequential in literature, comment and criticism."[42] But the younger literati were beginning to accord more respect to the monthly. Charles Angoff, in describing the effect of the *Smart Set* on his generation, claimed that the stories, poems, and articles seemed unlike those of any other magazine, "but it was H. L. Mencken's book reviews and George Jean Nathan's drama reviews that attracted most of the young people I knew. They were dazzlingly written, and they expressed the rebellion that we all felt."[43]

Mencken himself, however, could not maintain an unwavering conviction of the merits of the journal. On April 6, 1915, he asked Dreiser to observe his "progress during the past six months" in editing "a magazine that the civilized reader may peruse without damage to his stomach."[44] Dreiser's reply was so crushing that he sought no more encouragement from that quarter.[45] Dreiser's verdict was to remain unchanged for many years, and his opinions, and

[42] "A Note from the Editors," *SS*, LXVIII (Feb., 1922), 2. The editorial continues: "Take a glance at the magazine as it exists today. . . . [I]ts editors have introduced . . . the majority of the younger native writers who have subsequently . . . attracted the widest and most sober attention. . . . Among these . . . are F. Scott Fitzgerald . . . Harvey Fergusson . . . Ben Hecht . . . Sherwood Anderson . . . Floyd Dell. . . .

"The foremost of the young American dramatists, Eugene O'Neill, was introduced to the public through these pages. . . .

"Among English writers . . . the *Smart Set* was instrumental in introducing Lord Dunsany, W. S. Maugham, W. L. George, James Joyce, Aldous Huxley. . . .

"The *Smart Set* brought out part of 'Jurgen,' the masterpiece of James Branch Cabell, who received his first hearing in these pages. It has brought out Theodore Dreiser as a dramatist . . . Willa Sibert Cather's 'Youth and the Bright Medusa.'

"The Boston *Transcript*'s annual survey of American magazines for last year placed the *Smart Set* at the top of the list in the number of distinguished stories published." (Several of the above claims are not strictly true.)

[43] *A Portrait of Mencken from Memory* (New York, 1956), p. 19. Hereinafter cited as Angoff, *Portrait*.

[44] *Letters of Theodore Dreiser*, I, 186.

[45] "I wish I could say . . . that I liked the *Smart Set*. . . . [But] [u]nder you and Nathan the thing seems to have tamed down to a light, non-disturbing period[ical] of persiflage and badinage, which now and then is amusing but which not even the preachers of Keokuk will resent seriously. . . . Really the thing is too debonair, too Broadwayesque. . . . Everything, apparently, is to be done with a light, aloof touch, which to me is good but like a diet of soufflé" (*Letters of Theodore Dreiser*, I, 187-189). In Dreiser's letter, dated April 20, 1915, is a lengthy analysis of the monthly to show the editor how bad were the contents.

even his epithets, were eventually adopted by Mencken, as was Dreiser's suggestion: "There are splendid indictments to be drawn of a score of things before the world right now."[46]

Dreiser recognized that the harmonious co-operation between the two *Smart Set* editors did not indicate a lack of difference in temperament. Nathan, a believer in the doctrine of "Art for Art's sake," appeared to view his native land and all political phenomena without interest. Although he could write amusing epigrams on American foibles, his true love was the "magic lantern" of the stage, where artifice was the only reality.[47] Ezra Pound shared Dreiser's conviction that Mencken, however negative and flamboyant his sociology might be, provided a ballast needed to offset Nathan's haughty disdain toward mundane affairs.[48]

Mencken grew progressively less satisfied with the monthly. In 1916 he dismissed praise from Henry Sydnor Harrison, a well-known novelist of the day, by replying: " 'It rather startles me to hear that you have found anything worth reading in my *Smart Set* stuff, for on the whole it has had to be light and inconsequential. . . .' "[49] He did not realize that Harrison was not merely being polite, but owed a debt to the magazine for his success.[50] Later in 1916, Mencken became so unhappy with his editing that he wrote Pound that he was finally going to start a more ideal review, and Pound, then acting as an agent of sorts for the *Smart Set,* responded from England with encouragement and ad-

---

[46] *Ibid.,* I, 188.

[47] Charles Angoff, "Introduction," *The World of George Jean Nathan,* ed. Charles Angoff (New York, 1952), pp. xvi-xvii.

[48] Ezra Pound to Mencken, Sept. 27, 1916 (*Letters of Ezra Pound,* p. 98).

[49] Letter to Henry Sydnor Harrison printed in Frank Durham, "Mencken as Missionary," *American Literature,* XXIX (Jan., 1958), 480-482, 480.

[50] First, Harrison was "discovered" by the *Smart Set* of Colonel Mann: "Then I found a young man from Virginia, none other than Henry Sydnor Harrison, whose gay, satirical yarns captivated the whole staff. Years later . . . he told me that ours were the only acceptances he ever received in those days of first endeavor. . . . it must be remembered that the *Smart Set* found Harrison . . ." (Charles H. Towne, *Adventures in Editing* [New York, 1926], p. 60). Second, Mencken had written very favorably of Harrison's work ("Novels for Hot Afternoons," *SS,* XXXIV [July, 1911], 155).

vice.[51] Once again, however, the enterprise was postponed, and the editors busied themselves with launching what Mencken called "louse" publications—cheap "pulps" entitled *Parisienne, Saucy Stories,* and *Black Mask,* which were sufficiently profitable as financial ventures to enable the *Smart Set* to survive the war.

By 1923, despite some enthusiastic subscribers, the magazine was losing circulation.[52] According to Burton Rascoe, it was then becoming fashionable among the cognoscenti to sneer at the monthly.[53] Perhaps certain readers were convinced that the periodical had accomplished its task of liberating the beginning American writer—certainly the editors expressed publicly their opinion that their avowed mission was fulfilled.[54] Mencken's increasingly lower opinion of the magazine was stated to friends during the summer of 1923. He wrote to Sara Powell Haardt: "I am sick of the *Smart Set* after nine years of it, and eager to get rid of its title, history, advertising, bad paper, worse printing, etc."[55] Twenty days later he wrote to Ellery Sedgwick, then

[51] "Still the *country* U.S.A. is hopeless and may as well go to hell its own way. . . . Glad you are going to start a 'better' magazine. 'Better' is such a bloody ambiguous word. Seriously I think what is wrong is simply that neither England nor America have had an Eighteenth Century deist. . . .

"It's all very well your doing the light fantastic, but *you* (*you* H.L.M.) and a lot more of your friends will have to take art and freedom more seriously before you are done with the matter. 'Hell' in the person of Comstock's following, Sunday, and all the rest, will do you in, unless you get some heavy artillery.

"Perhaps the new magazine is intended to be a bit more 'weighty,' in which case you are on the right road" (letter of Sept. 27, 1916, *Letters of Ezra Pound,* pp. 97-98).

[52] The monthly had a circulation of about 50,000 during most of Mencken's and Nathan's editorship, but by 1923 there were less than 35,000 purchasers (Dolmetsch, "History of the *Smart Set,*" p. 72).

[53] ". . . the current custom of sneering at *The Smart Set.* . . . has been overdone. . . . [It is,] despite ignorant opinion to the contrary . . . not a mere vehicle for Mencken and Nathan. It publishes as high an average of good fiction as any magazine in the United States or England, and this goes for *The Dial* and *The Atlantic Monthly* . . ." ("The Case of *The Smart Set,*" *A Bookman's Daybook* [New York, 1929], p. 21).

[54] The American writer was considered sufficiently free and with a receptive enough audience to have no excuse for second-rate writing. The *Smart Set* is given credit for the emancipation of authors from Puritanical oppression (HLM, "Taking Stock," *SS,* LXVII [March, 1922], 138-144).

[55] HLM to Sara Powell Haardt, July 10, 1923. Copy in Princeton University Library Collection of H. L. Mencken Correspondence, hereinafter cited as P.M.C. (Mencken married Sara Haardt in 1930.)

editor of the *Atlantic,* that the *"Smart Set* is too trivial," adding that he had been trying to get rid of it for five years.[56]

Whether or not such magazines as the *Freeman* or *Broom* were providing competition for the *Smart Set* can perhaps not be known. It is possible that the ailing monthly was sharing a trend in the early twenties that saw far older and more distinguished monthlies steadily lose purchasers. The circulation of *Harper's* in 1922 was 70,986; by the next year 68,697, and by 1924 off to 66,694. The circulation of *Scribner's* in 1922 was 83,088, and by 1923 it had diminished to 73,036, and in 1924 reached 71,414.[57] This gradual erosion is even more significant when it is realized that the total of magazine readers was then increasing, partly because of population gains, partly because of more leisure time, and more generally because purchasers were better educated.[58]

MENCKEN'S JUDGMENTS OF MAGAZINES

MENCKEN's discussions of magazines before 1923 show a concern which was to help him define the role of the *Mercury.* He was acquainted with such of England's "more serious reviews" as the *Edinburgh Review, English Review,* and *Quarterly Review.*[59] Much of the time they received respectful comment, as when he praised the *Fortnightly Review,* the *Spectator, Saturday Review, Athenaeum,* and *Academy* for their favorable comments about Dreiser's novel *Sister Carrie.*[60] Less often he criticized English periodicals, including the *Nation,* Wyndham Lewis's *Blast,* and those magazines founded by Lord Northcliffe, which he de-

---

[56] HLM to Ellery Sedgwick, July 30, 1923. Copy in P.M.C.

[57] Ayer's *Directory,* 1923, 1924, 1925.

[58] Theodore Peterson, *Magazines in the Twentieth Century* (Urbana, Illinois, 1956), pp. 51-53. Hereinafter cited as Peterson, *Magazines.*

[59] "A Counterblast to Buncombe," *SS,* XL (Aug., 1913), 157.

[60] "The Plague of Books," *SS,* LII (June, 1917), 140.

scribed as "the most imbecile type," circulated in "the fashion of Barnum and Munyon."[61] After 1917, a shift away
from the English orbit is seen in his lashing of Americans
for publishing "heavy imitations of the *Athenaeum*," and
"warmed over *Spectators* or *Saturday Reviews*" and other
"imitations of English weeklies."[62] Independence is unmistakably declared: "Even Irving, for all his timorous colonial-
ism, finally mustered up enough courage to wrap himself
in the Star-Spangled Banner and defy the mighty Gifford,
editor and chief assassin of the *Quarterly Review*."[63] By
1919 the *Smart Set* had become anti-English, and soon Hugh
Walpole was debating with Mencken in the pages of the
Bookman over the new attitude.[64] Another Englishman
snapped: "America will be safe for Americans as long as
'The Smart Set' guards the frontiers."[65] This trend, combined with Mencken's steadfast refusal to counsel unhappy
Americans to embrace exile in Europe, casts doubt on Carl
Dolmetsch's assertion that the *Smart Set* helped foster the
migration to Europe, and that such a migration was a cause
of the declining circulation in 1922.[66]

Smart Set contributors were frequently satirical about
American magazines, but Mencken outdid them all (in

[61] "If a new Samuel Butler should print a new 'Erewhon' tomorrow, even
the *Nation* would be aware of it within a year" ("The Books of the Irish," *SS*,
LI [March, 1917], 143); "Notes on Books," *SS*, LXVI (Oct., 1921), 140;
"The Public Prints," *SS*, LV (July, 1918), 140.

[62] "The Coroner's Inquest," *SS*, LIX (July, 1919), 143; "Prof. Veblen and
the Cow," *SS*, LIX (May, 1919), 138.

[63] "Mainly Fiction," *SS*, LVIII (March, 1919), 139.

[64] "An Open Letter to H. L. Mencken," *Bookman*, LV (May, 1922), 225-
228 ("Aren't you conscious yourself of an increasing tinge of provincialism in
your critical utterances?" [*ibid.*, 228]) was answered by the American with
vigor: ". . . certain American journals . . . practise a puerile and slimy
Anglophilism. It has become a public nuisance, and when I deal with it at all
I treat it as such" ("Mr. Mencken Replies," *Bookman*, LV [June, 1922], 367).

[65] Simon Pure [pseud.], "The Londoner," *Bookman*, LV (Aug., 1922), 611.

[66] "History of the *Smart Set*," p. 119. In his first contribution, Mencken
expressed reservations about ". . . those queer, dreaming, unhappy Americans
who haunt the *pensions* of Florence and Pisa and try to convince themselves
that home is not sweet" ("The Good, the Bad, and the Best Sellers," *SS*, XXVI
[Nov., 1908], 159). Nor does he in his essay on politics for *Civilization in
the United States: An Inquiry by Thirty Americans*, ed. Harold Stearns (New
York, [1922]), suggest that exile is appropriate.

volume of criticism, though not in quality).[67] He found fault
with the *Little Review, Munsey's, Town Topics, Outlook,
Metropolitan, Harper's Weekly, Red Book,* and *Cosmopolitan.* His severest judgments, however, were directed toward
the *Dial, North American Review, New Republic, Freeman,
Bookman, Ladies Home Journal, Saturday Evening Post,*
and *Nation.*[68] The old *Critic* (later merged into *Putnam's*)
was found wanting, as were the *Scribner's* and *Century* of
the day.[69] Except for brief intervals, the monthly magazine
of the past was seen as "almost completely cut off from life,"
and only the brisk editing of Edgar Allan Poe drew a
tribute.[70] In fact, he imagined his editorial talents qualified
him as a modern equivalent to Poe.[71] Because he admired
the directness and vigor of Poe's magazine criticism, he
denounced the ponderous hesitancy of his contemporaries
on "the literary monthlies," especially when they begrudged
recognition to such writers as Joseph Conrad.[72] Another

[67] For instance, "Magazitis Americana—A Diagnosis," by John Gould
Fletcher, was a poetic indictment of several kinds of American magazines
(*SS,* XLIV [Sept., 1914], 47-49).

[68] The dissatisfaction was usually with bad reviewing, an excessive concern
with reform, pandering to popular tastes in fiction, and alliance with professors. Statements about the *Nation* from 1910 until 1921 could be quoted to
show how outspoken and sustained was his criticism, but a few must suffice.
"Just what is the matter with the sort of man who reads the *Nation?*" asked
Mencken in 1915 ("The Genealogy of Etiquette," *SS,* XLVII [Sept., 1915],
305). He did claim to know who wrote for the weekly: "Most of our native
critics, being Puritans themselves—consider, for example, the prim virgins,
male and female, of the . . . *Nation* . . ." ("The Literature of a Moral Republic,"
SS, XLVII [Oct., 1915], 152). Also denounced repeatedly was the ". . . insane
labeling and pidgeon[*sic*]-holing that passes for criticism among the gifted
Harvard boys of the . . . *Nation*" ("Criticism of Criticism of Criticism," *SS,* LII
[Aug., 1917], 139). An analysis of the *Nation* in 1918 concludes: "All that
remains . . . is for the *Nation* to be burnt by the public hangman" ("Seven
Pages about Books," *SS,* LIV [Jan., 1918], 143).

[69] "The Russians," *SS,* XLI (Dec., 1913), 153; "The Literary Shambles,"
SS, L (Dec., 1916), 138-139.

[70] "The American Magazine," *Prejudices: First Series* (New York, 1929),
pp. 172-173.

[71] Percy H. Boynton, *The Challenge of Modern Criticism* (Chicago, 1931),
pp. 29-39, gives a detailed comparison of the two editors which concludes:
"Poe dreamed for years of editing a national journal of his own, in which he
could discuss life and literature unhampered by an editorial overlord. He died
with his ambition unfulfilled. Mencken dreamed the same dream, and has
seen it come true in the *American Mercury*" (pp. 31-32).

[72] "Adventures among the New Novels," *SS,* XLIII (Aug., 1914), 153.

complaint was directed toward magazines whose high rates of payment for contributions were ruining otherwise promising writers. Christopher Morley was said to have been destroyed "when he took the shilling of the *Ladies Home Journal*," the "cheap (and rich) magazine" was declared to have "finished [Jack] London,"[73] and the *Saturday Evening Post* was repeatedly damned for seducing competent writers of fiction by excessive payments.[74] (He was later to modify his low estimate of the short stories in the *Saturday Evening Post*.)[75] Nor were the restrictions honored by editors satisfactory; he claimed that worthwhile literature had been kept unpublished because of cowardice on the part of editors and publishers.[76] If Lord Northcliffe's magazine enterprises in England dismayed Mencken, their "Hearst and Hearstoid" counterparts in America were equally condemned.[77] His strictures on magazines became so common that they came to shape his critical vocabulary.[78] If a writer was approved, his work was contrasted with that of "the magazine Hannah Mores"; if not, unfavorable parallels were drawn.[79]

[73] "More Notes from a Diary," *SS*, LXII (May, 1920), 144; "Literae Humaniores," *SS*, LIV (March, 1918), 140.

[74] "Observing the steady . . . descent of promising postulants in beautiful letters down the steep, greasy chutes of the *Saturday Evening Post* . . . we are too prone ass-like, to throw up our hands and bawl that all is lost . . ." ("Consolation," *SS*, LXIV [Jan., 1921], 138). Another attack is in "Taking Stock," *SS*, LXVII (March, 1922), 142, but his most interesting comments have remained unpublished. In his "Preface for a collection of American short stories to be translated into German," which was not published because of the currency deflation in Germany in 1923, he deplores the influence of the *Saturday Evening Post* on short fiction, and is especially scandalized that it "pays as much as $3,000 for a short story" ("Contributions to Books: H. L. Mencken: Typescripts: 1920-36," pp. 59-61, E.P.M.C.).

[75] HLM to Edmund Wilson, July 10, [1925]. Copy in P.M.C.

[76] "The Public Prints," *SS*, LV (July, 1918), 141.

[77] "Consolation," *SS*, LXIV (Jan., 1921), 138.

[78] "As for Dr. [William Dean] Howells, [he is] . . . a man vouched for by both the *Atlantic Monthly* and the *Ladies Home Journal*. . . . [A critical examination, however,] will show . . . a long row of uninspired and hollow books, with no more ideas in them than so many volumes of the *New Republic*" ("Suffering among Books," *SS*, LI [Jan., 1917], 266).

[79] In condemning William Lyon Phelps's *The Advance of the English Novel*, the reviewer said that "one can even imagine it following Dr. Mabie's 'White List of Books' in the *Ladies Home Journal*. . . . Now he is sicklied o'er with the pale cast of Harvard and the *Nation*" ("The Plague of Books," *SS*, LII [June, 1917], 138).

Satirical sketches of literary persons were made in terms of their taste in periodicals.[80]

Not all of his remarks, however, were negative. The constant "railing . . . at magazine editors"[81] was sometimes supplemented with free advice; in 1916 he suggested that a magazine be founded to counter the miasmatic muckraking idealism still lingering. In 1920 he expressed amazement that no American publisher had set up a counterpart to the English *Notes and Queries*: "In no other country in the world is there such a lush crop of lies and imbecilities crying aloud to be run down and disposed of."[82] (The word "debunking," probably coined in 1923,[83] was to be a timely help to critics of his own *Mercury,* but it would also have described the ferment in his mind during his earlier *Smart Set* days.)

In the South, the new *Reviewer, Double-Dealer,* and *All's Well* were praised as "*tendenz* magazines [that] announce valiantly . . . they are done with the past." Although Mencken commended his Southern colleagues for busying themselves with "slitting the throats of Timrod, Coogler, and Thomas Nelson Page," he still felt that the editors were soft-pedaling in their accounts of Southern life.[84] He was pleased with E. W. Howe's *Monthly*.[85] It is likely that he approved of Henry Holt's *Unpopular Review,* which had similarities to Ed Howe's periodical, and which, according to Charles and Mary Beard, was directed to the same au-

---

[80] Two Kansans were so characterized: William Allen White ("Water-Wagon Enchantments," *SS,* XLIV [Dec., 1914], 178) and E. W. Howe ("Business," *SS,* LIV [April, 1918], 138).

[81] "Taking Stock" *SS,* LXVII (March, 1922), 142.

[82] "The Literary Shambles," *SS,* L (Dec., 1916), 139; "Répétition Générale," *SS,* LXIII (Sept., 1920), 52.

[83] The word was popularized by William Woodward in his novel *Bunk* (New York, 1923). Woodward apparently originated the word as well (W. W. Woodward, "Debunk," *American Speech,* II [May, 1927], 374). The verb became so closely associated with Mencken that he was obliged to deny having invented it (*Supplement I: The American Language* [New York, 1945], p. 399 n.).

[84] "The South Begins to Mutter," *SS,* LXV (Aug., 1921), 139; "Notes on Books," *SS,* LXVI (Oct., 1921), 138; "Répétition Générale," *SS,* LXXII (Oct., 1923), 57-63.

[85] Tributes are printed in "Business," *SS,* LIV (April, 1918), 142, and in E. W. Howe, *Plain People* (New York, 1929), pp. 244-250.

dience that the *Mercury* courted.[86] And despite Mencken's diatribes against the *Nation,* he was named as a contributing editor in 1921. He wrote to Louise Pound: "I have joined the *Nation* as contributing editor. This is a joke, the significance of which escapes me. . . . My politics are anything but Liberal."[87] His occasional praise of liberal periodicals, however, might have given the impression to others that he was liberal.[88] He believed in the worth of magazine apprenticeship for aspiring writers: "Is it so soon forgotten that Willa Cather used to be one of the editors of *McClure's?* That Dreiser wrote editorials for the *Delineator* . . . ? That Huneker worked for the *Musical Courier?*" Comic and satiric weeklies of the early twenties, including *Life, Puck,* and *Judge,* were praised for exercising a "far more profound influence on the life of a community than the so-called serious weeklies."[89]

These many comments made during his *Smart Set* association helped to shape the editorial philosophy of a man soon to set out to become the "greatest ornament of his trade since Jeffrey."[90] His observation that "a new Poe would be deluged with adulation, and even money,"[91] perhaps indicates that he saw some possibility for a spirited editorship early in the decade that was to witness the establishment of the *Mercury.*

[86] "The Industrial Era," *The Rise of American Civilization* (2 vols.; New York, 1930), II, 766. Holt's *Unpopular Review* was characterized by "hatred of shams" (Henry Holt, *Garrulities of an Octogenarian Editor* [Boston, 1923], p. 40). When the title did not prove popular, it was changed to *Unpartizan Review* (*ibid.,* p. 244). The strongest approval expressed in the *Smart Set* was by Thomas Beer ("The Nietzschean Follies," *SS,* LXVII [March, 1922], 128-129).

[87] HLM to Dr. Louise Pound, May 11, [1921]. Louise Pound Collection, Duke University Library Manuscript Collection.

[88] Randolph Bourne and Van Wyck Brooks received qualified praise ("Sunrise on the Prairie," *SS,* LVIII [Feb., 1919], 138) and several other editors and liberal magazines are praised in "Notes on Books," LXVI (Oct., 1921), 138. Many of Mencken's opinions were shared by liberals in his pre-*Mercury* days, and in the twenties, "when [his] verbal antics stood out boldly, and his toryism did not," the confusion continued (Louis Kronenberger, "H. L. Mencken," *After the Genteel Tradition,* ed. Malcolm Cowley [New York, 1937], p. 106).

[89] "Consolation," *SS,* LXIV (Jan., 1921), 138; "Répétition Générale," *SS,* LXV (July, 1921), 38.

[90] "Memoirs," *Vanity Fair,* XLI, 16.

[91] "Taking Stock," *SS,* LXVII (March, 1922), 139.

3

THE ORIGINS OF THE *MERCURY* IN 1923

ALFRED KNOPF'S DESIRE FOR A MAGAZINE

By 1923 the publishing house founded by Alfred Knopf was looking about to find an editor for an undefined magazine enterprise. Mencken was an obvious possibility. He had known Alfred Knopf since 1913, when Knopf, then an employee of Doubleday, had discussed with him a proposed edition of the works of Joseph Conrad. Mencken's first impression, caused by Knopf's literary enthusiasm and apparent neglect of the expense of such an edition, was that Knopf was too idealistic.[1] This opinion was not to thaw entirely until 1924, but even before then Mencken began to admire the competence of the young publisher. Mencken had written for the *Smart Set* unusually appreciative notices of Knopf's books even before Knopf became his publisher in 1917.[2]

The house of Knopf might have noticed trends that would encourage their designs for a periodical. Several book publishers, desiring "house organs" for prestige, diversification, literary contacts, and cheap advertising for books, established magazines during the twenties.[3] As has been shown, the total number of periodical readers was steadily increasing. Many interesting magazines were founded dur-

---

[1] Kemler, *Mr. Mencken,* p. 117.
[2] As in "Shocking Stuff," *SS,* LII (May, 1917), 397-398.
[3] Peterson, *Magazines,* pp. 86-87. (Henry Holt's *Unpopular Review* was in no way a "house organ"; it was even published by another firm to remove any such suspicion.)

ing the first half of the twenties, several of them with success.[4]

Alfred Knopf approached Mencken early in 1923. His first suggestion was that Mencken alone edit some sort of new magazine, but Mencken prevailed on the publisher to bring Nathan in, just as Nathan's support had earlier brought Mencken into the *Smart Set* as co-editor. Nathan was induced to join, although with some misgivings.[5] The possibility that Alfred A. Knopf, Inc., might rehabilitate the *Smart Set* was considered, and such a rehabilitation nearly occurred. There were several points to recommend such a course. The magazine, while no money-maker, was by no means doomed; its readers included many who were very loyal, and the circulation prospects were not bad, as evidenced by the interest of William Randolph Hearst, who eventually purchased it for $60,000.[6] Another feature that would cut down the capital outlay necessary was the economy with which it was run. The editors had almost no office help, they paid very little for contributions, and their office was perhaps notable only for its profane decorations and low rent.[7] Last, and most important, Nathan strongly favored such a continuation. Nathan was the senior editor, and he was satisfied that his name always preceded Mencken's on the cover. The *Smart Set,* with its focus on New York and Western Europe and its emphasis on belles-lettres, was also satisfactory to him; in fact, he had already begun to resist an alarming tendency on the part of his co-editor to include political and economic articles in the monthly.[8] In any new venture he would not have the force of tradition to help him keep such materials at a minimum. He also sensed a "Messianic" aspect in Mencken's desire to

[4] The *Reader's Digest* first appeared in 1922, *Time* in 1923, and the *New Yorker* in 1925.
[5] Manchester, *Mencken,* p. 148.
[6] Kemler, *Mr. Mencken,* p. 165.
[7] Dolmetsch, "History of the *Smart Set,*" p. 55.
[8] Angoff, "Introduction," *The World of George Jean Nathan,* p. xxii.

establish a more pretentious new magazine, and this pre-
monition discomfited him.[9]

Several factors, however, made a continuation of the
Smart Set less likely than the establishment of a new review.
First, there was the flippant title, together with traditions
which chafed Mencken increasingly during his connection
with the magazine. Second, there were his unforgotten
dreams of such an ideal periodical as the "Blue Review,"
and these dreams were nourished by advice from correspondents like Pound and Dreiser. Third, his unusually
outspoken comment on magazines suggests a concern about
them which must have enhanced any desire to edit an
entirely new one himself.

In spite of Mencken's wishes, the talks among the
Knopfs, Nathan, and himself did not lead to any quick
abandonment of the old monthly. On March 5, 1923,
Mencken wrote to Alfred Knopf a report of a discussion in
New York with Samuel Knopf (Alfred's father), who was
to be the business manager of whatever periodical emerged
from the negotiations, and a plan for the Knopfs to take
over the *Smart Set* was then seriously considered.[10] There
was even an abortive announcement to Upton Sinclair, sent
June 15, that a reorganization of the *Smart Set* was in the
works.[11] Actually, Mencken must have been still trying to
convince the Knopfs that a new magazine was necessary,
and he may have been aided in this effort by Nathan's absence abroad. Eventually the Knopfs approached Eltinge F.
Warner, who in 1923 owned most of the stock in the
Smart Set, and offered to buy the ailing monthly. Warner,
however, did not find Knopf's offer sufficient, and therefore
any thought of converting it into a Knopf organ was
abandoned.[12] This interview between Knopf and Warner

[9] Kemler, *Mr. Mencken,* p. 165.
[10] HLM to Alfred Knopf, March 5, 1923. Copy in P.M.C. In a letter to
Ernest Boyd, Mencken describes further negotiations with Samuel Knopf, who
had come to Baltimore (April 23, 1923; letter in P.M.C.).
[11] HLM to Upton Sinclair, June 15, 1923. Copy in P.M.C.
[12] Dolmetsch, "History of the *Smart Set,*" p. 72.

must have occurred sometime between June 15 and July 10, because by the latter date it was agreed to found a new and more ambitious review.[13] The decision was to be kept secret for a time.

MENCKEN'S SEARCH FOR CONTRIBUTORS

BY July 26, 1923, Mencken began sending out confidential solicitations for manuscripts.[14] To Sara Haardt he sent a request for an article, promising that complete freedom of speech would prevail, especially when irritating to righteous citizens.[15] A statement of purpose regarding the fetal *Mercury* was included in Mencken's announcement to Theodore Dreiser: the magazine was meant to encompass such diverse fields as literature, science, politics, and economics.[16] Two days later Mencken showed signs of being carried away with his new idea, and informed Max Brödel that his review, although serious, would have shocking religious and cultural policies: atheism was stressed as a desirable means of stirring up the animals.[17]

In August his exertions to bring in manuscripts became more vigorous. He wrote to the talented Negro writer James Weldon Johnson, and upon an unresponsive Dreiser he again pressed his requests, using bait he probably considered irresistible: Dreiser was to be permitted to attack

[13] HLM to Sara Haardt, July 10, 1923. Copy in P.M.C.
[14] Robert F. Richards, in his *Concise Dictionary of American Literature* (New York, [1955]), p. 6, incorrectly claims that the *Mercury* was founded "with the avowed intentions of seeking manuscripts which had been rejected by other editors." Richards confuses the *Mercury* with the *Smart Set* in this respect, because Mencken had frequently solicited rejected manuscripts from other editors when on the earlier monthly (Dolmetsch, "History of the *Smart Set*," p. 46). (It should be pointed out that other editors waited in line for *Smart Set* rejects [Ezra Pound to Mencken, Aug. 12, 1917, *The Letters of Ezra Pound*, pp. 114-115]).
[15] HLM to Sara Haardt, July 26, 1923. Copy in P.M.C.
[16] HLM to Dreiser, July 28, 1923. Copy in P.M.C.
[17] HLM to Max Brödel, July 30, 1923. Copy in P.M.C. Mencken tried to tailor his announcements to fit the recipient: a letter to Ellery Sedgwick on the same day is meek enough.

by name the more evangelical Protestant sects.[18] In return, Dreiser promised some lyrical poems about "little flowers of love and wonder," and Mencken temporized by responding that the decision whether or not the new monthly would publish poetry had not been made, but that Dreiser should by all means forward the verse. He pressed anew a request for prose, and revealed more progress in defining the future magazine: it was said to be designed as a monthly resembling the *Mercure de France* and the *London Mercury,* but more saucy and amusing. The main purpose of the review was to outrage Anglo-Saxon decorum.[19] An interesting reminder of Mencken's earlier infatuation with H. G. Wells's "Blue Weekly" was his declaration that his new organ was intended to express an educated Toryism; he promised to print an article debunking the idol of democracy—Abraham Lincoln.[20] Perhaps the most princely announcement of all was directed to Carl Van Doren, and it includes an interesting speculation that the readers will include many from college faculties who resist Liberalism, yet who cannot stomach the dour *North American Review.* Mencken proudly pointed out that the first issue, which would appear in January, 1924, would be graced by Alfred Knopf's famous attention to details in format and printing.[21] Edmund Wilson was also asked to write for the projected monthly, as was Upton Sinclair, from whom Mencken requested some sort of reminiscent article about California for a genuinely quality magazine, printed on fine paper.[22]

The effect of the more boisterous trumpeting by Mencken was to discourage prospective contributors. One can

[18] HLM to Dreiser, Aug. 2, 1923. Copy in P.M.C.

[19] HLM to Dreiser, Aug. 10, 1923. Copy in P.M.C.

[20] HLM to Sara Haardt, Aug. 17, 1923. Copy in P.M.C.

[21] HLM to Carl Van Doren, Aug. 20, 1923. Copy in P.M.C.

[22] HLM to Upton Sinclair, Aug. 24, 1923. Printed in Upton Sinclair, *My Lifetime in Letters* (Columbia, Mo., [1960]), pp. 235-237. Hereinafter cited as Sinclair, *Letters.* To Edmund Wilson, Mencken wrote: "Confidentially . . . Knopf is setting up a new review. . . . Have you any ideas for the new one?" (Aug. 21, 1923; copy in P.M.C.). Mencken at this period was interested in Wilson, although he had to reject several of Wilson's stories contributed to the *Smart Set* because of the "Comstocks" and the Post Office.

easily understand the source of his complaint to Sara Haardt that he found it very difficult to line up writers. He found many of his acquaintances nervous and reluctant.[23] By September, however, the manuscripts began to flow in at a satisfactory rate, and the first issue of the *Mercury* began to take form.[24]

While Mencken was writing confidential notices to the better writers of his acquaintance, a debate had gone on about the title of the monthly. The differences of opinion among the principals is illuminating. Mencken and Nathan were satisfied with the "Blue Review," but Alfred Knopf ruled against it, despite the appeal to sentiment, on the grounds that it was too "arty."[25] A number of other possible titles were then produced, including "The Twentieth Century," "The Capital," "The Defender," "The Sovereign," "The Regent," "The Chancellor," "The Portfolio," "The Pendulum," "The Other Man's Monthly," "The Gray Monthly," "The Colonnade," "The Inter-Continental Review," "The Athenaeum," "The Colonial Review," "The New Review."[26] It was Nathan who eventually suggested "The American Mercury."[27] Mencken was immediately indignant, protesting that such a title would suggest a kinship with the *London Mercury,* which he thought very dull, or imitative of the *Mercure de France* or *Mercurio Peruano.*[28] When Knopf failed to heed such protests, Mencken allowed himself to be convinced that such a title was not only apt but was very good indeed, with a dignity like

[23] HLM to Sara Haardt, Aug. 24, 1923. Copy in P.M.C.
[24] To Ernest Boyd, Mencken wrote on Sept. 19, "Very fair stuff for the M. is beginning to come in," and on Sept. 28, "MSS are now pouring in from all directions. . . ." On Nov. 12, the editor wrote: "The Aesthete, barring acts of God, will surely go into the January number." Letters in P.M.C.
[25] Kemler, *Mr. Mencken,* p. 165.   [26] Manchester, *Mencken,* p. 149.
[27] Kemler, *Mr. Mencken,* p. 166.
[28] Manchester, *Mencken,* p. 149. At least one other writer shared Mencken's estimate of the *London Mercury*: "I think that *The London Mercury* is the dullest and least intelligent publication with pretensions in the English language" (Burton Rascoe, *A Bookman's Daybook,* p. 7). Mencken had been praised in the *Mercure de France,* CXXXI (Jan. 16, 1919), 249, and thus might have been aware of a resemblance, but the *Mercurio Peruano* parallel is so far-fetched as to suggest that it was added only after consultation with a periodical index.

Harper's and yet nearly as noncommittal.[29] The debate
would have ended there, but another crisis arose: on August
2, 1923, Mencken wrote of a tiff with the Post Office department about the title.[30] The difficulty was that someone
had copyrighted the name and still had rights to it. But a
cash settlement cleared the trouble away.[31] Only Theodore
Dreiser remained unhappy about "American Mercury," believing that something more subversive-sounding should be
chosen. Mencken's reply to Dreiser warned the novelist that
his suggested names would give the show away. Some outwardly respectable name might confuse people, but what
occurred on the stage inside the tent would be a different
matter. Mencken concluded his defense by reminding
Dreiser that P. T. Barnum was able to pass off burlesque
demonstrations by labeling them moral lectures.[32] As this
curious apology for the title suggested, Mencken's magazine
promised to be the most tempestuous "American Mercury"
since Andrew Bradford's *American Weekly Mercury,* an important colonial publication which first appeared on December 22, 1719.[33] Had Mencken known of the earlier *Mercury,*
and its relatively outspoken editor, he would probably have
further approved of his title.[34]

The attempt to keep the venture a secret was not very
successful (partly because Mencken sometimes forgot to
enjoin secrecy in his letters), and soon publicity became the
goal of the founders. Knopf was first to break the silence,
and he did so with a release to newspapers:

[29] Kemler, *Mr. Mencken,* p. 166.
[30] HLM to James Weldon Johnson, Aug. 2, [1923]. Copy in P.M.C.
[31] Interview with Charles Angoff, New York City, N. Y., Dec. 27, 1958.
[32] HLM to Dreiser, Sept. 10, 1923. Copy in P.M.C. (The list of Dreiser's
suggestions has apparently not been printed.)
[33] Anna J. DeArmond, "History of the *Mercury,*" *Andrew Bradford* (Newark,
Del., 1949), p. 39. Pages 39-222 of DeArmond's study are a thorough history
of the *American Weekly Mercury.*
[34] Bradford was repeatedly summoned before Pennsylvania authorities for
printing material deemed worthy of reprimand (L. N. Richardson, *A History of
Early American Magazines* [New York, 1931], pp. 15-16). Mencken might have
been reminded of the parallel in anon., "'The American Mercury': A New
Magazine Announced by Knopf," *Publishers' Weekly,* CIV (Aug. 18, 1923), 553.

The aim of The American Mercury will be to offer a comprehensive picture, critically presented, of the entire American scene. It will not confine itself to the fine arts; in addition, there will be constant consideration of American politics . . . , American industrial and social relations, and American science. The point of view . . . will be that of the civilized minority.

It will strive at all times to avoid succumbing to the current platitudes, and one of its fundamental purposes will be to develop writers in all fields competent to attack these platitudes in a realistic . . . manner.

It will cover a larger ground than [other magazines,] and it will diligently avoid the formal thinking that characterizes most of them. No cult or tendency will dominate its pages. . . .

The names of the editors offer assurance that, whatever its deficiencies otherwise, it will never be obvious or dull. . . .[35]

That the *New York Times* announcement was sandwiched between two panegyrics on the late President Harding, who had died on August 2, must have been grimly humorous to Mencken.[36] He had tried to print a caustic obituary of the dead President in the *Smart Set,* but Warner had opposed heatedly, declaring that he would sell the monthly as soon as possible rather than continue it under its existing set-up.[37]

Knopf's next bid for publicity was a large, regal announcement, beautifully printed and with richly scrolled margins, dated September, MCMXXIII. In this brochure he repeated that the new monthly would be the American counterpart of the English (*London*) *Mercury,* the *Mercure de France,* and Germany's *Neue Merkur,* and he stressed that it would not be "a rival to any existing American review."[38] Mencken, who was not at this early date fully reconciled to Knopf's "fancy whorehouse typography," wrote briskly to Harry Rickel: "Knopf is an idealist. The

[35] "Magazine to Cater to 'Civilized Minority,' " *New York Times,* Aug. 18, 1923, p. 2, col. 3.

[36] "Will Issue 300,000,000 of Harding Stamps—First Sheet of Memorial Postage to be Presented to his Widow," and "Predicted Harding's Rise—Kirby Forecast in 1915 and Facetious Reply Are Recalled" were the headlines of the articles (*ibid.,* p. 2, col. 3).

[37] Dolmetsch, "History of the *Smart Set,*" p. 73.

[38] "The American Miscellanea: 1923-1933," E.P.M.C.

second circular, to be issued December 1st, will be more business-like."[39] By October 10 Mencken and Nathan issued a broadside announcing their withdrawal from the *Smart Set* in readiness for their new duties with the *Mercury*.[40] Another editor was retained for the *Smart Set,* although he was apparently not informed of Warner's intention of selling the monthly as quickly as Hearst made a good offer.[41]

The financing of the new magazine was not nearly so difficult as present-day beginning publication is said to be.[42] Knopf, by obtaining credit at the printers, held the initial costs down.[43] There was no great expense with office help, and the temporary office itself, if more decorous than the old *Smart Set* office, was not much more plush. Mencken and Nathan signed an agreement whereby they were to enjoy complete freedom from interference by the publisher in their selection of material to be printed.[44] The co-editors were to own one-third of the stock in the periodical. Their salaries were fixed at $5,000 a year, to be paid during the first year by "shares of stock in The American Mercury, Incorporated."[45] Mencken was pleased with the "ironbound contract,"[46] and the delay in receiving a cash salary did not

[39] Angoff, *Portrait*, p. 199; HLM to Harry Rickel, Sept. 20, 1923. Copy in P.M.C.

[40] The reason stressed in the leaflet for their withdrawal was that the *Smart Set* mission was fulfilled; it had enabled them to break down some of the difficulties "which beset the American imaginative author, and particularly the beginning author . . . to set him free from the pull of the cheap, popular magazine on the one side and of the conventional 'quality' magazine, with its distressing dread of ideas, on the other . . ." ("The American Mercury: Miscellanea: 1923-1933," E.P.M.C.).

[41] Dolmetsch, "History of the *Smart Set*," p. 75. Morris Gilbert, the new editor, was able to publish five issues of a *Smart Set* that was restricted to fiction and which sold for ten cents.

[42] Peterson ("The Economic Structure of the Industry," *Magazines,* p. 76) estimates that the present-day cost of launching a magazine equivalent to the *Mercury* would, for an established publisher, be approximately two and one half to five million dollars. The odds against success, even at this investment, are cited as ten to one.

[43] HLM to Upton Sinclair, May 26, 1936: "Rather curiously, it took very little money to start the *American Mercury*. The printers offered credit for the first few numbers . . ." (copy in P.M.C.).

[44] Alfred A. Knopf to Singleton, Feb. 18, 1959.

[45] Kemler, *Mr. Mencken,* p. 167.   [46] Angoff, *Portrait,* p. 24.

at first greatly bother him—ownership of part of the stock in the *Smart Set* had proved profitable to its editors, and it appeared worth a temporary sacrifice to own a portion of the *Mercury*.[47]

The editors agreed to continue most of the *Smart Set* editorial arrangements. There was to be complete equality of authority in the selection of material: disapproval by either editor of a manuscript meant that it would not appear. Despite the expense and fatigue of the journey, Mencken was to continue to live in Baltimore and travel to New York City once or twice a month to help put the magazine together, and otherwise handle editorial business from Baltimore. A general rate was set of two cents a word in payment for prose,[48] and little occasion was found to pay more, even though other magazines offered several times that much during the twenties. The "relatively low"[49] rate showed that the publication would rely on its prestige to attract contributors, rather than on the size of its check. Such a policy was then being successfully followed by Ellery Sedgwick of the *Atlantic*.[50]

Despite Knopf's ease in securing credit at the printer's, there was a speculative side to the *Mercury,* a side reflected in the forced gaiety of Mencken's letters to Philip Goodman during the fall of 1923.[51] It was an expensive periodical to produce because of such factors as the quality paper. There were no assured sales: Mencken, writing of the possible number of purchasers, observed that "12,000 to start with would be wonderful."[52] It was only gradually that the

[47] Of the total sale price of $60,000 which Hearst paid for the *Smart Set,* Mencken and Nathan each received one-fourth, in addition to $40 per share for their stock in the monthly (Kemler, *Mr. Mencken,* p. 165).

[48] Interview with Charles Angoff, Dec. 27, 1958. Mencken and Nathan were responsible for setting this rate (Alfred Knopf to Singleton, Feb. 18, 1959).

[49] Angoff, *Portrait,* p. 196.

[50] Frederick Lewis Allen, "Sedgwick and the *Atlantic,*" *Outlook and Independent,* Dec. 26, 1928, p. 1406.

[51] "If we sell but 1,000,000 copies of the *Mercury* every month the second consolidated cumulative income bonds will earn 9⅜ per cent" ("H. L. Mencken: Letters to Philip Goodman: 1918-1933," 3 vols., E.P.M.C., I, 4. Sept. 12, 1923).

[52] HLM to Dreiser, Oct. 4, 1923. Copy in P.M.C.

principals in the undertaking became convinced that any long survival of the magazine was likely.

Nor could the editors have told much about the potential reception of the review from discussions in the press: there was too little agreement. As early as August 20, 1923, a rebuke was printed in the Bridgeport *Telegram*: "A new monthly review, edited by George Jean Nathan and Henry L. Mencken, is projected under the ambitious title of 'The American Mercury.' If the morals of the barnyard are the morals of America, and the manners of the feeding-trough are the manners of America, . . . then the magazine [will be thoroughly American and should be] a great success."[53] Sniffed a writer in the Columbus, Ohio, *Citizen*: "Mr. Mencken and Mr. G. J. Nathan are publishing a new magazine . . . we hear. We haven't seen it and won't be depressed if we never do."[54] Other comment was more favorable. There were approving notices in the *Nation,* the *Freeman,* and the *Bookman.*[55]

By the eve of publication the editors were understandably tense. A cynical composite portrait entitled "The Labor Leader," by James Mallahan Cain, so outraged the union printers of the press Knopf had chosen that they refused to print it. Something else was inserted in its stead, and preparations went ahead.[56] Mencken and Nathan differed about

[53] "Menckeniana: A Schimpflexicon," ed. Sara Haardt, 3 vols., I, 70, E.P.M.C. This collection was revised by Mencken and issued in abbreviated form as *Menckeniana: A Schimpflexicon* (New York, 1928).

[54] "Menckeniana: A Schimpflexicon," III, 172, E.P.M.C.

[55] Anon., "Editorial Paragraphs," *Nation,* CXVII (Aug. 29, 1923), 207: ". . . no two men are doing more to stir the youth in the colleges and out of them to independent critical, creative thinking than Mencken and Nathan." "[M]y understanding is that it will canvass the spiritual activities of mankind somewhat as the Freeman undertakes to do as a weekly" ("Journeyman," "Miscellany," *Freeman,* VIII [Sept. 19, 1923], 31). Anon., "The Gossip Shop," *Bookman,* LVIII (Oct., 1923), 223.

[56] This writer is indebted to James M. Cain for the following account of his essay: "The article left out of the first number of THE AMERICAN MERCURY, January, 1924, was by me, and titled THE LABOR LEADER. It appeared in the February issue, as the first of the magazine series called AMERICAN PORTRAITS. It was arranged at a lunch in Marconi's restaurant, Baltimore, in September, 1923, when Mencken told me of the new magazine and asked if I had any ideas for an article to go into the first number. I, writing of labor a great deal at that time, suggested this article, and he liked the idea. I was quite excited

the editorial presenting the aims and scope of the monthly. Mencken had originally written a vaunting promise: "The dramatic reviews will . . . cover the entire range of the American theatre," and Nathan had this changed to "The dramatic reviews will . . . cover the entire range of the New York theatre."[57] The magazine went to press about December 6,[58] and by December 20[59] Mencken was admiring the first of the one hundred and twenty issues he was to edit during the next ten years. It was distributed to the newsstands at least one day before Christmas.[60] Three thousand and thirty-three copies were mailed to "founder" subscribers, and two hundred large, rag paper copies were signed by the editors and sent to friends and advertisers.[61]

THE FIRST NUMBER OF THE *MERCURY*

PURCHASERS who paid the fifty cents for a single copy, or subscribers who paid five dollars for a year's subscription, found a handsome magazine. It was ten and three-sixteenth inches tall, seven inches wide, and one-half inch thick. The cover was Paris-green, with marginal scrolls by Elmer Adler, a noted typographer of the day. Printed in black, red, or blue, Adler's attractive marginal decorations and the green cover were to remain for many years. As its sewn construc-

---

at being in the first issue of so important a literary periodical, and badly disappointed when the January, 1924, issue appeared, with no article by me in it. Mencken told me, the next time I saw him, that the union printers, of the press Knopf had picked out to get the magazine out, had refused to set it up." Mr. Cain adds that Mencken, Knopf, and Nathan had at once changed printing establishments, " 'as [they] couldn't have printers dictating to [them] what [they] would publish' " (James M. Cain to Singleton, Feb. 1, 1959).

[57] "Editorials: H. L. Mencken: American Mercury," 3 vols., I, 6, E.P.M.C. The emendation of the typescript is not in Mencken's handwriting, and might be Nathan's.

[58] HLM to Ernest Boyd, Dec. 3, 1923. Letter in P.M.C.

[59] HLM to Philip Goodman, Dec. 20, 1923 ("Letters to Philip Goodman," I).

[60] The first account of the new review which this writer can discover is Burton Rascoe's, which was published Dec. 24 (*A Bookman's Daybook*, pp. 177-178).

[61] Bern Porter, *H. L. Mencken: A Bibliography* (Pasadena, Calif., 1957), p. 24.

tion promised, the magazine readily opened out flat like a
book. There were 128 pages in the January, 1924, issue, and
in all succeeding issues until 1936. As Adler later reported,
the type was chosen during a conference of the editors,
publisher, and printers, who met to discuss "the new magazine, and how best to express its ideas in type form."[62]
After considering several types, the decision was in favor of
Garamond, a type face based upon that used by Claude
Garamond in his attractive sixteenth-century French books.
The paper selected was the finest Scotch featherweight. It
was decided that there would be no illustrations. Certainly
the new monthly, at least in externals, should have satisfied
the fastidious Nathan, who disapproved of the definition of
a monthly magazine as something "halfway between a newspaper and a book." The only such periodical that interested
Nathan "editorially," he said, "is one which tends to be
nine-tenths book to but one-tenth newspaper."[63] As late as
1925 Mencken believed that to Alfred Knopf the *Mercury*
was "still visible primarily as a book."[64] In short, everyone
connected with the new review was proud of the distinctive
appearance which "set the *Mercury* apart from its tasteless
and gaudy newsstand neighbors" by striking "a new note of
elegance [in] the making of magazines." It was directed toward people who knew "the worth of a good magazine as
well as a Bellows portrait or a Tanagra figurine."[65]

The editorial in the first number, written largely by
Mencken, was only an elaboration of the many announcements made during the fall of 1923. The purpose of the
Mercury was declared to be the ascertaining and telling of
the truth, but the editors did not intend to conduct their
pursuit of truth with "messianic passion"; instead, their

[62] *Three Years*, p. 6.
[63] "On Monthly Magazines," *The World of George Jean Nathan*, p. 261.
See anon., "Made Like a Book" (adv.), *Publishers' Weekly*, CXV (April 27,
1929), 1, 989, for a more technical description.
[64] "Memorandum," *The Borzoi 1925: Being a Sort of Record of Ten Years of
Publishing* (New York, 1925), p. 141.
[65] *Three Years*, pp. 6, 30.

inquiries were to be skeptical. Although the world was described as "down with at least a score of painful diseases," no panaceas were possible, as the ills were "chronic and incurable." The Ku Klux Klan, the Anti-Saloon League, William Jennings Bryan, lodge-joiners, Methodists, "normalcy," Socialists, Capitalists, Greenwich Villagers, pedants, and Prohibition were threatened with exposure, with some effort to save "what is exhilarating in them, when all that is divine must be abandoned." Against such evils was juxtaposed "the normal, educated, well-disposed citizen of the middle minority," a reincarnation of the "civilized minority" of 1916 and before.[66] After defining the ideal reader, the editors promised to "keep to common sense . . . to belabor sham as agreeably as possible, to give a civilized entertainment," and to emphasize at all times the American scene. The reader was admonished that good work of all kinds "is always done in the middle ground" between the fringe of coteries, theorists, and sentimental idealisms.[67] The editorial, while somewhat turgid, sufficed as a vigorous statement of intentions.

The remaining contents were varied. The first article, by Isaac R. Pennypacker, was entitled "The Lincoln Legend." Pennypacker's essay was not what Mencken had earlier promised as a denunciation of Abraham Lincoln.[68] The author, an historian of the Civil War, was more interested in demolishing legends than in debunking. Although Lincoln was charged with limitations as a war leader and as an administrator, he was done the honor of disparagement by comparisons with such worthies as George Washington and William of Orange. Pennypacker tried to show that Lincoln's origins were not "so lowly" that, in accounting

[66] The caption on the *Smart Set* of April, 1916, was "The magazine of the civilized minority." Mencken's first use of such a phrase was apparently in "The Russians," *SS*, XLI (Dec., 1913), 155. Being described were the Russian intellectuals as confronted with Russian "medievalism."

[67] "Editorial," *American Mercury*, I (Jan., 1924), 27-30. Hereinafter *Mercury* articles will be identified by month and year.

[68] HLM to Sara Haardt, Aug. 17, 1923. Copy in P.M.C.

for his stature, they did violence "to the most elementary laws of heredity." Lincoln's ancestors, before the time of his father, were declared to have been people of "substance and local prominence," and the rail-splitter's rise was shown as natural in view of his solid ancestry. Pennypacker's closing was a nostalgic tribute, but his subject had been treated as a mortal.

The next offering was by Dreiser, then well-known as a radical in politics and as a naturalistic novelist. His contribution was poetry: four free-verse lyrical poems most remarkable for a mood of gentle pathos and traditional romantic imagery. Possibly the poet was unaware that one of the poems had previously appeared in the *Smart Set*; probably Mencken had forgotten.[69] No other verse was printed in the first number.

Following the poetry was an essay by Carl Van Doren entitled "Stephen Crane." Crane was presented as the first truly modern American writer. Other possible contenders for the honor, including Henry James, Mark Twain, Henry Adams, and William Dean Howells, were swiftly dismissed, and the footsteps of the "unduped yet affectionate spectator" were directed toward Crane. Van Doren's sweeping judgments and use of partial summaries of Crane's works would have appealed to readers hitherto ignorant of Crane.

A story which followed Van Doren's exposition was written by Ruth Suckow. Discovered by Mencken,[70] she was one of a number of *Smart Set* contributors who followed him to his new monthly.[71] "Four Generations" was a realistic description of the reunion of a German-American

---

[69] See p. 12, n. 5.

[70] Sinclair Lewis, writing to Alfred Harcourt on Jan. 20, 1922, quotes Mencken: " 'I lately unearthed a girl in Iowa, by name Ruth Suckow, who seems to me to be superb' " (*From Main Street to Stockholm: Letters of Sinclair Lewis,* ed. Harrison Smith [New York, 1952], p. 95; hereinafter cited as *Letters of Sinclair Lewis*).

[71] "Among the approximately 450 contributors to the *Mercury* during the next nine years (1924-1933), eighty-five were former *Smart Set* writers who, by that time, had become fairly well-established authors" (Dolmetsch, "History of the *Smart Set,*" p. 143).

family in the Midwest. The author used the contrasts between the Old World and America, as embodied in the
several generations, to develop her tale. There followed a
series of letters by James Gibbons Huneker to his friends
and publisher. Printed as "Huneker on Huneker," these
letters gave examples of the epistolary style of a noted musical and literary critic who was one of Mencken's heroes.

Harry Elmer Barnes, in "The Drool Method in History,"
criticized the tendency of teachers and writers of history
to succumb to sectional, racial, and nationalistic bias. Barnes,
a professor of sociology, vindicated "the Sneer Method, with
all its admitted defects, as an infinitely more salutary and
healthy approach to history than . . . the Drool Method."
He approved of such historians as Charles Beard and belittled the work of others, ranging from John Church
Hamilton to H. J. Eckenrode.

Samuel C. Chew, a professor of English, contributed a
record of a conversation between himself and George Moore,
the English novelist. "Mr. Moore and Mr. Chew" reported
the thoughts of the two men on Thomas Hardy, travel
writings, and the health of Mrs. Chew. The dialogue showed
the sensibilities of the two men of letters in an attractive
manner.

After "Mr. Moore and Mr. Chew" came a feature of the
Mercury labeled "Americana," a standard department which
had its origins in the *Smart Set*.[72] The form for "Americana"
listings almost never varied; first a state was mentioned,
then followed a brief, ironical introduction by the editor
further defining the source of the folly, and then a passage
of stupidity or prejudice was quoted from a newspaper, a

---

[72] The earliest form of "Americana" was "The Purling of the Platitudinarians"
and "More Purlings," which appeared in *SS*, XLIV (Dec., 1914), 206, 216.
Excerpts from foolish speeches, sermons, and books were reprinted often after
1914, but it was not until 1922 that they were presented as "Americana." The
first arrangement under that heading was by Milnes Levick (*SS*, LXIX [Nov.,
1922], 117-119). In May of 1923 "Major Owen Hatteras, D.S.O." (Mencken's
and Nathan's joint pseudonym) began the "Americana" that was transferred,
without change, to the *Mercury* after the December number of the *Smart Set*.

sermon, a political speech, or the like. Some examples from the first number include:

ARIZONA

From an harangue delivered to the Chamber of Commerce of Tucson by the Hon. H. B. Titcomb:

> The person who objects to the ringing of cracked bells from a church-tower I do not believe is a good citizen of any community.

The culprits whose utterances or deeds earned them a hearing in "Americana" were often introduced with pomp, an effective device of burlesque, illustrated in the following item:

TEXAS

Speciman of literary criticism by Prof. Dr. Leonard Doughty, a favorite pedagogue of the republic of Texas, where the great open spaces breed a race of men with hair on their chests and red blood in their veins:

> It might have been thought of the Teuton that he had reached earth's nadir of stupid badness and graceless shame in Hauptmann and Sudermann. . . . But . . . the stain of that yellow, bastard blood is upon much of the 'authorship' of the United States. . . .

Mencken's choice of Doughty was not wholly random; he had been feuding with the Texan.[73] Nor was the editor above inserting a "plug" for his good friends in introductions to the "Americana" items:

KANSAS

Latest triumph of the Higher Patriotism in Kansas, as reported by E. W. Howe in his interesting *Monthly*:

> The attorney general of Kansas has ruled that if a child in school refuses to repeat the flag pledge, its parents may be arrested and fined. A good many children are

[73] A portion of this "Americana" entry had been printed in "Nordic Blond Art," *SS*, LXXXI (May, 1923), 139, 141. Not only had Mencken damned Doughty then, but he had also attacked him in the New York *Evening Post* for November 24, 1923. Doughty was not actually connected with the academic world, but was rather a lawyer (L. Doughty, "On Pre-Adamic Hottentots, Mencken, The Nation, and Others," *Nation,* CXVIII [March 19, 1924], 316).

tired of repeating the flag pledge every day, which is as
follows. . . . The pledge was invented . . . by an old
maid engaged in welfare work.

(Howe, a Mencken partisan, reciprocated with an emphatic
tribute: "The best thing that ever happened to our literature is *The American Mercury*.")[74] Other "Americana"
items exposed naïveté, credulity, smugness, illiteracy, bigotry, or the blending of business into religion. The quotations
seemed audacious because they usually were prefaced by
names and sources. The department was to give more an-
noyance than any other portion of the magazine.

"The Tragic Hiram," by John W. Owens, a colleague
of Mencken on the Baltimore *Sun,* was a gently satirical
portrait of Hiram Johnson, one-time Governor of California
and a Republican aspirant to the presidency. Mencken
chose Owens to write the study of Johnson partly because
the editor recognized something true of the twenties that is
still perhaps valid: ". . . one often encounters middle-rank
journalists who are more politically alert than top sociolo-
gists, economists, or political scientists."[75] Two articles on
military affairs also appeared in the first number of the
Mercury, both by authors who chose to conceal their names.
The first, entitled "Two Years of Disarmament," was an
appraisal of contemporary efforts to balance military power
among the nations. Emphasis was placed on the Japanese
naval situation. After a disquieting account of the fortunes
of the Chosiu, or war party, the author suggested that the
fortification of Guam was imperative. The other military
article, "On a Second-Rate War," was intended to show that
World War I witnessed some clumsy and unimaginative
generalship. The war was belittled, and it was claimed that
"the inevitable next war will show combat so transformed
and reformed that the struggle of 1914-1918 will seem, by
comparison, little more than a clash 'between barbaric

[74] *Three Years,* p. 43.
[75] C. Wright Mills, *White Collar* (New York, 1951), p. 136.

hordes.'" Inadequacies in military training were explained
by the anonymous critic as factors in the second-rate performance of American forces early in the war.

In a section of the *Mercury* labeled "The Arts and Sciences" came several short essays. Under the "Archictecture"
subheading the prominent architect C. Grant La Farge discussed the legal and architectural problems of building skyscrapers in an essay entitled "The New Sky-Line." Under
the "Medicine" subheading was an account of "The Pother
about Glands," by L. M. Hussey. Hussey, a chemist and
pharmacologist, had some restraining remarks to make concerning gland surgery. George Philip Krapp, a distinguished
student of the English language, wrote the "Philology"
division of the "Arts and Sciences." His essay was a general
statement of problems of usage met by philologists.

After Krapp's article appeared a light, humorous essay
by Leonard Lanson Cline, a newspaper reporter. Cline's
"Sweeney's Grail" was a mocking defense of the much
criticized policeman: "Thus the cops dream, and we con-
temn them, never realizing that their reticence is of dignity
and not of dulness, and their obscene outbursts those of
spirits tormented rather than vulgar." Another offering in
light humor was a short story by John McClure, who, like
Ruth Suckow, had been a *Smart Set* contributor. McClure,
then an editor of the *Double-Dealer* in New Orleans, entitled his comic phantasy "The Weaver's Tale."[76] James
Oneal's "The Communist Hoax" was an essay attacking the
notion that a "red scare" was justified. Oneal, an historian
of the labor movement, traced the many factions of the
Communists, Socialists, and I.W.W. to 1923, and concluded
that there were fewer radicals than alarmists believed, that
those few spent most of their energy in internecine strife,
and that therefore fears of a conspiracy against the government were ridiculous.

[76] McClure's story was essentially a reworking of a tale he had had printed
in the *Smart Set* in 1922 and 1923.

Two more offerings from the academic world were printed in the first issue. Margaret Münsterberg, daughter of Hugo Münsterberg of Harvard, wrote an account of George Santayana's stay at that university. "Santayana at Cambridge" was followed by an essay by Woodbridge Riley, whose discussion of Mormonism and Christian Science had recently been suppressed from the *Cambridge History of American Literature*. Riley, a professor of philosophy, found solace by criticizing Unity, Christian Science, and less organized manifestations of what he classified as "new thought."

Three other departments in the monthly were largely written by the editors. "The Theatre" was of course Nathan's province, as it had been in the *Smart Set*. Nathan interpreted an admittedly second-rate performance by the actress Eleonora Duse as a joke deliberately perpetrated by a genius upon "a lot of American boobs" who would not know better than to applaud. Nathan then indulged in some theorizing: "The greatest moments of any drama are . . . the spaces of silence between the speaking of one character and the speaking of another"; "Drama is pantomime adorned and embellished with literary graces"; "Drama is emotion," etc. The critic approved of a performance of *Cyrano de Bergerac,* disparaged some Theatre Guild productions of foreign comedies, reviewed favorably *Queen Victoria,* by David Carb and Walter P. Eaton, and found John Drinkwater's *Robert E. Lee* inferior. Zoe Akins was sermonized for the failure of her most recent play to match her earlier ones, and a production of Melchior Lengyel's *Sancho Panza* was also found lacking.

Mencken was assisted in "The Library" by James Branch Cabell, Ernest Boyd, and Isaac Goldberg. Boyd, a noted student of the Irish literary scene, reviewed Georg Brandes's *Main Currents in Nineteenth Century Literature* and Benedetto Croce's *Poesia e non Poesia*. Cabell discussed Robert Nichols's *Fantastica: Being the Smile of the Sphinx and*

Other Tales of Imagination. Goldberg, soon to write biographies of both *Mercury* editors, wrote about *Patria Nova,* by Mario Pinto Serva, a Brazilian. Mencken's reviews were of Nikolay Rimsky-Korsakoff's *My Musical Life,* John W. Burgess's *Recent Changes in American Constitutional Theory,* and Charles Josey's *Race and National Solidarity.* In the reviews (which averaged about eight hundred words apiece), only one Knopf book was examined.

The co-editors compiled the "Clinical Notes," their continuation of the *Smart Set's* "Répétition Générale."[77] The first "Clinical Notes" were varied. There were brief essays claiming that "One horse laugh is worth ten thousand syllogisms," that hedonism "is the only sound and practical doctrine of faith for the intelligent man," and that polytheism is more adequate than monotheism as an explanation of the origin of man's shortcomings. There were epigrams: "Toward men, ever an aristocrat; toward women, ever a commoner—that way lies success"; "Among men, women admire most those who have all the attributes and qualities of an actor and yet are not actors by profession." Some of the items in "Clinical Notes" might have as well have appeared in "Americana."[78]

The foregoing is a brief description of the contents of the first issue except for an article by Ernest Boyd—"Aesthete: Model 1924." The reception of this provides a good introduction to the unusual public response to the new periodical. Boyd's essay was a composite portrait of the creator of the worst of avant-garde writings[79] and identified the typical aesthete as a product of Harvard. His education was described as superficial at college, and after graduation his association with sophisticates resulted in his recruitment

---

[77] The "Répétition Générale" department was born in 1919 (*SS,* LVIII [April, 1919], 49-53). The title was apparently suggested to Mencken by an experience of Huneker ("A Literary Behemoth," *SS,* XLVII [Dec., 1915], 156).

[78] The last page of the first number was devoted to the identification of the contributors. "The American Mercury Authors" was a permanent feature.

[79] Boyd's omnivorous reading habits are described by Rascoe in "Ernest Boyd: Elegant Reading Machine," *A Bookman's Daybook,* pp. 178-182.

into the avant-garde. Boyd described the aesthete's enthusiasms as skimmed from the pages of the *Masses* and the *Little Review*. The "lofty rhetoric" of the *New Republic* was declared to have led the aesthete to France, where he soon suffered disillusionment about the "Wilsonian storming of Valhalla." While in France, however, he commenced a ridiculous literary and social life, and stayed in Paris after the war to admire Dadaists and other modernists. Upon his return to America, the perfected aesthete settled in Greenwich Village and began to write prose and verse "remarkable chiefly for typographical and syntactical eccentricities, and a high pressure of unidiomatic, misprinted French to the square inch." Boyd, himself "a leading figure in the Algonquin circle,"[80] then satirized coterie criticism. Displays of arid learning, use of a critical vocabulary made up of stock phrases, worship of the "altogether contemporary," and excessive attention "to the arts adored by the crowd, the 'lively arts,' Mr. Seldes calls them," are exposed as absurd tendencies. The portrait ended with an account of the aesthete's return to orthodoxy. Boyd's essay, in a style "entirely in harmony with his point of view,"[81] was more than simply a "deft bit of kidding."[82] It was to occasion, in its author's words, "a display of literary manners" suitable to a "Ku Kluxing, Fascista world."[83]

THE GREENWICH VILLAGE RESPONSE

WITHIN hours after the first issue was placed on sale, news of Boyd's lampoon spread about in Greenwich Village. The literati there bought all available copies, read the attack, and were outraged. They felt themselves to be

[80] Hunter Stagg, "Mr. Boyd's Portraits," *Reviewer*, V (Jan., 1925), 90.
[81] *Ibid.*, 93.
[82] Rascoe, " 'Aesthete: Model 1924'—Timeless and Universal," *A Bookman's Daybook*, p. 177.
[83] "Enter the Author," *Portraits: Real and Imaginary* (London, [1924]). p. 153.

the butt of the satire—either individually or collectively—
and prepared to counter-attack. Burton Rascoe, the chroni-
cler of the uprising, heard on Christmas Eve from Edmund
Wilson that "Malcolm Cowley and Matthew Josephson
were much cut up about Boyd's skit in the *American
Mercury*."[84] This first report proved an understatement:
"The whole literary left wing, which had hitherto been
disorganized . . . solidified against the perpetrator of the
article. Obsure poets and art theorists who had never been
heard of before began collaring people and calling them up
on the phone, saying that Boyd had themselves specially in
mind when he wrote the piece and that they meant to have
his blood." The sensitive writers swarmed over to the East
Nineteenth Street habitat of Boyd. When he emerged, he
was greeted "with a fusillade of ripe tomatoes, . . . eggs,
sticks, stones, and copies of S4N," and the elderly critic
barely escaped back into his house. Rascoe tells of three days
of imprisonment while "Dadaists pushed his door bell, kept
his telephone abuzz," and cast unpleasant items through his
windows.[85] From a loud-speaker set up outside his house,
derogatory broadcasts were amplified over the neighbor-
hood.[86]

Malcolm Cowley, in his *Exile's Return,* has also cast light
on the disturbance. Cowley, at the time an editor of *Broom,*
admitted being "harried and combative," "like Aubrey
Beardsley forced to defend his masculinity against whispers."
In such a state of mind, he found in Boyd's article slanders
which it "did not contain." Cowley admitted that he had
been mistaken to feel that the essay made imputations of
homosexuality, but he did feel that Boyd's caricature was
drawn from the "early careers of Gilbert Seldes, Kenneth
Burke, Edmund Wilson and Matthew Josephson, with
touches borrowed . . . from John Dos Passos, E. E. Cum-

---

[84] " 'Aesthete: Model 1924'—Timeless and Universal," *A Bookman's Daybook,* p. 177.
[85] "Ernest Boyd: Elegant Reading Machine," *ibid.,* p. 183.
[86] Kemler, *Mr. Mencken,* p. 168.

mings, myself, Gorham B. Munson and John Farrar."[87]
Cowley asserted that Boyd had written an unfair and libel-
ous attack because of commercial competition from the
Villagers, but he could hardly excuse his own conduct toward the wretched satirist.[88] Nor were Cowley's assaults to
diminish; they merely changed form, and he remained opposed, not always to Boyd, but to the *Mercury*. His bitter-
ness encouraged him to lead in denunciation of the review's
"philistinism,"[89] and later even to charge that the *Smart
Set* had been edited for "drugstore cowboys."[90]

Perhaps the wrath of the Villagers was in part generated
by fears that the new monthly would lower the chances for
survival of the struggling *Broom*.[91] Another cause has been
advanced: "Boyd's article amounted to a blanket repudia-
tion of all that the editors had done in behalf of European
letters during the previous decade. The reaction of their
young followers . . . was violent and decisive."[92] It was
likely that some of the former *Smart Set* readers had not
understood that the editors' quarrel in that monthly had
never been with the middle class as such, but "only its booby-
hood."[93] Such writers as Gilbert Seldes mentioned in Boyd's
essay had indeed been recent *Smart Set* contributors.[94]

[87] (New York, [1934]), p. 198.

[88] Cowley telephoned Boyd, demanding an interview, and when Boyd refused to speak with him, Cowley delivered a profane diatribe over the telephone.
When his listener pretended that the outburst was the recitation of a Dadaist
poem, Cowley lost all control and threatened to "beat up" his antagonist.
Eventually Cowley sent Boyd a graceless apology. (Cowley's account of the
conflict is in *Exile's Return*, pp. 200-201, whereas Boyd's narrative is in
Portraits: Real and Imaginary, pp. 153-155.)

[89] *Exile's Return*, p. 205.

[90] "Smart Set Legend," *New Republic*, LXXXI (Jan. 16, 1935), 281.

[91] Both monthlies cost fifty cents a copy and five dollars a year. "Aesthete:
Model 1924" was an indictment of some of the editorial policies of *Broom*
as well as of the editors.

[92] Dolmetsch, "History of the *Smart Set*," p. 124.

[93] Lionel Trilling, "Eugene O'Neill," *After the Genteel Tradition*, p. 132.

[94] Seldes contributed a study of Harvard to part four of a series entitled
"The Higher Learning in America." His article was printed in *SS*, LXVII
(Feb., 1922), 59-63. Cowley tells of a 1924 encounter between Seldes
and Boyd: "Once, in the street, [Boyd met] Gilbert Seldes, a writer whose
features were included in the portrait of the imaginary Esthete. Seldes harbored
no grudge and raised his walking stick in friendly greeting. Mr. Boyd, however,
interpreted this gesture as a threat and walked hurriedly away. Seldes followed
him, having a message to deliver. . . . It is easy to imagine the spectacle of

Nevertheless, the *Mercury*'s drift away from the literary left was only a continuation of tendencies that had been apparent in the earlier monthly, and the drift should have surprised no one by December, 1923.[95] As J. K. Hutchins has said, it is hard not to smile now "at the furore Ernest Boyd set up. . . . The row was silly, but in fact it says something about the period that so trivial a piece of literary business was a matter of public interest."[96]

THE PUBLIC APPROVES

BY the close of December the *Mercury* staff was jubilant. The public had greeted their magazine with "a sales reception which boggled the wildest expectations of the editors."[97] After the subscribers and advertisers had received their part of the 5,000-copy first printing, the remaining copies were sent to the newsstands, where they sold out soon after arrival. By December 28 a second printing was being prepared; Mencken wrote to Philip Goodman: "We have word this morning that the subscription department was 670 subscribers behind—that is, behind in entering them up. Knopf has bought 30 new yellow neckties and has taken a

---

these two prominent critics, both of them sedentary and peaceful by disposition, one fleeing with terror . . . the other pursuing with the most amicable intentions" (*Exile's Return*, p. 202).

[95] Mencken had criticized *Broom* in his parting editorial in *SS*, LXXII (Dec., 1923), 142, and a general lack of sympathy with Villagers was consistently one of his prejudices. He had been roundly scored by the leftists because of his attack on Thorstein Veblen: "Mr. Mencken . . . has made a hit with the American bourgeoisie as a keen satirist of the intelligentsia.

"Over, if Mr. Mencken so chooses, are the days when he had to scintillate in the pages of the *Smart Set* for country school-teachers, adolescents and other appreciators of almost-naughtiness. Now he may write for the *American Magazine*. . . .

"If he survives this storm of popularity, I will confess . . . but not until I am assured that I will not find him next year featured on the Pollyanna circuit" ([Floyd Dell], "Popularity," *Liberator*, Dec., 1919, p. 42).

[96] "A Note on the Nineteen Twenties," *The American Twenties*, pp. 16-17. (Another curious aspect of the tiff was that Rascoe had sharply attacked *Broom*, and especially Matthew Josephson, in an article for the New York *Herald Tribune* of Sept. 17, 1923, and no retaliation was then proposed ["Josephson and the Modern Aesthetic," *A Bookman's Daybook*, pp. 138-141]).

[97] "Ernest Boyd: Elegant Reading Machine," *ibid.*, p. 184.

place in Westchester County to breed Assyrian wolf-hounds."[98] The second printing, and then a third, a total of about 15,000 copies, were quickly sold.[99] It should be recalled that Mencken had written Dreiser that as many as 12,000 purchasers would delight him, yet about 3,000 more than that number had flocked under his green standard. The price of the January, 1924 number soon soared to ten, then twenty-five, and perhaps even fifty dollars.[100]

The *Mercury* was approved by an essayist for the *New York Times Book Review* who especially admired its "attractive dress."[101] The *Nation* expressed strong approbation in its editorial columns: "Beautiful in form, stimulating in the variety of its matter, it is frankly iconoclastic, avowedly concerned with 'proving to all men that doubt, after all, is safe.' Its credo is consciously, carefully different from that of any of its rivals and predecessors." The only criticisms expressed were of an imagined "loss of tempo": "The Clinical Notes suffer by comparison with the Répétition Générale of the old *Smart Set*. There are surprising sobernesses here and there. But these after all are minor points when 'Castor and Pollux are out again.' "[102]

Other responses were less enthusiastic. The *Outlook* recalled Mencken's pro-Germanism: "Mr. Mencken has announced his passion for liberty, and liberty in his scheme of thought dwells, or did dwell, in Berlin"; having discharged his warning, the critic admitted that the first issue was "a well-printed and interesting magazine, independent, and disrespectful alike to stodgy conservative and freakish radi-

---

[98] HLM to Goodman, Dec. 28, 1923. "Letters to Philip Goodman," I.

[99] Goldberg, *The Man Mencken*, p. 203, states that 17,500 copies were sold. Bachman, *et al., Three Years*, p. 8, declares only that the "January issue exceeded 14,000." The editors estimated that a total of 15,500 was sold (H[erbert] R[ead], "Foreign Reviews: American Periodicals," *Criterion*, V [June, 1927], 373).

[100] Anon., "The American Mercury," *New Republic*, XXXVII (Feb. 6, 1924), 274; Goldberg, *The Man Mencken*, p. 203; Irene and Allen Cleaton, *Books & Battles: American Literature, 1920-1930* (Boston, 1937), p. 185.

[101] Anon., "Current Magazines," *New York Times Book Review*, Dec. 30, 1923, p. 10.

[102] Anon., "The American Mercury . . . ," *Nation*, CXVIII (Jan. 9, 1924), 23.

cal."[103] Reservations were also expressed in the *New Republic*. It was denied that the editors of the "beautiful green and black tandem steamroller" were truly iconoclastic: "A better word will have to be invented to describe someone who loves to hear the crash of empty bottles quite as much as that of ikons, who often can't tell the difference . . . the resulting noise is so loud as almost to sound like a philosophical system." Mencken was pictured as a mere name-caller concerned only with "the atrocities and imperfections" of America. The tendency to use equally emphatic epithets "whether speaking of a deep cancer or of a surface rash" was scored.[104] There were even rumors that George Horace Lorimer, then editor of the mighty *Saturday Evening Post,* had been startled.[105] A Massachusetts reader, however, declared that "the voice of Jeremiah is silent and the result is a book as staid as the *Atlantic* and not as interesting."[106] An Oklahoman did not share that calming verdict. Mencken's launching of the *Mercury* was said to make "the shout of alarm ever more imperative. Nothing American is safe from his curious probing and prescription."[107]

On December 31, 1923, however, the opposition (except toward poor Boyd) was temporarily inarticulate. And many persons whose opinions the editors respected felt that, when the "first number of the *American Mercury* appeared in 1923, it was like a fresh gale blowing through the horsehair-furnitured parlor of convention."[108] Mencken faced the future with boyish excitement, writing on the last day of the year: "By No. 6 we should be in the hands of the Department of Justice."[109]

[103] Anon., "The 'American Mercury,'" *Outlook,* CXXXVI (Jan. 16, 1924), 90.

[104] Anon., "The American Mercury," *New Republic,* XXXVII, 274.

[105] This hearsay is by John E. Rosser ("H. L. Mencken," *Real America* [Chicago, 1933], n.p. In "Articles about H. L. Mencken: Clippings: 1919-1933," E.P.M.C.).

[106] From the Springfield, Mass., *Union,* Jan., 1924, in Sara Haardt's "Menckeniana: A Schimpflexicon," I, 70, E.P.M.C.

[107] From the Muscogee *Phoenix,* May 4, 1924, in "Menckeniana: A Schimpflexicon," II, 107, E.P.M.C.

[108] Henry Morton Robinson, *Fantastic Interim* (New York, 1943), p. 82.

[109] To Hamilton Owens, Dec. 31, 1923. Copy in P.M.C.

4

MENCKEN AS EDITOR

EDITORIAL CONSOLIDATION

I N January, 1924, Alfred Knopf sponsored a series of literary parties to celebrate his "unusually prompt success"[1] as a magazine publisher. To these affairs his Baltimore editor went with reluctance—when he could not avoid them—for he was not always happy at such functions in New York City. Besides, he was a busy man. As the acclaim which greeted the January issue increased with each month in 1924, Mencken saw that various consolidations had to be effected.

On February 17, the office was moved from 220 West 42nd Street into a part of Alfred Knopf's new suite in the Heckscher building, which was located at Fifty-Seventh Street.[2] The offices, while "luxurious, [were] business-like, with black and white tiled floor, well upholstered library, and neatly arranged desks."[3] An office staff, with Edith Lustgarten as secretary and with ten advertising and circulation clerks, was retained.[4]

Although these arrangements helped in the conduct of the monthly, Mencken began to have difficulties of another sort. He tried to do most of the editorial chores at 1524

[1] Anon., "Knopf Offices Move to Fifty-Seventh Street," *Publishers' Weekly,* CV (Feb. 23, 1924), 601.

[2] Information from Mencken's note on a letter to Sara Haardt, Feb. 12, 1924. Copy in P.M.C. The mailing address of the review was 730 Fifth Avenue.

[3] Anon., "The Publishers and the New Season," *Bookman,* LXI (April, 1925), 212.

[4] Manchester, *Mencken,* p. 151.

Hollins Street in Baltimore, but frequent trips to New York, where he lodged in the Algonquin Hotel, were a necessary ordeal. The work was hard and time-consuming, it interfered with his writing of books and Baltimore *Sun* articles, and there was no immediate pay from Knopf.[5] Moreover, tension between the co-editors was fast increasing. Their differences were to affect greatly the literary mission of the magazine.

Whereas Mencken believed that the *Mercury* should be a general magazine, with literary concerns subordinated to other interests, Nathan held an opposite opinion. Late in his life Nathan wrote that "a magazine worth its salt should forego the common editorial preoccupation with journalistic immediacy and devote itself instead to those materials of art and life that are not necessarily bound strictly by the clock and that deepen, whether seriously or lightly, a reader's understanding of his surroundings, of himself, and of his fellows."[6] It had been Nathan who obtained the conversation by Samuel Chew entitled "Mr. Moore and Mr. Chew" as well as other more belletristic contributions to the first number of the monthly.[7] This approach contrasted to the growing tendency of Mencken to eschew art for a record of the antics of boobs. As early as 1920, Mencken could write that whether a Dreiser heroine "does this or that is of less importance to a comprehension of him as an artist than

---

[5] Mencken, quoted by Isaac Goldberg, "Notes used by Dr. Isaac Goldberg [for *The Man Mencken*]," New York Public Library H. L. Mencken Collection, p. 65. Hereinafter cited as N.Y.M.C.

[6] "On Monthly Magazines," *The World of George Jean Nathan*, p. 261. As the above-quoted essay was written about 1951, a less idealistic and earlier statement should be mentioned to give a full picture: "A magazine, to me—and to my associate, friend, and partner Mencken no less—is a toy, something with which to amuse ourselves. . . . It provides us with the pleasure of unloading certain of our ideas. . . . A new idea needs trying out, as a new tennis racket does.

"As an editor, I have . . . no wish to elevate my fellow man. . . . The world is quite all right, so far as I am concerned, as it is . . ." ("The Editor and His Public," *Bookman*, LXI [May, 1925], 275-276).

[7] Kemler, *Mr. Mencken*, p. 170. Kemler implies that Nathan obtained Van Doren's study of Stephen Crane without encouragement from his fellow editor, but in light of the flourishing correspondence between Mencken and Van Doren during this period, such an implication seems unwarranted.

the fact that the average American is a Methodist, and regards a baseball pitcher as the superior of Beethoven. . . ."[8] Mencken had seriously believed that the dramatic critic would eventually succumb to such a doctrine. The debate, at first genial, continued until the end of their *Smart Set* days, often with Nathan sounding the more plausible.[9]

The first discernible limitation imposed on the Baltimore editor was in his phrasing of the opening editorial, when Nathan restricted his responsibility for reviewing the stage to the New York area rather than to all of the United States.[10] Mencken believed that this approach showed an ignorance of the matters the *Mercury* was meant to deal with: "his mind was focused on New York, and especially on Broadway. I therefore had to drop him. . . ."[11] This statement, written years later, was an oversimplification; the conflict lasted longer than a year.

When Eugene O'Neill wrote the play *All God's Chillun Got Wings* especially for his friend Nathan, offering it for publication in the *Mercury* before its New York production, and when Nathan considered the piece an editorial windfall, Mencken became angry. Although the drama was printed, Alfred Knopf, who was to arbitrate any severe differences between the editors, had to intervene on the side of Nathan. The debate had been so warm that Mencken resolved to see whose views would dominate. He felt that the O'Neill work did not cast light on the workings of American democracy, and therefore it did not belong in the magazine.[12]

---

[8] "Criticism," "Répétition Générale," *SS*, LXII (May, 1920), 34.

[9] As in "Conversations: IV. On Politics," *SS*, LXIV (Feb., 1921), 93-98.

[10] "Editorials in the American Mercury. . . ," I, 6, E.P.M.C. The handwriting on the emendation is apparently Nathan's.

[11] "Introduction," "The 'Hatrack' Case: 1926-1927, The American Mercury vs. The New England Watch and Ward Society, The Postmaster-General of the United States, *et al.*," 8 vols., I, 100 n., E.P.M.C. Hereinafter cited as "The 'Hatrack' Case."

[12] It was claimed that the February, 1924, number, because of "All God's Chillun Got Wings," sold for as much as ten dollars (*Three Years*, p. 27). Later advertising brochures prominently listed O'Neill, who made no further contributions as a *Mercury* author.

In the summer of 1924 the strife grew too intense to be eased by Knopf's arbitration. Mencken charged his partner with incompetence in matters of magazine finance,[13] and repeatedly charged that Nathan was not doing his share of the drudgery.[14] By the fall of 1924, Mencken was so chagrined that he confronted Knopf with an ultimatum: "One or the other of us must leave. You can be sure that if you fire me it will not oppress me. . . . Besides, if Nathan has his way, you will probably sell more magazines."[15] Knopf chose to support Mencken, his original choice as editor, and Nathan was persuaded to vacate his co-editorship.[16] This change was announced on February 19, 1925, together with the information that he was to remain as a contributing editor. Because Nathan pretended that no feud existed and lost no opportunity to pay tribute to Mencken,[17] and because all public statements of his change in status were careful to say that he withdrew "because of his desire to be free from the technological details of editing,"[18] the public never knew the depth of the schism. For Mencken's part, the "Nathan divorce proceedings," as he termed them,[19] were conducted with surprising zeal. His former partner was relegated to an obscure desk among the clerks,[20] and

[13] G. J. Nathan, *The Intimate Notebooks of George Jean Nathan* (New York, 1932), p. 95. Hereinafter cited as Nathan, *Intimate Notebooks*.

[14] Angoff, *Portrait*, p. 29; "Introduction," "The 'Hatrack' Case," I, 100 n. Isaac Goldberg (*The Theatre of George Jean Nathan* [New York, 1926], p. 10) defends Nathan, finding him "a serious if not a hard worker. . . . He is at the *Mercury* offices every morning at nine, remaining there until noon, and at his desk in his apartment five or six hours daily, with a heap of finely sharpened lead-pencils ready for instant use."

[15] Kemler, *Mr. Mencken*, p. 171.

[16] Angoff claims that Nathan's desire to be free was augmented by a cash settlement arranged in 1925 by Samuel Knopf, business manager of the monthly until his death in 1932 (interview, New York City, Dec. 27, 1958).

[17] Two statements made in 1930 are typical: "Said Nathan of Mencken: 'I respect him, and am his friend, because he is one of the very few Americans I know who is entirely free of cheapness, toadyism and hypocrisy. . . . He is the best fighter I have ever met. And he is the fairest, the cleanest, and the most relentless'" (quoted in "Mencken and God," *Time*, XV [March 17, 1930], 80); "'My friend Mencken is the *Mercury*'s ideal editor'" (quoted in "Nathan and Mencken Part," *New York Times*, March 1, 1930, p. 12, col. 2).

[18] *Three Years*, p. 4.

[19] HLM to Goodman, April 28, 1925. "Letters to Philip Goodman," I, n.p.

[20] According to August Mencken, Knopf was responsible for the desk assignment (interview, Baltimore, Maryland, Dec. 23, 1958).

he was allowed to contribute only "Clinical Notes" and
theater reviews. In March, 1930, Mencken and Knopf purchased his stock in "The American Mercury, Inc.,"[21] and he
was "fired." His association for the five years after 1925
was allowed only "to save his face."[22] This aspect of the
editorial consolidation insured unity in the direction of the
periodical, but, as will be seen, it was to lessen its literary
importance considerably.

As Nathan's duties diminished, the increased work began
to wear Mencken down, and he began to look for help in
dealing with the six or seven hundred manuscripts which
arrived each month. A well-timed inquiry from Charles
Angoff, recently graduated from Harvard and then writing
for an obscure Massachusetts newspaper, resulted in the offer
of a position on the *Mercury*. Within three days after reporting for work, Angoff was left to handle the affairs of
the magazine, and he was, understandably, "terrified."[24]
The new assistant, soon to be managing editor and much
later editor, evidently gave satisfaction, for his employer
wrote, Angoff "turns out to be very good. He has already
relieved me of much routine drudgery, and I hope to put
even more on him."[25]

The directions left with the bewildered assistant show
the typical editorial routine. He was to look through the
manuscripts as they arrived, and, if he saw something
promising, forward it to Baltimore; otherwise, he was to
reject it. If changes were desired, instructions were to be
included with the returned manuscript. Such important
chores as proofreading were his. He was told to handle the
manuscripts with speed, whether they were to be accepted
or not. This efficiency was praised both by contributors and
by other editors.[26]

[21] "Nathan and Mencken Part," *New York Times,* March 1, 1930, p. 12, col. 2.

[22] Alfred Knopf to Singleton, Feb. 18, 1959.

[23] Mencken, "Introduction," "The 'Hatrack' Case," I, 101 n.

[24] Angoff, *Portrait,* p. 29.

[25] HLM to Goodman, Feb. 4, 1925. "Letters to Philip Goodman," I.

[26] Benjamin DeCasseres, a frequent contributor, wrote that "anyone who has

Angoff soon learned other facts about the monthly. For instance, the buying policy did not permit the accumulation of manuscripts for possible later use: no more stories or articles were to be purchased than were needed for the immediate future.[27] Nor was he to buy serial features or essays dealing exclusively with non-American matters. A knowledge of legal restrictions on the republication of *Mercury* material was acquired.[28] He became familiar with Mencken's habits in arranging the format early every month.[29] Most important, he became sensitive to his boss's personal preferences, and he tried assiduously to follow them.[30]

---

dealt with Mencken in his capacity as editor of the *American Mercury* knows that he has not only introduced a new kind of magazine to America but he has also introduced a new kind of editor . . . one who gives immediate attention to your manuscript, pays spot cash, encloses return stamped envelope with the proofs and gives you second serial rights without asking" (*Mencken and Shaw: The Anatomy of America's Voltaire and England's Other John Bull* [New York, 1930], pp. 66-67). Edmund Wilson's tribute appeared in "The Literary Worker's Polonius: A Brief Guide for Authors and Editors," *The Shores of Light: A Literary Chronicle of the Twenties and Thirties* (New York, [1952]), p. 595.

[27] "We buy from hand to mouth deliberately and have done so since our first issue. The moment an editor begins to accumulate manuscripts he begins to accumulate losses. Some of them . . . get out of date, and others succumb to changes in policy" (HLM to Bob Brown, Nov. 1, 1932. Letter in N.Y.M.C.).

[28] As late as 1929 the *Mercury* retained all rights "for thirty days after publication, and during that time reprinting is forbidden without credit to the magazine. . . . Then all rights are transferred to the author, and thereafter we have no rights at all" (HLM to Miss Valverda Milliken, June 19, 1929. Copy in P.M.C.). Eventually the thirty-day period was extended to six months.

[29] The regular mailing date was the fifteenth of every month (James Branch Cabell, *Let Me Lie* [New York, 1947], p. 226).

[30] Angoff's *Portrait* emphasizes his independence as an associate on the *Mercury* at the expense of his general docility. He also claims that he sometimes "cut out passages that seemed in especially bad taste" without consulting Mencken ("The Inside View of Mencken's Mercury," *New Republic*, CXXXI [Sept. 13, 1954], 19). He has claimed further that he was sometimes responsible for the printing of liberal articles, such as contributions by Emma Goldman, etc. (interview, Dec. 27, 1958, New York City). Since Mencken was a personal acquaintance and greatly respected Emma Goldman, visiting her in Europe after her deportation, acceptance of her work—none of her contributions were doctrinaire—must not have been difficult. In view of the controversial nature of *Portrait*, Mencken's statement should be given: ". . . he had no control in my time over what went into the magazine" ("Introduction," "The 'Hatrack' Case," I, 101 n.).

THE IRON EDITOR

IF Mencken's attacks on the professors were partly inspired by an eighteenth-century German ancestor's writings, his approach to editing the *Mercury* seems to have been influenced by his great admiration for another German kinsman—Bismarck.[31] He felt that a magazine should be a "dictatorship. . . . [It cannot] be run by a committee or a board of editors. A board of editors only means that [it] satisfies the least civilized on the board, generally a woman or a former minister."[32] It should reflect the prejudices, however violent, of its editor. Nor were the wishes of the readers to be a primary consideration; he viewed polls or surveys as editorial prostitution, and Nathan agreed.[33]

An important factor in his domination of the monthly was his insistence that much of the contents had to be rewritten until it was "an integral part of the expression of his personality."[34] Writers soon learned that the magazine was to be its editor's "mouthpiece"; authors found their manuscripts repeatedly returned until they gave an article the proper slant and salted it with Menckenese.[35] Contributors found their essays graced with German words—a favorite Mencken prose affectation—or pointed up to be more

[31] Mencken collected copies of Johann Burckhard Mencke, *De Charlataneria Eruditorum* . . . (Leipzig, 1715), an erudite professor of history's attack on the "charlatanry of the learned." G. Van Roosbroek, *The Reincarnation of H. L. Mencken* (n.p., 1925), explains the editor's fascination with his ancestor, while Quincy Howe, *A World History of Our Own Times* (New York, 1949), p. 5, tells of the kinship of Bismarck and Mencken. In the early twenties Mencken's room in 1524 Hollins Street was decorated with "pictures of Cabell, Bismarck, and his Leipzig ancestors" (Manchester, *Mencken*, p. 139).

[32] Angoff, *Portrait*, p. 187.

[33] Nathan to HLM, [New York], n.d. Letter printed in *Intimate Notebooks*, pp. 100-101.

[34] Manchester, *Mencken*, p. 153.

[35] "Back the manuscripts would go, again and again, with notes . . . winding up with an embellished request for another try. In the end, authors generally got the idea: everything which came under Mencken's pencil had to have something of him in it before it could get his . . . approval" (*ibid.*, p. 154).

satirical than originally intended.[36] If a writer discovered the changes in time and protested, the changes would be removed, but often the essay had already been printed.[37] Although the *Mercury* was open to all writers, it was more hospitable to those who shared something of its editor's interests, such as Gerald W. Johnson.[38] More meretricious writers, such as Benjamin DeCasseres, who could easily learn the desired formulae, were also in an advantageous position.[39] The editor's departments, including "The Library," the earlier "Clinical Notes," and the editorials, helped strengthen the all-pervading presence of H. L. Mencken. His opinions were nowhere contradicted, since the expressed policy of the monthly was to avoid printing "the other side" of any controversy, whether it be prohibition or literary criticism. In short, critics have agreed that the *Mercury* and its editor were virtually one.[40] Such an intimate relationship between an editor and a quality monthly was unusual, but it was believed that the editor's

[36] Harry Hansen quoted a *Mercury* contributor as follows: " 'I saw my article appear in print colored with such words as privatdozent, geheimrat, bierbruder, and hasenpfeffer, which mystified my friends because I don't know German' " ("Hazlitt for Mencken," *Time,* XXII [Oct. 16, 1933], 43).

[37] "[W]hen the reader began an article by an unknown journalist, he knew in advance not only how it was going to be written but how the fallacy under examination was to be exploded. If young contributors did not adhere to the formula, they were told to, and surprised writers found, upon receiving proofs of their articles, that they had been pointed up to be more devastating than intended. (When they objected, they were permitted to say exactly what they wanted to say)" (Cleaton, *Books & Battles,* p. 187).

[38] Johnson, originally with the Greensboro, North Carolina, *Daily News* and a contributor to Emily Clark's *Reviewer,* caught Mencken's attention and was elevated to the Baltimore *Sun* and the *Mercury.* Johnson, however, felt obliged to deny that he was simply joining a "school," and stated that he would continue to "write of Main Street from his own point of view" (quoted in anon., "Things in General," *Reviewer,* IV [April, 1924], 233).

[39] "[N]o suggestion for a projected article went out without detailed instructions for its writing. When, for example, he asked Benjamin DeCasseres to do a sketch of New York saloons . . . he sent along a complete outline, including the saloons to be discussed, and named specific anecdotes for inclusion" (Manchester, *Mencken,* pp. 153-154).

[40] A sample comment is John E. Drewry, "American Magazines Today," *Sewanee Review,* XXXVI (July, 1928), 349-350: "*The Mercury,* of course, is but an extension and amplification of the personality of H. L. Mencken. . . ." (In Chapter VI of this study, this generally accepted dictum will be modified somewhat.)

personal point of view was what justified the magazine and made it unique.

Before a survey of the early years of the periodical is undertaken, Mencken's basic practicality should be pointed out. Despite an elaborate pose, he had emerged from his *Smart Set* experiences a practical editor. His 1924 request sent to Ellery Sedgwick was probably no more than a kind of compliment: "Have you such a thing as a Style Sheet for the *Atlantic?* The magazine always looks clean and well edited. I have been wobbling along since *The American Mercury* began in a sort of day to day manner."[41] Actually the new monthly showed the labors of a perfectionist who had already helped write two booklets on his editorial technique.[42] Equally misleading was his claim that he "seldom read . . . magazines that touch, in any way, the field" of the *Mercury*;[43] he was more thorough and appreciative as a student of other magazines than his diatribes in the *Smart Set* had hinted.[44] Another sign of astuteness was his ability to avoid for many years the "Comstocks" and other censors. Such survival would not have been remarkable had he printed staid and uncontroversial material, but censors were alert to the *Mercury,* partly because of its running attack on "snouters," "wowsers," and "Pecksniffs." His avoidance of legal interference until 1926 was noteworthy during a period when several magazines were suppressed.[45] (The

[41] HLM to Sedgwick, Dec. 7, 1924. Copy in P.M.C.
[42] *A Personal Word* (New York, 1922) and *Pistols for Two* (New York, 1917), were by Mencken and Nathan in collaboration.
[43] Goldberg, "Notes used . . . [for *The Man Mencken*]," N.Y.M.C., p. 65.
[44] His omnivorous reading of magazines was described in *Prejudices: Fifth Series* (New York, [1926]), pp. 255-262. His judgments were more lenient in 1926 than earlier, and by 1941 he had waxed nostalgic about the very periodicals scored in the *Smart Set* (*Newspaper Days* [New York, 1941], pp. 66-69). During the first years of the *Mercury* he was on friendly terms with several other editors, especially Oswald Garrison Villard of the *Nation*: "I'd rather be editor of the *Nation* than . . . any of the other journals," wrote Mencken in 1925 ("H. L. Mencken on The Nation," reprinted from the Baltimore *Sun* for July 6, 1925, "Pamphlets and Leaflets: H. L. Mencken: 1924-36," E.P.M.C.).
[45] For instance, Malcolm Cowley's and Matthew Josephson's *Broom* was put out of business by the post office early in 1924. The editors, perhaps exhausted by their assaults on Boyd, were unable or unwilling to fight the suppression (Cowley, *Exile's Return*, p. 205).

"Hatrack" episode was an exception to years of caution toward censors.)[46] Most important, however, was his recognition that an audience would respond to his particular variety of irreverent, swashbuckling journalism. He "met a new demand for ideas," and when his "explosive, debunking" *Mercury* became known, buyers appeared in increasing numbers.[47]

THE CIRCULATION, 1924-1925

THE January, 1924, number sold approximately 15,000 copies, and the February number 21,870. The circulation thereafter gradually increased: March, 26,287; April, 36,634; October, 45,561; December, 42,614. In 1925, although "no unusual or sensational methods were employed to put the magazine before the public," the growth continued: January, 44,330; February, 46,505; July, 47,634; August, 51,331; October, 55,084; November, 58,418; December, 62,323.[48] For the period ending June 30, 1924, the official average circulation was 24,367; for the period ending June 30, 1925, 46,679.[49] The monthly, then, increasingly appealed to buyers. A survey of its typical contents, as shaped to its editor's prejudices, will partly show why.

[46] A constant refrain in both his *Smart Set* and *Mercury* correspondence was expressive of this fear, which did not diminish after 1926. Upton Sinclair, planning a new magazine in California, was warned: "You will be barred from the mails if you are not careful" (HLM to Sinclair, Feb. 26, [1930?]. Copy in P.M.C.). But Mencken was also wary for the sake of the *Mercury:* "This is an excellent story, but printing it in this great Christian country, at least in a magazine that goes through the mails, is impossible. The Postoffice wowsers would give three cheers, and declare a public holiday" (HLM to James T. Farrell, Nov. 21, [1932?]. Copy in P.M.C.).

[47] Cecil E. Shuford, "An Evaluation of the Influence of H. L. Mencken and *The American Mercury* upon American Thought," unpublished Master's thesis (Northwestern, 1929), p. 50.

[48] Information from *Three Years,* pp. 8-10.

[49] Ayer's *Directory,* 1925, 1926.

POLITICS: THE COOLIDGE ERA

DEBUNKING and satirical essays constituted about 34 per cent of the contents of the *Mercury* from 1924 to 1929, a relatively high percentage for a serious monthly. These debunking essays were to many readers characteristic of the editor's interest in presenting "the obvious in terms of the scandalous."[50] Although no muckraker, Mencken took a newspaper reporter's delight in exposing, without the slightest belief in the possibility or desirability of reform, the machinations of politicians.[51] His own political theory during the early twenties was that of a "libertarian," a believer in liberty "in its widest imaginable sense—liberty up to the extreme limits of the feasible and tolerable." He was "against forbidding anybody to do anything . . . so long as it was at all possible to imagine a habitable world." "The burden of proof" was said always to rest upon advocates of control, "upon the policeman . . . the lawmaker, the theologian, the right-thinker."[52]

The *Mercury*'s negative politics are best seen in its treatment of Calvin Coolidge, President from 1923 to 1929. When once asked whether he read the *Mercury,* Coolidge said that he did not, as he had heard that it was against him.[53] A look at a single issue, that of August, 1924, gives examples enough to prove the President's analysis correct. The first article, "Mr. Coolidge," by Frank Kent, a political writer for the Baltimore *Sun,* was an indictment of the

[50] Mencken apparently first used this phrase to identify the "general formula of George Bernard Shaw" ("The Ulster Polonius," *SS,* XLIX [Aug., 1916], 138).

[51] Mencken, writing about William Salisbury, defined his own political views as early as 1908: "His philosophy, a sort of aloof pessimism, is unmistakably that of the average reflective journalist. He sees the public as an ass. . . . He sees all this and gently deplores it, but he harbors no fantastic yearnings to reform the world. On the contrary . . ." ("The Good, the Bad, and the Best Sellers," *SS,* XXVI [Nov., 1908], 157).

[52] HLM, "H. L. Mencken," *Nation,* CXVII (Dec. 5, 1923), 647.

[53] Kemler, *Mr. Mencken,* p. 210.

Washington press for its part in keeping "from the people the facts about public men." After a discussion of the tendency of journalists to praise and protect politicians, Kent calls attention to Coolidge, whom he declares to have profited extraordinarily from coddling by reporters:

. . . without it he would long ago have become a sort of sad political joke. Look at the facts for a moment. Here was the dullest and most ignored and obscure Vice-President in history, suddenly pitchforked into the presidency. As Governor of Massachusetts and as Vice-President he had been a laughing stock for those who watched him function—a thoroughly commonplace, colorless person with a neat little one cylinder intellect and a thoroughly precinct mind . . . [a] docile product of the Murray Crane machine. . . . Regularly, the insignificant, insipid, almost meaningless remarks of Mr. Coolidge are vitalized by the correspondents to seem human, forceful, and thoughtful. The inanity and inadequacy of the man are never revealed.

Turning a few more pages of the August, 1924, number, one finds the following "Americana" item:

MASSACHUSETTS

From the learned and distinguished Springfield *Republican*:

A firm belief that Calvin Coolidge became President in accordance with a divine plan and that he should be maintained in office in order that the plan may be carried through forms the keynote of Mayor Edwin F. Leonard's campaign. . . . In the mayor's opinion, any attempt to sidetrack Coolidge now would be a deliberate effort to frustrate the plans of Almighty God and would be attended by certain disaster.

Mencken had no editorial in the August, 1924, issue, but he aired his thoughts in "Utopia No. 7,368," printed in the "Clinical Notes":

At the first election at which the women of America could vote the vast majority of them voted for the late Harding, the most incompetent donkey ever seen in the White House since the dull days between the Jackson dynasty and the Civil War. Now the majority of them are preparing to vote for Coolidge, perhaps the only man in . . . this imperial land of whom it may be said with any plausibility that he is actually worse than Harding.

And again in his "Heroes" essay in the same department: "Is there any sign of superiority in Coolidge?" asked Mencken, and answered that he "is a cheap, sordid, and grasping politician, a seeker of jobs all his life, willing to do almost anything imaginable to get them." In his "Democracy in Practice," also in "Clinical Notes," he asks of the electorate why they have faith "in so transparent and puerile a mountebank as the Hon. Mr. Coolidge?" In "The Inquiring Mind," by Zechariah Chafee, Jr., a Harvard Law School professor, a remark by Coolidge to the Filipinos is criticized. Even in the end-papers, a joint advertisement for the *Nation* and the *Mercury* quotes Mencken: "The *Nation* is a periodical that addressed itself exclusively to the intelligentsia. One could no more imagine a Follies girl reading it than one could imagine a . . . subway ticket-chopper or the Hon. Calvin Coolidge reading it." This sort of criticism, during a period when "Coolidge Prosperity" seemed triumphant and "Silent Cal" enjoyed great esteem, continued, perhaps reaching its climax when Mencken specially commissioned Sinclair Lewis to write "The Man Who Knew Coolidge" in 1927,[54] paying much more than his customary two cents per word for the monologue of a Babbitt who had called on Coolidge in the White House.[55]

Lesser political figures, many of them Democrats, suffered a similar treatment. "Hylan," by William Bullock, published in the April, 1924, *Mercury,* was a portrait of the incumbent mayor of New York City. It is sharply critical of the mayor's political past, tracing his petty skulduggeries before his elevation to the mayoralty by Tammany. Bullock's "Hylan," which avoided the name-calling that marred other

[54] Lewis to Alfred Harcourt, Sept. 30, 1927, Oct. 25, 1927, and Nov. 12, 1927, trace the writing and the editors' reception of the essay (*Letters of Sinclair Lewis,* pp. 251, 255, 258).

[55] Angoff to Singleton, Jan. 11, 1959. Angoff recalls $750.00 as payment for "The Man Who Knew Coolidge."

political studies, is an example of the kind of essay that Angoff claims the *New Yorker* adapted into its well-known "profile."[56] Much of the time the articles on political figures were derogatory. When a "Washington Correspondent" rather cruelly ridiculed Charles Curtis, Vice-President from 1929 until 1933, in an August, 1929, essay, the Vice-President was stung by the sarcastic portrayal and its flippant title: "Heap Big Chief." Curtis, who was of Indian descent, publicly denounced the anonymous author.[57]

Of the political biases of the monthly, none was more prominent or consistent than its opposition to Prohibition. The editor's assumption was that Prohibition, which lasted from 1920 until 1933, was a contemptible effort, largely by rural Methodists and Baptists, to strip the civilized urban man of his liberties. This attitude toward legislated morality, shared by certain other magazine editors, was greatly strengthened in the *Mercury* by Mencken's deep personal nostalgia for the saloon and his antipathy toward snooping and spying among the citizenry. The monthly steadily published frontal attacks such as Clarence Darrow's "The Ordeal of Prohibition," August, 1924; C. W. Alvord's "Musings of an Inebriated Historian," August, 1925; and Raymond Pearl's "Alcohol and the Duration of Life," February, 1924, wherein the biologist stated that "moderate drinkers show a superior average of duration of life as compared with the abstainers." A bootlegger who concealed his identity behind the pseudonym "C. G. John" wrote "Reflections of a Bootician" for the April, 1928, number ("bootician" was a coinage designed to elevate the trade of bootlegging to a level with the newly labeled "beauticians" and "realtors.")[58] It was not surprising that the

---

[56] *Portrait*, p. 10. This claim will be further discussed in Chapter VII, "The *Mercury* as a Journalistic Influence."

[57] "Declares Narrative is Full of Untruths," *New York Times*, July 29, 1929, p. 11, col. 2: "'It is full of willful and deliberate misrepresentations and statements that could be made only by a coward,'" stated Curtis.

[58] Mencken invented the word ("Philological Note," "Clinical Notes," April, 1925).

rumor grew that the *Mercury* was subsidized by the liquor trust.[59]

Other political forces ridiculed by the periodical included the powerful American Legion, as in O. L. Warr's "The Heroes' Union," February, 1928. The Ku Klux Klan, a great force even in non-southern areas in the middle twenties, was opposed, as were more refined societies: the Daughters of the American Revolution were criticized in Margaret Cobb's "The Soviet of Lady Patriots" (September, 1928). In addition to specifically defined issues, such as Prohibition, individual politicians, or organizations, there were a number of satires of political types, such as Harvey Fergusson's "The Washington Job-Holder" (March, 1924) and James M. Cain's "Politician: Female" (November, 1924).

The magazine did view some governmental figures with favor. The most praised living politician was James A. Reed, of Missouri. (Senator Reed was persuaded by Mencken to contribute "The Pestilence of Fanaticism" to the May, 1925, issue.) The rare politician who received favorable treatment should have been gratified; the *Mercury*'s approval was sufficiently brisk and matter-of-fact to be convincing, as in Frank Kent's "Couzens of Michigan," May, 1927, or Duff Gilfond's "LaGuardia of Harlem," June, 1925. These laudatory articles were frequently concerned with figures of the eighteenth and nineteenth centuries. Despite the popular impression that Mencken's monthly sneered at everything, its political enemies of the twenties were often subtly juxtaposed to early Americans. For instance, in the same issue

[59] Upton Sinclair encouraged the rumor: "A second time I was invited, and submitted a sketch of Jack London. . . . this article is full of meat, as interesting a study of a man of letters as the 'American Mercury' has ever published. But it came back; and why? Because the life of Jack London happens to illustrate the devastating effects of alcohol upon genius. . . . My friend Mencken wrote me: 'This magazine is committed to the policy of the return of the American saloon.' I tried to argue with him; surely it is the duty of a wise and tolerant editor to give both sides a hearing. . . . But Mencken answered that the question was one which did not permit of discussion. . . .

"Shall I be crude, and suggest that this editor is subsidized by the liquor interests? I have heard this said, and Mencken has heard it also . . ." (*Money Writes!* [New York, 1927], pp. 34-37). See also Sinclair, *Letters*, pp. 239-241.

with Kent's "Mr. Coolidge" appeared "A Forgotten American Statesman," by Milledge L. Bonham, Jr. The "statesman" therein eulogized was Edward Livingston, the early American jurist. In other articles the founding fathers were presented as socially graceful and as alert politicians, discoveries intended as approval, but often misunderstood by readers to be debunking. Actually Nathan and Mencken thought well of the early Presidents.[60]

Also treated with respect by the *Mercury* was another group of men: the hardy, individualistic, freethinking, free drinking inhabitants of the nineteenth-century city. These cities of the unstandardized old timers, as, for example, Owen P. White's "El Paso" (August, 1924), were wholesomely provided with such physiological outlets as bawdy houses and saloons. The *Mercury* often contrasted the more colorful bygone figures (such as Ward McAllister) with the post-World-War-I American: a standardized boob, without dignity or honor. The reader was, however, not assumed to be indignant at the spectacle, but rather detached and amused.

These were, in brief, the *Mercury*'s chief political contents as molded by its editor's prejudices during its first five years. There were many variations on his basically simple themes, but few contradictions. The results made lively reading.

RELIGION: THE ANTI-PURITAN

A LTHOUGH the political heresies of the monthly might be deplored by many Americans in the mid-twenties, they were, after all, no worse than those of many other magazines. Americans, however, sensed that the monthly, from a religious point of view, was quite diabolic, and this belief gave rise to hysterical opposition.

[60] As in "Editorial," July, 1926.

The assumptions underlying the *Mercury*'s handling of religion were not designed to comfort the orthodox. Mencken was not only completely agnostic in his opinions, but outspokenly so, and his contributors, before the Depression, eagerly orchestrated his robust skepticism. He believed neither in immortality nor in any "higher" purpose inherent in life. Of the supposed benefits of organized Christianity, or any religious group, he was doubtful, especially as he hacked at the Protestants' most ambitious political flower—Prohibition. He was entertained by the naïve and often gross alliance between business and religion so noticeable during the prosperous twenties.

The reader was assumed to be convinced of the soundness of this general approach because he was assumed to be of the minority which held that science had discredited religion, viewed the modernist compromises with hospitality, and considered religious orthodoxy one of the nastier accouterments of "Victorianism." So confident were the contributors of their position that most of the articles about religion were calmly on the offensive, like Arthur Ficke's "Reflections of a Bible-Reader" (March, 1924). Ficke, after discussing the Old Testament, concluded that "the reading of the Bible should be quietly discouraged; and that the ingenuity of our intellectual leaders should be directed toward that end." The freethinking essayist conceded that the Bible should be made "readily available for the scholar."

The various Christian sects were examined, almost always with disrelish. The Methodists, who were held culpable for the rash of morality legislation which followed World War I, were accorded the most severe treatment, as in Herbert Asbury's "Up From Methodism" (February, 1925). Asbury, related to an early Virginia bishop of the Methodist Church, was thoroughly disillusioned with his inherited faith. The Baptists, Lutherans, Mormons, and other sects were found wanting, and the Roman Catholics, despite Mencken and Nathan's agreement that sophisticates did not criticize the Catholic Church,[61] received some attacks. Angoff's "Boston Twilight" (December, 1925) angered the Catholics of Boston, and was said to have contributed toward the Watch and Ward action against the *Mercury* in 1926. The Catholic press, however, had to concede that "Catholics . . . emerge somewhat better than our Protestant brethren"[62] from the scrutiny of the periodical.

Writings by the editors strengthened the other criticisms of religion. As will be seen, Mencken's editorial calls for an anticlerical party, and Nathan's lighter and more urbane comments in his "Clinical Notes," were as influential in defining the *Mercury*'s iconoclasm as the efforts of their worldly contributors. A result of these combined attacks on the religious sentiments held by most Americans was the encouragement of the secular tradition in American thought; also benefited was the Modernist movement, partly defined by such articles as "A New God for America" (March, 1926), by Herbert Parrish, an Episcopal clergyman. Another result was that anti-Fundamentalist freethinkers, such as Maynard Shipley, had a better place to display their articles than the seedy and obscure rationalist publications of the day. The combination of freethinking contributors and editorial jibes at religion helped the *Mercury* to support a lively agnosticism acceptable to many readers, especially

---

[61] The efforts of Mencken and Nathan to change manuscripts so that they would offend Protestants rather than Catholics are traceable in the correspondence printed in *Intimate Notebooks,* pp. 102-106. Mencken's basis for preference of Catholics over Protestants is discussed in "Holy Writ," *SS,* LXXII (Oct., 1923), 141-142. He habitually revised the rough drafts of his "Clinical Notes" so as to soften his criticisms of the Catholic Church, and many instances of revision detrimental to Protestants are to be found in the typescripts:

"Religious Prejudice— . . . The Church bears criticism very badly, and frequently hits below the belt in its rejoinders. This is especially true in America, where the heirarchy [*sic*] is largely made up of low-caste Germans and Irishmen." (This statement was amended to read "men unfamiliar with the punctilio" instead of "low-caste Germans and Irishmen.")

"The Champion— . . . San Francisco, once the home of Mark Twain and Bret Harte, is now ravaged by Prohibition enforcement officers." (Mencken inserted "Baptist dervishes and" before "Prohibition enforcement officers.") ("Clinical Notes: H. L. Mencken: The American Mercury 1924-25," E.P.M.C., pp. 83, 94, 96.)

[62] J. A. Daly, "Mencken and Einstein Look at Religion" (New York, n.d.), p. 7 ("Pamphlets on H. L. Mencken, 1917-30," E.P.M.C.).

college students. It was amusing to examine John Roach Straton's New York Baptist church through the cynical eyes of Stanley Walker ("The Fundamentalist Pope," July, 1926): "The visitor looks about him and perceives that the congregation bears none of the loathsome stigmata of great wealth or high social position. He concludes that they are just folks." Walker ends his account of the outspoken Fundamentalist in a way to please the sophisticated, claiming that New York City would be the poorer without its Straton: "The new Gomorrah loves him in much the same fashion that a smaller town loves and takes pride in the village atheist. He is unusual, and he gives a good show."

The larger urban centers of the United States were undisturbed by the Menckenian panorama of religion as charlatanry, but in less knowing regions the early *Mercury* was said to be "a publication that is usually handed around with fire tongs."[63]

LITERATURE: FICTION

BEFORE 1920 Mencken had often encouraged Theodore Dreiser, Sherwood Anderson, and Sinclair Lewis, partly because of their "realism." Their success, early in the twenties, led the Baltimore critic to celebrate prematurely the obsolescence of the Anglo-Saxon author in America.[64] Present-day opinion is less generous toward Mencken's protégés than that of the twenties, and, moreover, a situation has developed that one Mencken partisan laments: the twenties are today frequently "described in terms of exaggerated and distorted hindsight. . . . many writers have and give the impression that F. Scott Fitzgerald and Ernest

[63] Anon., quoted from *The Mountain View Leader* (California) before 1929, *Menckeniana: A Schimpflexicon*, p. 69.
[64] HLM, "Notes and Queries," *SS*, LXIII (Sept., 1920), 142; "Preface for a collection of American short stories . . ." [unpubl.], "Contributions to Books: H. L. Mencken: Typescripts: 1920-36," E.P.M.C., pp. 62-64.

Hemingway were the most influential writers of those years. Actually, Mencken was a more dominant figure. . . . So also, were Dreiser, Anderson, and Lewis."[65] These shifts in reputation are important in relation to the *Mercury,* not so much because these three writers occasionally appeared in the early years of the monthly, but because Mencken's selection of short stories was shaped by his esteem for their kind of writing, and the most typical contributors of fiction to the *Mercury* were lesser writers who today appear to have been followers of Dreiser, Anderson, and Lewis.

It was such minor figures as Winifred Sanford, Charles Sampson, and Ruth Suckow who wrote the most characteristic "Mercury" fiction before 1929. And if Mencken's estimates of some of them seem too high,[66] tributes to the uniformity of worth in *Mercury* fiction are not wanting: according to Frances Newman, after the "epoch making and rare and valuable first number . . . stories like Sherwood Anderson's and like Ruth Suckow's 'Four Generations' and like Daniel Merrill Anderson's 'Play a Waltz' have been the only stories it has printed."[67] And one critic became so enthusiastic as to claim that Mencken had invented a *"new form of literary magazine,"*[68] although the monthly was simply a general magazine which, if anything, neglected belles-lettres.[69]

[65] James T. Farrell, *Reflections at Fifty and Other Essays* (New York, [1954]), p. 47 n.

[66] "The American short story leads the world; the American etching is rapidly forging to the modern front rank. . . . And to return briefly to the shorter form of fiction, there is not a writer in Europe today doing better work than the American Ruth Suckow" (HLM, "Répétition Générale," *SS,* LXXI [June, 1923], 36).

[67] "The American Short Story in the First Twenty-Five Years of the Twentieth Century," *Bookman,* LXIII (April, 1926), 191.

[68] J. D. Logan, "A Literary Chameleon: A New Estimate of Mr. H. L. Mencken" (Milwaukee, Wis., 1926), p. 19 ("Pamphlets on H. L. Mencken, 1917-30," E.P.M.C.). C. E. Shuford goes to another extreme: "*The American Mercury* usually buys but one short story a month, but that story is of high quality artistically. It is not surprising, however, that it is realistic, and occasionally almost naturalistic" ("An Evaluation of the Influence of H. L. Mencken and *The American Mercury* upon American Thought," pp. 118-119.) Actually, an average of two short stories per issue appeared between 1924 and 1929.

[69] Nathan had wanted a fifty-fifty balance between literature and general

Prospective contributors were often aware of the editor's preference for realism. Dreiser, submitting "The Mercy of God," which appeared in August, 1924, wrote Mencken that the story was "right out of life & should have appealed" to him.[70] When Thomas Wolfe sent sections of *Look Homeward, Angel* to the *Mercury,* hoping that they would be published as short stories before their appearance in the novel, he "deliberately chose for Mr. Mencken scenes that are simply and clearly written, because [he] thought [Mencken] would like these better, but they seem too elementary to the subtle moderns who edit *The Dial.*"[71]

One result of the stress on realism and "slices of life" was that autobiographical essays and fiction were often hard to tell apart. What began as an essay would sometimes blend into fiction, and such "fiction" as Herbert Asbury's famous "Hatrack," printed in April, 1926, was later declared to have been nonfiction.[72] A claim that the periodical used "confession" stories has been made,[73] but these narratives were merely autobiographical sketches by disillusioned people. Mencken had a high regard for the painfully honest biogra-

---

material. Between 1924 and 1929, however, an average of seven times as many general essays as short stories appeared. Of literary folk, Kemler claims that the *Mercury,* "contrary to general opinion . . . was not even literary enough to please them. . . . Behind the scenes there were . . . signs of discontent—Willa Cather, for example—predicted that the *Mercury* would be bankrupt within a few months and advised Knopf to abandon the enterprise entirely" (*Mr. Mencken,* p. 169). Alfred Knopf denies that Willa Cather gave any such advice: ". . . I can assure you that she never expressed any opinion of the prospects of the *Mercury* and certainly did not advise me to abandon it" (Knopf to Singleton, June 2, 1959).

[70] Dreiser to Mencken, May 12, 1924, *Letters of Theodore Dreiser,* II, 426-427.

[71] Wolfe to Madeleine Boyd, Feb. 15, 1929, *The Letters of Thomas Wolfe,* ed. Elizabeth Nowell (New York, [1956]), p. 125. Mencken rejected the manuscript with a polite note.

[72] "Hatrack" was included in *Up from Methodism,* published by Knopf in 1926, as a chapter in Asbury's Autobiography. The *Mercury,* in its legal squabble about the story, emphasized its authenticity.

[73] C. E. Shuford, "An Evaluation of the Influence of H. L. Mencken and *The American Mercury* upon American Thought," p. 92: "The principle back of *Mercurian* 'debunking' is significant. That principle is the old Menckenian skepticism seeking to make a romantic nation turn to realism. In this battle Mencken is clever enough to employ the 'confession story,' the popularity of which elsewhere proves it . . . effective: Herbert Asbury's "Up from Methodism" is perhaps the best example of a *Mercury* Confessional."

phy, but printed no "confessionals" in the sense of those in today's *True Confessions* magazine.[74]

The policy of "discovery," for which the *Mercury* became well known,[75] began early, and stories appeared by James Stevens, formerly a Washington sawmill hand,[76] Winifred Sanford, a housewife from Wichita Falls, Texas,[77] and Robert Joyce Tasker, an inmate of San Quentin Prison.[78] Together with the "discoveries" were a few professionals, such as Chester T. Crowell, but these established writers were usually not sufficiently well paid to compete very fiercely with the amateurs and newspapermen who wrote much of the fiction.[79] Such prominent writers of the twenties as Fitzgerald, Lewis, Cabell, Dreiser, and Anderson contributed not more than two short stories apiece.

Whenever the fiction touched the political or religious realms, it reinforced the magazine's attitudes. Lewis's "The Man Who Knew Coolidge" was no more severe, and far less artful, than Leonard Hall's "The Bishop is Tired," a

[74] Most autobiographical sketches dealt with youth or childhood, and almost all expressed disenchantment with their inherited creed, e.g., Malvina Lindsay's "A Methodist Childhood," Nov., 1929; Neil B. Musser, "A Mormon Boyhood," Jan., 1930; and Samuel Yellen, "A Socialist Boyhood," Oct. 1930.

[75] In one of its early announcements the monthly was advertised under the slogan "Many a talented amateur has had his stuff printed for the first time in The American Mercury" ("The American Mercury Miscellanea, 1923-1933," E.P.M.C.).

[76] "[I]f H. L. Mencken had not hauled me out of the woods I'd still be sweating away there, heaving timber for eight hours a day" (quoted by Jim Tully, *College Humor,* Oct., 1927, n.p. ["Articles about H. L. Mencken: Clippings: 1919-1933," E.P.M.C.]).

[77] Winifred Sanford is the woman described in Angoff, *Portrait,* pp. 111-113. Nothing else is known of the author, whose stories were among the best in the *Mercury.*

[78] Nowhere was Mencken's humanity as an editor more apparent than in his dealings with convicts. He once wrote Tasker the following advice: "You spend too much time thinking about yourself. Give yourself four or five years to get into *The American Mercury* and don't be impatient" (quoted by Jim Tully, *College Humor* (Oct., 1927), n.p. ["Articles About H. L. Mencken: Clippings: 1919-1933," E.P.M.C.]).

[79] When an especially desirable story, such as Jim Tully's "Shanty Irish," was wanted for the magazine, the two cents per word rate was raised: "I got $750 from the *Mercury* for what was used of 'Shanty Irish.' I knew the editors of *Liberty* were Irish and that it would or might please them at three or four times the money, but I thought the *Mercury* was the best show-window, that good work remained and was of definite commercial value later" (Tully to Nathan, n.d., *Intimate Notebooks,* p. 71).

fictional portrayal of an aged Episcopal bishop through his thoughts about his career (December, 1928). The selection of the characteristic *Mercury* material can be traced in the editorial correspondence: "unfortunately, this story is a bit too sentimental for the American Mercury . . .";[80] "an imaginary visit of Jesus would not fit into The American Mercury,"[81] etc. The prospective contributor was encouraged to send fiction that dealt realistically with some segment of life, however homely, that the author knew well. Above all, the writer was cautioned to avoid "rubber stamp" characterizations, surprise endings, and other stereotypes.[82]

In general, the fiction in the early *Mercury* was rarely very imaginative. Instead, most of the stories were quietly realistic selections from the personal experiences of minor writers, writers whose heads no longer show above the waters now that Lewis, Anderson, and Dreiser are submerged up to their necks. Yet the "middle minority" to whom the periodical was directed was satisfied. The subordination of fiction to essays, the dearth of imaginative and romantic fiction, and the comparative absence of "big names" seemed like small prices to pay for the realistic tour of America that was conducted. As for Mencken, his interest in creative writing continued to diminish after 1924, but his monthly's success was partly based on the respectable, though rarely brilliant, fiction which it printed.

[80] HLM to Bob Brown, March 15, 1930. Letter in N.Y.M.C.

[81] HLM to ——— Lowman, Aug. 10, 1928. Letter in N.Y.M.C. (The editor had earlier asked Lowman to write something for the periodical: "We pay enormous honoraria" (Dec. 23, [1927?]. Letter in N.Y.M.C.).

[82] Mencken denied that Poe invented the short story form, and Bret Harte was blamed for "all the dull mechanics who now fill the cheap American magazines with short stories so trite, so nearly alike and so obvious." O. Henry was found a bad influence because of his surprise endings ("Preface for a collection of American short stories . . . [unpubl.], "Contributions to Books: H. L. Mencken: Typescripts: 1920-36," E.P.M.C., pp. 59-61).

LITERATURE: POETRY AND DRAMA

MENCKEN's attitude toward poetry explains the failure of the *Mercury* to publish much good verse. The editor only reluctantly decided to print any poetry in the new journal. One of his reasons for his decision appears cynical: "It tones up the magazine . . . and we need tone to get away with the rough stuff."[83] An average of about two poems per issue appeared during the first five years, and many of these poems recalled those of the *Smart Set* because of their conservatism in form and content.[84]

The editor made no secret of his conservative attitude, giving, in the Chicago *Sunday Tribune* in 1924, a compact statement of his ideas.[85] He believed that his position was "simply poll-parroting, of course, though in less decorous terms, Matthew Arnold, Johann Wolfgang Goethe and all the other old masters,"[86] although his opinions were sometimes more worthy of the popular Eddie Guest, who was often ridiculed in the *Mercury*.

With such a romantic theory, in an editor whose approval was necessary for every accepted poem, it was not

[83] Angoff, *Portrait*, p. 84.

[84] Dolmetsch ("History of the *Smart Set*," p. 91) describes the verse in the review as "curiously old-fashioned in its adherence to traditional lyric forms and its insistence on statement rather than suggestion."

[85] The pre-World War I new poetry revival was seen as quite over. In fact, poetry was less inhibited in 1885 than in 1924 because of the "imbecility" of the Greenwich Village revolt against form: "the poet is strictly forbidden to use any of the traditional materials of his craft. . . . He must eschew rhyme, he must eschew all regular rhythms, and he must eschew all direct attack upon the emotions. In other words, he must eschew poetry." The poetry of the day was considered "bizarre, unearthly," and "too cerebral." "Poetry has nothing to do with the intellect," but rather should "conceal and obliterate harsher realities." Concluding that poetry should reach "the generality of the literate," he damns the "intellectual aristocracy" who "detach themselves from the ordinary flow of American ideas." Except for a few "old fashioned poets, notably Miss Reese and Miss Teasdale," "the real poetry of our era has been written, not by poets at all but by. . . . the earnest rhetoricians who roam the chautauquas and the Kiwanis clubs, waving the banner of idealism" ("Poetry in America," Chicago *Sunday Tribune*, Nov. 30, 1924, Part Five, p. 1, cols. 1-2).

[86] "Notices of Books," *SS*, LXXI (June, 1923), 140.

surprising that little experimental poetry was printed. Toward the younger professional poets, the *Mercury* was usually only polite. Babette Deutsch, becoming known in 1926 as a promising young poet, was invited to submit, not poetry, but rather a prose essay entitled "The Plight of the Poet" (May, 1926). The magazine was more hospitable toward amateurs whose brief lyrics could be assembled into regional symposiums, and nearly a quarter of the early *Mercury*'s verse was written by such unknowns as those who appeared in "Oklahoma Poets" (May, 1926) or "Oregon Poets" (November, 1926).

Several better-known poets occasionally made an appearance, including Carl Sandburg, Edgar Lee Masters, and Vachel Lindsay. But their offerings were not large, and often these offerings represented their weaker performances. This latter limitation was especially true of Masters' verse; he found it impossible to match his earlier *Spoon River Anthology* accomplishment.[87] Almost all of Masters' poetry printed in the review appeared in 1925 under the general title of "Lichee-Nut Poems" (January, 1925) and "More Lichee-Nut Poems" (June, 1925). Thereafter his *Mercury* writings showed more interest in reminiscence, and after 1926 he subsided largely into prose. Lindsay's "The Trial of the Dead Cleopatra" (August, 1924) and "The Virginians Are Coming Again" (July, 1928) were his only verse contributions. The first poem was an eight-page review of Cleopatra's life; the second was an attack on the spirit of Babbittry. Sandburg's "M'Liss and Louie" (July, 1924), "Santa Fé Sketches" (March, 1927), "Many Hats" (August, 1928), and "Destroyers," "Foolish About Windows," "Epistle," and "Baby Boy" (October, 1928), showed a diminishing talent. The best of these poems were perhaps "Sante Fé Sketches"; the weakest were those in the October, 1928 number.

[87] Mencken was forced to admit the decline in "The Library," June, 1924, and Oct., 1925.

The most uniformly successful poems in the *Mercury* were the literary ballads. The editor responded to the strong rhythms and simple narratives of his friend George Sterling, his "discovery" John McClure, and Stanley Vestal, Edwin Markham, and James Weldon Johnson. Sterling's amusing "Ballad of the Swabs" (October, 1925) was followed by "The Ballad of the Ghost-Arrow" (February, 1927). Nearly as accomplished were Vestal's "Ballads of Kit Carson" (July, 1925). McClure's ballads included the "Rhymes of Gay Thomas" (November, 1925) and "Three Poems" (April, 1927), but he shared Masters' decline into prose, and before long was writing essays in dialogue, such as "Ballad Making" (February, 1928). "The Ballad of the Gallows-Bird," by Edwin Markham, had been rejected by Mencken before the arrival of Angoff. After the new managing editor heard of the manuscript, he traveled over to its author's Staten Island residence and retrieved it. After some editing, the ten-page ballad was printed in August, 1926. The gothic narrative often echoes Coleridge's *Ancient Mariner,* but Markham's unrelentingly bitter theme is also suggestive of Ambrose Bierce. The hero stabs an enemy and is caught and hanged, but, finding himself apparently alive, slips to the ground and experiences a long, nightmarish odyssey which ends back at his gallows, where he discovers himself swinging, and realizes that he was a damned spirit. Markham's ballad is too long and only intermittently successful, but it was more imaginative and ambitious than most of the poems in the *Mercury.* James Weldon Johnson's "Go Down, Death!" was, however, perhaps the most striking poem to appear in the monthly. Johnson, a Negro, described the death of a Negress and her ascension with the help of a "personified" Death sent by God.

Still, the verse was usually not remarkable, and the editorial of December, 1928, devoted to summarizing and celebrating the fifth anniversary of the *Mercury,* was obliged to describe the monthly's poetic accomplishment with relative modesty: "The magazine, more than once, has printed passable poetry. It will print better when better is written."

As for drama, after the publication of O'Neill's "All God's Chillun Got Wings" (February, 1924), a justly famous drama on miscegenation, almost no more plays were printed. There were a few short pieces by James M. Cain, including "Servants of the People" (April, 1925), "The Hero" (September, 1925), "Trial by Jury" (January, 1928), and "Theological Interlude" (July, 1928). Even more "hard-boiled" than these trim little dialogues was Robert Blake's "The Law Takes Its Toll" (July, 1929). Its author, a condemned convict, set down as exactly as possible the conversation of his fellow prisoners in the cells of the condemned. Blake was himself executed one week after completing the stark drama.[88]

"THE LIBRARY"

AFTER the first few numbers, Mencken carried on his book review department without outside help. The books selected were varied; certainly, despite the frequent reviewing of Knopf's books, the claim that the *Mercury* was a Knopf "house organ" was false.[89] The works discussed in "The Library" were not very often literary, for, as Ernest Boyd wrote in 1925, the "new trend in Mr. Mencken's interests" caused belles-lettres to be "relegated to the background, and both his editorials and his critical articles [to be] concerned with ideas rather than with pure literature."[90] His reviews had never been self-consciously

[88] "The Law Takes Its Toll" was eventually dramatized as "The Last Mile," by John Wexley (Lawrence E. Spivak, *The American Mercury Reader: A Selection of Distinguished Articles, Stories, and Poems Published in The American Mercury During the Past 20 Years, 1924-1944*, ed. Lawrence E. Spivak and Charles Angoff [New York, 1944], p. 42 n.). Hereinafter cited as *The Mercury Reader*.

[89] Leon Whipple, "The Revolution on Quality Street, Part II," *Survey*, LVII (Jan. 1, 1927), 427.

[90] Ernest Boyd, *H. L. Mencken* (New York, 1925), p. 81.

"literary"; in fact, there was persistent questioning whether he was a critic at all.[91] His book review department showed him primarily a critic of ideas. Books brought ideas into "The Library," and the reviewer would state them, then evaluate them. Because poorer books made a more entertaining show, they often received the most lingering attention. Mencken's comments did not amount to a formal, objective review in many instances, and efforts to endow him with an erudite or systematic approach have not been convincing.[92] Sometimes one is reminded of an early warning addressed to him regarding his impressionistic criticism: "Don't write so much about yourself. Stick to the books."[93]

His lack of interest in creative literature was shown by the great amount of attention given books treating political, religious, psychological, medical, and journalistic subjects. After a three-page long attack on an apparently dull book concerned with journalistic ethics (July, 1925), Fitzgerald's *The Great Gatsby* received only a few perfunctory remarks. After five pages of commentary about books on politics and

---

[91] Stuart Sherman once observed that the "unsympathetic person might say" of Mencken's writing that "it is not criticism at all, but mere scurrility and blackguardism" ("Beautifying American Literature," *Nation*, CV [Nov. 29, 1917], 594). Louis Bromfield also denied that the editor was a critic, "believing him far more a politician" ("The New Yorker," *Bookman*, LXI [July, 1925], 582). Edmund Wilson found him "perhaps a prophet rather than a critic" ("The All-Star Literary Vaudeville," *New Republic*, XLVIII [June 30, 1926], 159); but the less generous John Farrar had a lower estimate: he cannot "by any stretch of the imagination be called a literary critic. He is purely and simply a mustard plaster!" ("Mustard Plaster Mencken," *Bookman*, LXIV [Dec., 1926], 389). Benjamin DeCasseres made another effort: "He is not a critic at all. He is an advocate, a prosecuting attorney" (*Mencken and Shaw*, p. 92).

[92] One such effort is Ivan J. Kramoris, "The Principles of Literary Criticism of H. L. Mencken," unpublished master's thesis (Marquette University, Milwaukee, Wis., 1928). More illuminating is the judgment of William Manchester, Jr., "A Critical Study of the Work of H. L. Mencken as Literary Critic for the Smart Set Magazine, 1908-1914," unpublished master's thesis (University of Missouri, 1947), which concludes: "The most impressive characteristics of Mencken's early [criticism are] its obviousness, its tenacity, and its complete lack of elasticity" (p. 212). Also suggestive is Goldberg's claim that "after you strip Mencken of such externalities as sociological, political and philosophical wrappings, you find in him essentially the creative critic . . . who creates his works out of other men's books" (*The Man Mencken*, p. 251).

[93] Anon. letter, reprinted in Mencken, "Novels Bad, Half Bad, and Very Bad," *SS*, XXXVIII (Nov., 1912), 153.

religion (October, 1924), the reader finds a mere announcement of Shaw's *Saint Joan*. Despite his pioneering study of
Shaw, Mencken was content to hold his review to one
sentence: "The Old Master, at 68, breaks out with one of the
best plays that he has done since 'Caesar and Cleopatra,'
and the best preface, by long odds, since that to 'Androcles
and the Lion.'" There was, however, more elaborate praise
of his friend Sinclair Lewis, whose *Babbitt* was declared
"the very model of a modern novel." *Arrowsmith* was approved (April, 1925), as was *Elmer Gantry* (April, 1927).
Herbert Read, commenting on an exchange copy of that
number sent to the office of Eliot's *Criterion,* was startled:
"Mr. Mencken goes plump off into the deep end for
'Elmer Gantry,' without a thought of literary standards."[94]
The editor's enthusiasm for *Elmer Gantry* was significant: "Here is a truly immense accumulation of observation. . . . The labor of putting all that stuff together
must have been enormous. . . . No other American novelist
. . . has ever come to closer grips with the essential Americano, or depicted him with more ferocious brilliancy. . . .
His colleagues spend themselves upon riddles of personality.
He depicts a civilization." The same premises underlay his
repeated praise of Ring Lardner, who was hailed in June,
1926, because "his portrait gallery is as extensive as Sinclair
Lewis's. . . . He is trying to do something that no other
fictioneer has tried to do. Without wasting any wind upon
statements of highfalutin aesthetic or ethical purpose, he is
trying to get the low-down Americano between covers."
(Lardner appreciated the approval of both Mencken and
Nathan, but found, ironically enough, that his efforts to
"crash the *Mercury*" were futile.)[95]

There were only isolated protests against Mencken's

[94] "Foreign Reviews: American Periodicals," *Criterion,* VI (Dec., 1927). I am
indebted to Sir Herbert Read for the identification of several contributors to
Criterion who discussed the *Mercury* in unsigned departments and essays.
[95] Donald Elder, *Ring Lardner: A Biography* (Garden City, N. Y., 1956),
pp. 368, 371.

theories of fiction before 1927,[96] and only a few complaints about his more obvious prejudices, such as the anti-English bias that led him to underestimate severely the works of Katherine Mansfield.[97] His reviews of poetry, at the height of the resurgence of American poetry during the mid-twenties, were usually unappreciative: in an October, 1925, review of twenty-nine volumes of verse he confessed to boredom, announcing that "we are passing into an era of flabby stuff . . . the fine frenzy which seized the poet fifteen years ago has spent itself." Much of the review was dedicated to a celebration of the good old days.[98] Even his benevolent reviews of poetry seemed off-hand, as when he cryptically examined sixty-one volumes of verse in the June, 1926, issue.

Many of his "reviews" were frank efforts to amuse the reader, and for these purposes inferior works, preferably by

[96] For instance, Isabel Paterson, "Reading with Tears," *Bookman,* LXIV (Oct., 1926), 196: "A 'character' tends to become a 'case.' H. L. Mencken is so immersed in this fascinating job of noting and classifying specimens of a genus that he has actually forgotten, if he ever knew, the elementary distinction between a 'character' and a 'type.' With magnificent unreason, he demands that the novelists create characters, and suggests types for them to draw from! He says that 'a first rate novel is always a character sketch, of an individual . . . Becky Sharp. And then he proposes that something . . . be done with 'the American University President, politician . . .' and a dozen other—types! Is it possible that Mr. Mencken thinks Thackeray meant Becky Sharp as a composite portrait of an English governess?"

[97] "All sorts of third-rate stuff is dumped upon the . . . Yankee by English log-rollers. I . . . point to the short stories of Katherine Mansfield. A few years ago all the literati who tour our bucolic women's clubs were speaking of them with bated breath. The plain fact is that most of them were as hollow as jugs. Their people were simply animated sticks. All the 'profound' observation in them was imaginary. . . . Who reads the stories of Miss Mansfield today? The same persons who also read William. J. Locke" (Dec., 1925). In the December, 1925, *Bookman* was also a reply by Mencken to Hugh Walpole's recent defense of Katherine Mansfield and English writing. Walpole, writing of an earlier attack by Mencken had charged: "If you think [Mansfield's] short stories to be as 'devoid of genuine imaginative passion as so many bond circulars' then I tell you (and here there is a personal assertion naked and unashamed) you don't know what genuine imaginative passion is" ("My Dear Mencken," *Bookman,* LXII [Nov., 1925], 248).

[98] "It was something of an adventure . . . even so lately as five years ago— to review the current verse. There was an immense earnestness in it, and a great deal of originality, some of it almost hair-raising. Sandburg's yawp resounded through the land, and the deep bellow of Masters, and Amy's shrill hullabaloo, and Vachel Lindsay's jazzy tunes, and Frost's melancholy moans. . . . And in the rubbish there were some pearls.

"But I can find none in the volumes now under review. . . . the old glow is gone."

eminent but aged professors, were admirably suited. The best of these tours de force, such as his review of Henry van Dyke's *Six Days of the Week: A Book of Thoughts About Life and Religion*,[99] were collected and reprinted in the *Prejudices*. In fact, the more foolish the book, the more delightedly the editor toyed with it, stunning it, batting it about, like a cat with a mouse, before dispatching it.[100] It was only rarely that he would arouse his waning literary enthusiasms and remembrances to write such reviews as those in the April, 1925, number. In that issue he discussed three recent works on Joseph Conrad with a persuasive show of authority. There followed a review of Lewis's *Arrowsmith* which was illumined by genuine interest. The last review was of *Barrett Wendell and His Letters,* by M. A. D. Howe. Wendell had been a Harvard professor, which fact opened him to the possibility of irreverent jocosities, but Mencken's essay is a surprisingly mellow and informed tribute. He was most predictably cordial when reviewing autobiographies, and he frequently lauded that literary

[99] The review of March, 1925, begins:

I offer a specimen:
As living beings we are part of a universe of life.
A second:
Unless we men resolve to be good, the world will never be better.
A third:
Behind Christianity there is Christ.
A fourth:
If Washington had not liberated the American Republic, Lincoln would have had no Union to save.
A fifth:
Some people say that a revolution is coming on in our own age and country. It is possible.
A sixth:
God made us all.
A seventh:
It is a well-known fact that men can lie, and that very frequently they do.

After quoting Van Dyke's declaration that "a whole life spent with God is better than half a life" and that "anything out of the ordinary line will attract notice," the reviewer concluded: "Tupper *est mort! Hoch* Tupper! *Hoch, hoch! Dreimal hoch!*"

[100] A three-page-long review of Wilbur Abbott's *The New Barbarians* (May, 1925), begins: "It would be easy to poke fun at this disorderly and indignant tract; even, perhaps, to denounce the learned author, in a lofty manner, as a mere cream-puff. His argument, at more than one place, is so shaky that it tempts ribaldry with a powerful lure, almost a suction," etc.

form.[101] The most sordid life story he considered an achievement somehow notable.[102]

But in general one wonders, in view of the lack of sensitive and concerned literary analysis, the reliance on such journalistic phraseology as "the deep bellow of Masters" and "Frost's melancholy moans," and the consistent emphasis on books that lent themselves to ridicule or jest, how a literary history of 1931 could end with the following announcement: "The most influential practitioner of the critical art from 1920-1930 was H. L. Mencken. . . . by far the most influential literary critic in the American field."[103]

Mencken was a prominent critic partly because the literary analysis in "The Library" was not the basic charm of that department. Most of the books reviewed were non-literary, and yet the discussions of these other works invoked great interest, first, because Mencken discoursed freely in what was considered "the most forceful prose style now written in English."[104] Second, in addition to his lively prose, he had an impressive general grasp of the American scene. Third, what he lacked in subtlety was more than

[101] "Who ever heard of a bad autobiography? That is, a bad *honest* one? I can scarcely imagine it. Even the story of . . . a bookkeeper chained to his stool . . . done simply and with candor, would hold the reader as no novel save the best could hold him. For there is a dreadful fascination about the truth. It alarms and annoys the absurd bladders who rove and pollute the earth . . . but at the same time it arrests and enchants them. They simply cannot resist it, hideous though it be" (Nov., 1926).

[102] An autobiography by Gertrude Beasley, entitled *My First Thirty Years* and published in Paris because of the fear of censorship, had a vivid portrait of her mother: "The old woman is done unsparingly and almost appallingly. We are made privy to her profound and bellicose ignorance, her incurable frowsiness, her banal pride in her obscure and ignoble family, her frantic hatred of her recreant husband's relatives, her lascivious delight in witless and malicious scandal-mongering. But there is something heroic in her, too. Her struggle to cadge a living for her squirming litter takes on a quality that is almost dignity. She is shrewd, unscrupulous, full of oblique resource. Her battles with her husband, and particularly with him in his capacity as chronic father, often have gaudy drama in them. Consider her final and only effective device for birth control: a loaded shot-gun beside her bed! One longs to meet the old gal, and shake her red hand. She is obscene, but she is also curiously admirable" (Jan., 1926).

[103] Russell Blankenship, *American Literature as an Expression of the National Mind* (New York, [1931]), pp. 723-724.

[104] F. Scott Fitzgerald, "How to Waste Material: A Note on My Generation," *Bookman*, LXIII (May, 1926), 263.

balanced, in the eyes of many of his contemporaries, by a
Rabelaisian acceptance of the libertarian beliefs then typical
of intellectuals.[105] Consider, for example, his defense of
science, in a decade when science enjoyed very high prestige,
against the strictures of a moralist fearful of its encroach-
ments. C. E. Ayre's lamentations in his *Science: The False
Messiah* were humorously paraphrased by the reviewer:
"What if the electron reveals itself as a speck of vacuum
performing a witless and eternal Charleston? What if
epinephrin is synthesized, and even Gordon gin?" Psychology, especially the behaviorist school, has "turned Man
into a teetotum, not unlike the electron." "Nothing in any
of these triumphs of science," admitted the reviewer, "will
help a man to determine whether, having $50 to invest, he
will do better to put it in the missionary box or buy some
worthy girl a pocket-flask and a set of necking tools." A
paean to science was then gradually unfolded, and jibes
were made at metaphysicians, philosophers, and moralists;
science was exalted as "amoral by its very nature: the minute
it begins separating facts into the two categories of good
ones and bad ones it ceases to be science and becomes a mere
nuisance, like theology."[106] Equally entertaining were brisk
descriptions of the "good old days" scattered in the book
reviews.[107] And liberals must have found palatable the

---

[105] A summary of these beliefs is in Frederick Lewis Allen's *Only Yesterday*,
pp. 165-168.

[106] September, 1927. In December of 1927 Edmund Wilson challenged
Mencken as an arbiter of science and poetry: "The new 'Prejudices' [Sixth
Series] include . . . the usual animadversions on poetry—which, as usual, is
described as a mellifluous lie designed to console us for the ghastly reality.
Mencken elsewhere in the same volume confesses an inability to take philosophy
seriously; and his incapacity for dealing with even the simplest philosophical
problems—that is, his incapacity for rigorous and subtle thinking—is actually
his principal, and serious, weakness. . . . One was about to say that Mencken's
scientific ideas were old-fashioned; but the fact is that there has never been a
period when the profounder men of science held the views which Mencken
takes for granted as unassailable premises" ("Cabell and Colloids," *New
Republic*, LIII [Dec. 7, 1927], 75).

[107] "It was the end of the Civil War that started the great show, and it went
on in ever-increasing *crescendo* for thirty years—a whole generation. Then,
suddenly and as if by some unintelligible act of God, there came a halt and a
reconsideration—and *Katzenjammer* followed. The American people, it seems
to me, have never been genuinely happy since. Today they are rich, and if the

championship of native liberalism in the South in reviews attacking staid professors and celebrating progressive ones.[108] In short, Mencken usually editorialized more than he reviewed.

"CLINICAL NOTES" AND EDITORIALS

THE "Clinical Notes" department was originally conducted jointly by Mencken and Nathan, but Mencken's last contribution was printed in the July, 1925, number, and thereafter the department was written by Nathan until its abandonment in 1930. As their contributions were not signed, it has hitherto been necessary for critics to guess the authorship of notes before August, 1925.[109]

Mencken's brief essays and comments in the "Clinical Notes" ranged from miniature editorials to brief epigrams. Like reviews from "The Library," some of them were revised and issued in his *Prejudices*. His eighty-odd contributions were rarely as light and witty as Nathan's, but they often showed ingenuity. Many of his notes were the result

---

laws are to be believed they are virtuous, but all the old goatish joy has gone out of their lives. Compare Coal Oil Johnny to young John D. Rockefeller. Compare Jim Fiske to the current J. Pierpont Morgan. Or General Nelson A. Miles to General Pershing. Or Chester A. Arthur to the dull and preposterous Coolidge. Or even Anthony Comstock to his unhappy heirs and assigns. Something is surely missing. Life among us is no longer the grand and dazzling adventure it once was. The Americano no longer dances gorgeously with arms and legs. He has become civilized, which is to say, he has joined a country club. His father roared in the stews and saloons" (July, 1926).

[108] Edwin Mims's *The Advancing South* was an excuse for an essay on the South (August, 1926) in which Mims is sharply criticized. Howard W. Odum's *Rainbow Round My Shoulder* provided an occasion for a panegyric of the professor in the University of North Carolina (September, 1928). Mencken persistently praised the University of North Carolina as "by long odds the most enterprising and ambitious of all Southern institutions of learning. It has somehow managed to throw off the pox of barnyard theology that menaces most of the other colleges in the Confederate States" (Oct., 1926).

[109] Some critics, unfortunately, have guessed badly. For instance, Alfred Kazin, in his *On Native Grounds* (Garden City, N. Y., 1956), p. 158, quotes *Nathan's* "The Smart American Taste" (Sept. 1924) to help show how frivolous was *Mencken*. A list of Mencken's contributions to "Clinical Notes" is to be found in my "History of the *American Mercury* under the Editorship of Henry Mencken, 1924 to 1933," pp. 386-387.

of humorous reflection on philological matters, such as "Give a Dog, Etc.," which deplored the change of the name "Bohemia" to the more cacophonous "Czecho-Slovakia" (March, 1924). Others of the notes were anti-Christian, like the "Definition" printed in April, 1924: "Christendom may be defined briefly as that part of the world in which, if any man stands up in public and solemnly swears that he is a Christian, all his auditors will laugh"—a remark reminiscent of Ambrose Bierce. Equally cynical was his essay about the motives that induce young men to become clergymen ("The Ghostly Fraternity," June, 1924). Several of the notes are romantic appreciations of sea-borne bootleggers, who are praised for giving a refuge to Liberty after she was driven from the land by the "Methodist White Terror" ("The New Galahad," April, 1924). A variant on this theme appeared in February, 1925, entitled "Misfits": "What superb sailors for the American fleet the daring fellows of Rum Row would make, and how beautifully some of the current admirals of the Navy would fit into the pants business!"

Some positive suggestions were thrown out, including "Needed Books" (May, 1924), "Literary Tip" (December, 1924), and "Market Tip" (June, 1924). A plea in favor of plastic surgery included a characteristic dig at Prohibition:

If the Hippocratic Oath obliges a surgeon to trephine the skull of a Prohibition enforcement officer who has fallen a victim to the just wrath of a *posse comitatus,* then why should it forbid him to relieve the agony of a young woman whose nose, in saggital section, is like a clam shell, or whose ears stick out like studding sails? . . . nothing, it must be obvious, is more depressing than the spectacle of a human virgin without physical charm. She is a walking futility; a tragedy in one long, lugubrious act.[110]

Occasionally a note would concern the social scene, as in "The Master Illusion" (March, 1925):

In America servants are seldom servile, and when they are they are almost always foreigners—and their masters are Episcopalians

[110] May, 1924.

who were hard-shell Baptists until 1917. When I go into a house, and the door-opener inquires affably how my rheumatism is coming along and tells me what his sister's husband's aunt took for hers, I am always certain, at least, of one thing: that the mistress of the mansion was born a lady. When the fellow cringes I never mention anything, at dinner, that happened before the year 1900. Nor do I venture to discuss Methodism, cabbage or the pants business.

The "Clinical Notes" of Mencken showed him in a relaxed mood, writing to amuse himself as well as his readers.

The editorials, however, showed the editor at his most combative and audacious, and represented, early in the history of the *Mercury,* both his best and his worst writing. Several of his best-known editorials were cruelly satirical, and others were stinging attacks on citadels cherished by many of his countrymen. Perhaps the most severe editorial was an obituary of William Jennings Bryan, whom Mencken had observed at the Scopes trial when reporting the affair for the Baltimore *Sun.* Since it helped contribute to the popular image of the *Mercury,* the editorial should be amply quoted:

Has it been marked by historians that the late William Jennings Bryan's last secular act on this earth was to catch flies? A curious detail, and not without its sardonic overtones. He was the most sedulous flycatcher in American history, and by long odds the most successful. His quarry, of course, was not *Musca domestica* but *Homo neandertalensis.* For forty years he tracked it with snare and blunderbuss, up and down the backways of the Republic. Wherever the flambeaux of Chautauqua smoked and guttered, and the bilge of Idealism ran in the veins, and Baptist pastors dammed the brooks with the saved, and men gathered who were weary and heavy laden, and their wives who were unyieldingly multiparous and full of Peruna—there the indefatigable Jennings set up his traps and spread his bait. He knew every forlorn country town in the South and West, and he could crowd the most remote of them to suffocation by simply winding his horn. The city proletariat, transiently flustered by him in 1896, quickly penetrated his buncombe and would have no more of him; the gallery jeered him at every Democratic national

convention for twenty-five years. But out where the grass grows
high, and the horned cattle dream away the lazy days, and men
still fear the powers and principalities of the air—out there between the corn-rows he held his old puissance to the end. There
was no need of beaters to drive in his game. The news that he
was coming was enough. For miles the flivver dust would
choke the roads. . . .

There was something peculiarly fitting . . . that his last days
were spent in a one-horse Tennessee village, and that death found
him there. The man felt at home in such scenes. He liked people
who sweated freely, and were not debauched by the refinements
of the toilet. Making his progress up and down the Main street
of little Dayton, surrounded by gaping primates from the up-
land valleys of the Cumberland Range, his coat laid aside, his
bare arms and hairy chest shining damply, his bald head
sprinkled with dust—so accoutred and on display, he was obviously happy. He liked getting up early in the morning, to the tune
of cocks crowing on the dunghill. He liked the heavy, greasy
victuals of the farmhouse kitchen. He liked . . . all country
people. I believe that this liking was sincere—perhaps the only
sincere thing in the man. His nose showed no uneasiness when
a hillman in faded overalls and hickory shirt accosted him on
the street, and besought him for light upon some mystery of
Holy Writ. The simian gabble of a country town was not gabble
to him, but wisdom of an occult and superior sort. In the presence of city folks he was palpably uneasy. Their clothes, I suspect,
annoyed him, and he was suspicious of their too delicate manners. He knew all the while that they were laughing at him—if
not at his baroque theology, then at least at his alpaca pantaloons.
But the yokels never laughed at him. . . . His place in the Tennessee hagiocracy is secure. If the village barber saved any of his
hair, then it is curing gall-stones down there today.

II

But what label will he bear in more urbane regions? One,
I fear, of a far less flattering kind. Bryan lived too long, and descended too deeply into the mud, to be taken seriously hereafter
by fully literate men, even of the kind who write school-
books. . . . He was born with a roaring voice, and it had the trick
of inflaming halfwits. . . . What moved him, at bottom, was
simply hatred of the city men who had laughed at him so

long. . . . He went far beyond the bounds of any merely religious frenzy, however inordinate. When he began denouncing the notion that man is a mammal even some of the hinds at Dayton were agape. And when, brought upon Darrow's cruel hook, he writhed and tossed in a very fury of malignancy, bawling against the baldest elements of sense and decency like a man frantic—when he came to that tragic climax there were snickers among the hinds as well as hosannas.

Upon that hook, in truth, Bryan committed suicide, as a legend as well as in the body. He staggered from the rustic court ready to die, and he staggered from it ready to be forgotten, save as a character in a third-rate farce, witless and in execrable taste.

Toward the end of the editorial, Mencken discussed Bryan's legacy to his native land:

Heave an egg out of a Pullman window, and you will hit a Fundamentalist almost anywhere in the United States today. They swarm in the country towns, inflamed by their pastors, and with a saint, now, to venerate. They are thick in the mean streets behind the gas-works. They are everywhere that learning is too heavy a burden for mortal minds, even the vague, pathetic learning on tap in little red schoolhouses. They march with the Klan, with the Christian Endeavor Society, with the Junior Order of United American Mechanics, with the Epworth League, with all the rococo bands that poor and unhappy folk organize to bring some light of purpose into their lives.

The Bryan editorial, which appeared in October, 1925, attracted attention, but should not have surprised *Mercury* readers, who had read comparable editorials before. In March, 1924, the farmer was attacked in language as extravagant as that used in the Bryan essay. Mencken protested the rural "jehad against what remains of American intelligence, already beleaguered in a few walled towns." The desire of country people to impose the "Wesleyan code of rural Kansas and Mississippi" is described as

. . . a Utopia dreamed by seven millions of Christian husbandmen, far-flung in forty-eight sovereign States. They dream it on their long journeys down the twelve billion furrows of their seven million farms, up hill and down dale in the heat of the day. They dream it behind the stove on winter nights, their boots off and their socks scorching, Holy Writ in their hands. They dream it as they commune with *Bos taurus, Sus scrofa, Mephitis mephitis,* the Methodist pastor, the Ford agent. It floats before their eyes as they scan the Sears-Roebuck catalogue for horse liniment, porous plasters and Bordeaux mixture; it rises before them when they assemble in their Little Bethels to be instructed in the Word of God, the plots of the Pope, the crimes of atheists and Jews. . . . This Utopia haunts and tortures them; they long to make it real. They have tried prayer, and it has failed; they now turn to the secular arm. The dung-fork glitters in the sun as the host prepares to march. . . .

Before 1927 (when the editor began to mellow somewhat), other editorials calculated to "stir up the animals" were published. Prohibition, of course, received many such denunciations, as did Coolidge, the Anti-Saloon League, and organized religion. There was to be no flinching from Mencken's opinions. When the osteopaths demanded space in the *Mercury* to answer the editor's campaign against them, he replied tersely that the monthly "does not pretend to any austere judicial spirit. . . . This magazine, in brief, is not dedicated to such debates as go on in country barbershops."[111] The Common Man, was, of course, considered a boob:

Let a lone Red arise to annoy a barroom full of Michigan lumber-jacks, and at once the fire alarm sounds and the full military . . . power of the nation is summoned to put down the outrage. But how many Americanos would the Reds convert to their rubbish, even supposing them free to spout it on every street-corner? Probably not enough, all told, to make a day's hunting for a regiment of militia. The American moron's mind simply does not run in that direction; he wants to keep his Ford, even at the cost of losing the Bill of Rights. But the stuff that the Baptist and Methodist dervishes have on tap is very much to his taste; he gulps it eagerly and rubs his tummy. I suggest that it might be well to make a scientific inquiry into the nature of it. The existing agencies of sociological snooting seem to be busy

[111] June, 1924.

in the other direction. There are elaborate surveys of some of the large cities, showing . . . how many children a normal Polish woman has every year. Why not a survey of the rustic areas, where men are he and God still reigns? Why not an attempt to find out just what the Baptist dominies have drilled into the heads of the Tennesseeans, Arkansans and Nebraskans? It would be amusing—and instructive.

The excerpt above, from an editorial of November, 1925, is indicative of the editor's irreverent view of God and the average citizen. Nor were foreign nations exempt: in June, 1926, England and her leaders, including Churchill, Asquith, Baldwin, King George V, and the Prince of Wales, were so thoroughly ridiculed that a representative in the Canadian House of Commons read aloud the offending editorial to his fellow legislators, demanding to know if "that kind of magazine was to be permitted entrance into Canada."[112]

Nevertheless, if most of the editorials had relied on mere name-calling and invective, however skilful, the reader would soon have ignored them. Fortunately, the editor could write better modulated editorials than his Bryan, farmer, and Fundamentalist ones. There was, for instance, an imaginary history of the development of fire and its use by mankind (August, 1927) that recalls the irony of Anatole France. Another editorial of March, 1925, shows that the Baltimore agnostic could write an amusing and genuinely provocative essay about Protestantism in America. A slightly more acid but still urbane editorial of April, 1926, on education in the United States, was a discussion of whether the purpose of formal education is to "set the young mind upon

---

[112] "Canada Acts on Mercury: Premier Orders Scrutiny of Editorial Criticizing the King," *New York Times,* June 12, 1926, p. 2, col. 5: "The American Mercury, one of whose issues recently was barred from the mails in the United States, is now to come under the scrutiny of the Canadian Minister of Customs. . . .

"Premier King assured Mr. Hocken that the Minister of Customs would consider whether the editorial is of such a character that the magazine should be barred. He suggested with a smile that Canada was not anxious 'to make this a casus belli in any way.'"

a track, and keep it running there in all decorum." Nor was the editor wholly without "constructive" suggestions. One editorial was dedicated to the need for a "suave and soothing burial service for the admittedly damned." Mencken went through *Who's Who in America* and found that "Frost, George Sterling, Robinson, Sandburg, and Masters keep suspiciously mum" about their religious opinions; therefore he suggested "that they meet in some quiet saloon and draw up the ritual I advocate." The December, 1926, editorial also called for a marriage service for the damned. Other suggestions were perhaps deliberately irresponsible; for example, his advocacy of swift and dire punishment for delinquent public officials in the June, 1924, *Mercury*: "My scheme would restore to the art of putting down crime something of the fine bounce and gusto that it had in the Middle Ages."

The more commendable serious editorials usually dealt with the state of journalism or the American's neglected heritage of liberty. The editorial of July, 1926, one of the best, was an artful and moving praise of liberty. Another serious essay (May, 1926) lectured the "scofflaw" of the twenties on his responsibility to grapple forthrightly "with the underlying indecency" of Prohibition: "The American, played upon for years by a stream of jackass legislation, takes refuge in frank skulking. He first dodges the laws, and then he dodges the duty of protesting against them. His life becomes a process of sneaking." A visible mellowing after 1927 perhaps reached its peak in the November, 1928, issue, where there appeared a loving appreciation of Franz Schubert, who had died on November 19, 1828. In other editorials were sown pleas for honesty, decency, and dignity.

The increasing tendency to call for "dignity" was ironic; Mencken was himself an expert at denying dignity to others. The contradiction did not bother the editor. His magazine provided a good show, and his editorials played a part, helping make the monthly one of the foremost satirical journals of the decade.[113]

"AMERICANA"

Very few critics have seen the significance of the "Americana" department of the *Mercury*. Angoff, one of whose jobs was to assist in compiling the foolish remarks reprinted in the department, declares that the "American[a] department was all froth, and nobody realized it better than Mencken himself."[114] Neither claim, however, is true. It had been Mencken who transplanted the department from the *Smart Set* with affectionate care, and it was his artful if brief introductions to the items which made them seem so ridiculous. He also oversaw the reprinting of "Americana" in book form, writing the following introduction to the first annual collection:

They . . . offer a singularly intimate and revelatory insight into the daily life and thought of the American people. No sociological inquiry, however elaborately planned, could get as near to the folk. Here are the things that Americans of the vast majority read every day. Here are the ideas presented to them. Here are the impromptu, unposed portraits of the prophets and sorcerers who lead them. Superficially, the collection may seem to belong to humor. As printed from month to month in *The American Mercury* it has unquestionably caused some cackles. . . . But those who see only humor in these fantastic paragraphs see only half that is in them. Fundamentally, nine tenths of them are serious in intent, and they are all presented here for a quite serious purpose. The purpose, one of the main aims of *The American Mercury,* is to make the enlightened minority of Americans familiar, by documentary evidence, with what is going on in the minds of the masses—the great herd of undif-

---

[113] Mencken had no editorials in the following issues before 1929: Aug., 1924; Jan., 1925; April, 1925; May, 1925; June, 1925; July, 1925; Aug., 1925; Sept., 1925; Feb., 1926; Jan., 1927; and Dec., 1927.

[114] Angoff, "The Inside View of Mencken's Mercury," *New Republic*, CXXXI, p. 19.

ferentiated good-humored, goose-stepping, superstitious, sentimental, credulous, striving, romantic American people. [The
collection] is thoroughly and representatively American. . . . It
drips with the juices of Kiwanis, the American Legion, the Ku
Klux, Rotary, the Mystic Shrine, Elks, the Sons of the Revolution and the Y.M.C.A.

If the present collection wins any esteem among scholars it
will be followed by others at intervals of a year or two.[115]

Nor was the editor's belief that the material was of serious
importance to flag soon; in *Americana 1926* "scholars" are
again directed to work in the "copious and highly significant
literature."[116]

If the average reader of the *Mercury* was more interested
in amusement than in sociological lore when perusing the
monthly "Americana" offerings, he probably found enough
humor to satisfy himself. The department was very probably
"the most popular feature of the magazine."[117] Moreover,
it was the feature, as will be seen, most widely copied by
other periodicals.

"Americana" also made a major contribution to folklore: "The world of Babbitt exists in perfect form only in
the pages of Sinclair Lewis and in the 'Americana' items
enshrined in the faded issues of Mencken's *American
Mercury.*"[118] To help create this mythological world such
writers as Ezra Pound and Eugene O'Neill sent in suggestions.[119] It was reported that Mencken had a spy bureau
"which collects for him illustrations of the absurdities of
democracy, and he sorts them out by states, and once a
month they appear between the arsenical green covers."[120]
Actually, about half the clippings were sent in by readers,

[115] HLM, "Introduction," *Americana 1925* (New York, 1925), pp. v-vi.
[116] HLM, "Introduction," *Americana 1926* (New York, 1926), p. v.
[117] Cleaton, *Books & Battles,* p. 186.
[118] Max Lerner, *America as a Civilization* (New York, 1957), p. 638.
[119] Pound to Mencken, April 27, 1927 (*Letters of Ezra Pound,* p. 211);
O'Neill to Nathan, April 17, 1926 (Goldberg, *The Theatre of George Jean
Nathan,* pp. 160-162).
[120] Upton Sinclair, "Mr. Mencken Calls on Me," *Bookman,* LXVI (Oct.,
1927), 254.

and the remainder came from the editor's friends and "more or less serious students of American psychology at the universities."[121]

From the inchoate batches of clippings emerged fairly well-marked patterns; an experienced reader could often anticipate, by a glance at the brief heading, what was coming. For instance, in the editor's introductions to reports of the unseemly or undignified recreations of fraternal, civic, or veterans organizations, one could expect to find parodies of the cant of the day:

ILLINOIS

How captains of industry in the faubourgs of Chicago relax from the strains of Service, as reported by the patriotic Southtown *Economist*:

> Englewood Kiwanians . . . starred in the gentle art of rolling popcorn balls with their noses.[122]

Occasionally two items would be linked into a sequence:

OHIO

The Cincinnati *Times-Star* in defense of the county's men of vision:

> It is too bad to record . . . that . . . there is a rising tide of antagonism to the luncheon clubs in which American business men meet once a week to discuss over a rather simple meal matters of interest to them and their communities. Rotarians, Kiwanians and similar groups writhe under the lash of the 'younger intellectuals'; . . . Why are the younger intellectuals so scornful? Only on the surface is the matter puzzling. Sit in at one of these luncheons and you have the answer. The men you meet there are successful men with a bent to practical. . . . No wild women dance on the table. No synthetic gin is served. If there is a piano in the room and the custom of choral singing, the songs in which the members join are likely to be standard things, with little jazz stuff and almost no 'blues.' They tell no off-color stories. They do not read Ben Hecht, or James Joyce. . . .

[121] HLM, "Introduction," *Americana 1926*, p. v.
[122] May, 1925.

Actual behavior of the same men of vision in Ohio, as revealed by a letter in the *Buckeye,* official bulletin of the State Kiwanis District:

> At the Youngstown meet . . . some of the visitors acted as though the Eighteenth Amendment were not a part of the law. In addition to general rowdyism, throwing of food, putting water into toy balloons, and spewing on the floor . . . they had a noise producing instrument which was an absolute nuisance. . . . At one meeting in Alliance the members of one visiting club wrecked the industrial exhibit and the cloak room, pushing the attendants aside and throwing all apparel not theirs on the floor in heaps.[123]

A favorite source of quotations for "Americana" was the *Iowa Legionnaire,* whose editor was of course deeply opposed to Mencken:[124]

Refined activities of the stalwart he-men of the Iowa American Legion, in convention assembled at Cedar Rapids, as reported by that great journal, the *Iowa Legionnaire*:

> A haughty woman who high-nosed a group of Legionnaires on the Montrose corner got the jolt of her life when one of the fellows ran up, seized the head of a fox fur she was wearing, opened its mouth and squirted milk from a nippled bottle down its throat.
>
> One comrade had a dressed wax woman he carried around with him. Bystanders who didn't know she was wax were horrified when he "beat up on her." One night the police were called when he was seen to start undressing her, putting in a wallop occasionally before an open window at the Roosevelt.[125]

In addition to solicitous coverage of the "recreations of the Men of Vision" were collections of dicta resulting from the organizations' rhetorical efforts to deepen the specious idealism of their groups. Most of these eruptions showed an in-

[123] July, 1925.
[124] Mencken had sharply denounced Frank F. Miles, editor of the *Iowa Legionnaire,* and Miles had replied in kind, shortly before the *Mercury* was established (HLM, "Hoch Iowisch," *Nation,* CXVI [Jan. 17, 1923], 72; HLM, "From an Editor and a Gentleman," *Nation,* CXVI [Jan. 24, 1923], 151).
[125] Dec., 1928.

fluence of Bruce Barton, whose popularizations of Christian heroes were then widely read: "There must have been something divine in the origin of Rotary," speculated one speaker, and scores of others agreed.[126] Businessmen, athletic coaches, and others rushed to share in the discovery that the traditions of the Western World were not opposed to their various activities.[127]

Another area of concern for "Americana" was the apparent resurgence of sentiment for "blue laws" and other forms of puritanical meddling after the passage of Prohibition. Mencken's libertarianism was assumed to be correct, and the reader was expected to respond with thoughtful laughter to the following incidents:

NEW JERSEY

Progress of the New Morality in Jersey City:

> Mrs. Mary Grieco was found guilty of violating the vice and immorality act by Acting Judge William McGovern in the Second Criminal Court. . . . Mrs. Grieco early Sunday erected a clothespole in her back yard.[128]

COLORADO

Progress of the New Morality in Denver:

> Allen Schultz and his wife, Dorothy, were fined $5 and costs for kissing in a parked automobile. Schultz maintained that a man could kiss his wife when he pleased, but the judge had different views.[129]

KANSAS

Progress of the New Morality on the steppes, as revealed by the enterprising Kinsley *Graphic*:

[126] June, 1927. Other statements included "Jesus Christ is the greatest Rotarian," "Benjamin Franklin was the first Rotarian," "Comets should be given the distinction of being the first Rotarians," "Tolstoy was an unconscious Kiwanian," "St. Patrick was the first real Kiwanian of the Celtic race," "God is a regular fellow," "Jesus Christ was the first and *the only perfect* Rotarian," "Lincoln was a born Rotarian," etc.

[127] Their claims included "Football is the highest form of spiritual exercise," "Cain and Abel were probably the first realtors," "Jesus was the first Chautauqua orator," "David was the first Boy Scout," "Aristotle was the Judge Gary of his day," etc.

[128] March, 1926.   [129] Feb., 1926.

Boys are forbidden to play marbles in McPherson, because it teaches them gambling.[130]

DISTRICT OF COLUMBIA

From the police regulations of the capitol of the Republic:

Any one playing immoral music shall be liable to arrest.[131]

NEW YORK

Proof that Manhattan is the most civilized spot on the globe:

Miss Frances Rathowitz, of First Avenue, who stopped to roll her stockings opposite the statue of George Washington that proclaims liberty to Union Square, went to the House of the Good Shepherd for three months today because a policeman saw her knees. Girl and policeman fought it out before Magistrate Oberwager in the Tombs Court—and the policeman won. "Women should not roll their stockings in public," the magistrate decided.[132]

The "Americana" department sympathized with the victims of academic repression:

CONNECTICUT

Progress of academic freedom in Hartford, as revealed by the *Times*:

For criticising Dean Edward Treffingwell Troxell's recent Trinity chapel address, in which the dean was quoted as saying that 'it is our duty in college to disregard the individual and to turn out a Trinity type,' Malcolm Stevenson, managing editor of *Tripod*, the weekly college paper, has been suspended from Trinity for a month.[133]

---

[130] July, 1925.   [131] Aug., 1925.
[132] Nov., 1926. An item of December, 1927, from Oregon, helped complete the image:

The mind of the American policeman, as disclosed by a Corvallis dispatch: Although authorities in the city are holding James Parker on suspicion that he may be Harry Hill, wanted at Streator, Illinois, for killing his mother, doubt that he is the Chicago youth was expressed today as description of him shows that he is two inches shorter than Hill. Police believe, however, that he is wanted in Chicago for something, basing this opinion on his unwillingness to talk.

[133] March, 1926. Another instance of "Americana" taking the side of the

Partisans of Mencken in the colleges received direct encouragement:

NORTH CAROLINA

Bitter Reflection of the editors of the *Carolina Magazine,* organ of the more literate students at the State University:

> North Carolina has less alien blood per square inch than any other State in the Union. That is one good reason why she also has less writers, less painters, less sculptors and, above all, less musicians than practically any other State of equal resource; certainly any other State of equal bombast.[134]

Another important emphasis in "Americana" was its recording of brutality, especially in the South:

TEXAS

Progress of fundamentalist jurisprudence in the great Republic of Texas. . . .

> At Bishop, Texas, one Smith, a colored physician, was burned to death after his hands and feet had been cut off. It was alleged that Dr. Smith, while riding in his automobile, collided with a car occupied by whites.[135]

MISSISSIPPI

From the archives of the Committee on the Judiciary of the House of Representatives. . . .

---

students against the faculty is in the March, 1925, number:

CONNECTICUT

Dispatch from Middletown, seat of Berkeley Divinity School, the State Hospital for the Insane, the State Industrial School for Girls, and Wesleyan University:

> Asserting that there is technically no such thing as a highball, Professor Karl P. Harrington, head of the Latin department at Wesleyan, has asked for the suppression of the college song, "Drink a Highball at Nightfall."

[134] Feb., 1925. Students must have been amused by the frequent descriptions of college officials engaged in puerile frolic, as in a September, 1927, item from Iowa:

> The recreations of the dons at Simpson College, as described by the Des Moines *Register*:
>
> Dr. John L. Hillman, president of the college, will doff his academic robes and encase his figure in a track suit tomorrow afternoon in a celebrity race, a feature of the annual intramural meet. President Hillman and three faculty members . . . will propel four kiddy-cars down a 100-yard stretch, the winner to receive a lead medal. . . .

[135] April, 1924.

Pickens, Miss.: An 18-year-old colored girl was shot by a mob which was in search of her brother, who was said to have borrowed 50 cents from a white man and refused to pay him 10 cents interest.[136]

GEORGIA

Progress of lawlessness among the Oglethorpe county blackamoors, as reported . . . to the Atlanta prints:

Singlehanded, W. T. Patton, well known Oglethorpe county farmer, Monday afternoon held off a crowd of white citizens who demanded that he turn over to them Bab Waller and Julie Wise, two Negroes who earlier in the day *had prevented two white men from robbing them.*[137]

The more medieval suggestions about punishment were dutifully imbedded in the amber of "Americana":

MISSISSIPPI

Brother J. L. Williams, of Enterprise, describes the Law Enforcement ideal in the eminent *Baptist Record,* of Jackson:

If what our missionaries tell us is true, and I do not doubt it, we would learn a valuable lesson in the execution of law from dark, benighted Africa. Over there the accused is held guilty until he proves his innocence. If he fails to prove he is not guilty there is only one penalty—his head is cut off, stuck on a long pole, hoisted in a public place, and remains there thirty days.[138]

There also appeared many foolish literary judgments:

ILLINOIS

Rousing literary note from a critical reader of the Chicago *Tribune*:

Michael Arlen . . . is greater than Shakespeare, greater than all—and the greatest goes unnoticed. Wake up, you would-be intellectuals, and strain your throats in demand for the genius of all the ages![139]

[136] April, 1924. [137] July, 1925.
[138] Nov., 1928. [139] July, 1925.

MASSACHUSETTS

Why Boston is the dramatic capital of the Republic, as revealed in the cultured Boston *Herald*:

> 'What Price Glory?' will open at the Wilbur Theatre without a line of the profanity which lent much of the realism to its war-time scenes. The management agreed to the elimination of the strong language after an ultimatum by Mayor Curley that the play could not be produced here if the marines did not speak in the stage trenches as they would before their mothers and sisters. The mayor . . . was moved to remark, however, that the play was not as bad as Walt Whitman's poems. This comment was occasioned by his having found on his livingroom table yesterday morning a copy of Whitman which he had hidden behind the books in a bookcase. He brought the book in to the City Hall to destroy it for his family's protection, but on hearing a prominent city official remark that he was curious to read it the mayor gave him the volume.[140]

OREGON

Specimen of red-blooded dramatic criticism from the eminent Eugene *Daily Guard*:

> Shakespeare is almost as bad as Ibsen, and it takes a morbid or primitive nature to enjoy a play of that kind.[141]

ILLINOIS

Literary judgment attributed to the Right Rev. Edwin Holt Hughes, A.B., A.M., S.T.B., S.T.D., D.D., LL.D., ordinary of the Methodist archdiocese of Chicago:

> Edgar A. Guest is the poet-laureate of God.[142]

OHIO

The eminent *Press,* of the rising town of Huron, advises its readers on a literary subject:

> Don't fail to see 'Les Miserables' at the Huron Theatre tonight. Although it has the same name, 'Les Miser-

[140] Jan., 1926.   [141] April, 1926.   [142] Oct., 1926.

ables,' the picture is quite different from the book. The book is not recommended.[143]

Nor was avant-garde creative literature ignored:

IN PARTIBUS INFIDELIUM

Advanced prose from *transition,* the organ of the exiles of the Left Bank:

Faula and Flona
by Theo Rutra

The lilygushes rang and ting the bilbels in the ively. Lilools sart slingslongdang into the clish of sun. The pool dries must. The morlowlei loors in the meaves. The sardinewungs flir flar and meere. . . .[144]

Not surprisingly, many of the forty-odd items which were presented in the average "Americana" concerned religion:

NEW YORK

From a public bull by the Right Rev. William T. Manning, S.T.D., LL.D., D.D., chevalier of the Legion of Honor, officer of the Order of the Crown of Italy, and ordinary of the diocese of New York:

Religion is as natural as playing polo or hockey, and is thoroughly in touch with those games.[145]

MARYLAND FREE STATE

Romish orgies among the high-toned Baltimore Methodists, as described by a gaping reporter of the eminent *Evening News*:

Watch night services will be held at the Mount Vernon Place Methodist Episcopal Church, beginning at 11:55 o'clock tonight. At that time the church will be darkened, with the exception of a single lighted taper on the altar. At midnight twelve men of the congregation, representing the Twelve Apostles, will stand before the altar rail and receive light from the taper. They then will communicate the light to candles held by the worshipers.[146]

[143] Nov., 1928.   [144] Nov., 1929.
[145] June, 1926.   [146] April, 1927.

Of the thousands of clippings citing religious phenomena, much attention was given to the less dignified alliances between religion and business:

CONNECTICUT

Incident of the sacerdotal life in South Manchester, from an eminent Hartford print:

> The 500 ministers attending the Methodist Conference at South Manchester were presented with black silk ties, and a booklet on silk manufacturing, by Cheney Brothers. Announcement of the gift suggested the singing of the hymn, 'Blest Be The Tie That Binds,' which was done enthusiastically.[147]

Although Catholics were not often represented in the department, several New Jersey miracles were recorded, as were selected teachings of the Church:

NEW YORK

Theological dictum from an article in *America* by the Rev. Wilfrid Parsons, S. J.:

> How do we know that this particular miracle of the Virgin Birth happened? We know that it happened *because the Catholic Church teaches that it happened.* This is in itself complete, absolute, and final proof of this doctrine.[148]

The great majority, however, of "Americana" insertions were simply random instances of human stupidity cited without malice. As pointed out by an anonymous essayist, the project "would have delighted Flaubert, who always had an ambition to write an Encyclopedia of Human Stupidity."[149] Nor was the conduct of the department other than democratic; rich and poor, northerner and southerner, city jake and country yokel, all took a turn in the stocks:

NEW YORK

News imparted to a palpitating world over the sign manual of the Hon. Arthur Brisbane:

---

[147] Oct., 1926.   [148] April, 1924.
[149] "Are We More Banal Than Others?" *Literary Digest*, LXXXVIII (Jan. 23, 1926), 29.

The Rev. Dr. John Roach Straton, the New York Fundamentalist, says Christ's coming will eclipse even Lindberg's reception.[150]

MASSACHUSETTS

Effects of Woman Suffrage in this State, as disclosed by the Lynn *Telegram-News,* a great intellectual and moral organ:

> Many of the village belles . . . of Danvers . . . have started wearing dog collars. Dog collars are not only being worn by school girls, but are even worn by teachers. . . . The girls do not always buy their dog collars. That fact was brought to light when many complaints were heard from dog owners to the effect that dogs have mysteriously lost their neck pieces.[151]

NEW YORK

From a list of prizes offered for solid contributions to the fine arts:

> SEVEN THOUSAND DOLLARS, donated to the Art Center of New York by Mrs. John D. Rockefeller, Jr., will be used to provide prizes for the best architectural suggestions for improved hot dog stands.[152]

FLORIDA

The Rev. Golightly Morrill, speaking before the St. Petersburg Advertising Club, as reported by the *Evening Independent* of the same great town:

> God was the First Advertiser and the world is His billboard.[153]

ARIZONA

Patriotic dictum attributed to Capt. Cloyd Heck Marvin, B.A., M.A., Ph.D., president of the University of Arizona, by the *Daily Star* of Tucson:

> We cannot accept European music as the basis of our music, because it is founded on monarchial and aristocratic notions.[154]

[150] Oct., 1927. [151] June, 1925. [152] Dec., 1927.
[153] March, 1928. [154] Oct., 1925.

MISSISSIPPI

From an address to the Kiwanis Club of Columbus, a rising town on the Tombigbee river, by the Rev. W. F. Powell, a gifted exhorter of those parts:

> God was the first Kiwanian.[155]

NEW YORK

Humorous note in the *Monroe Legionnaire,* published at Rochester:

> Thanks to divine guidance, the American Legion is as free of hypocrites as it is humanly possible to be.[156]

MASSACHUSETTS

Obiter dictum of the erudite editor of the *Hampshire Gazette,* published in Northampton, Cal's home town:

> Property is all there is to civilization.[157]

NEBRASKA

Note on a democracy's uses of the fine arts, from the *Editor and Publisher*:

> A statue of Andy Gump, comic strip character created by Sydney Smith of the Chicago *Tribune,* was unveiled on the front steps of the Douglas County Courthouse in Omaha.[158]

CALIFORNIA

News item in the Davis *Enterprise*:

> We have learned of a news item of local interest, but which we are not at liberty to use, as the deal has not yet gone through.[159]

One entry, of unusual merit, more moving and challenging than most of the quotations, is one of the masterpieces of "Americana" sensibility:

SOUTH CAROLINA

Contribution to a history of industrial progress in the South, from the fair city of Columbia:

[155] March, 1925.   [156] Oct., 1926.   [157] May, 1927.
[158] Aug., 1925.   [159] April, 1927.

Sixty-two long years in cotton mills and yet spry, proud and cheerful at 88—this is the record of Miss Epsie Scott, one of the first women ever to be employed in a textile mill in the South. She lives contentedly here in a little room that is bed-room, kitchen and parlor.

"Pleasures! I have none," she answered to a question, "I didn't have time in my life for any pleasures. I never even knew about Santa Claus. I hung my stockings up once or twice just for fun, but—shucks, it didn't do no good, so I stopped."

In 1854, when she was a little girl of 10, her father died, leaving her to help support younger brothers and sisters. From that year until 1915 Miss Epsie Scott was a cotton mill worker. When the Northern soldiers burned the Saluda Cotton Mills she went to Georgia, but in later years gradually retraced her way to the mills of South Carolina, working here and there. She worked in one mill so long that "three times the floor wore out under where I stood and they had to put a new floor on." Not a penny did she save while working. There appeared to be so many nieces and nephews needing help. So when a few years ago she became too feeble to do anything but sit in her little room there was some talk of sending her to the almshouse. But no almshouse for proud Miss Epsie! Compromise resulted in her being given enough money to live alone.[160]

The occasional appearance of such vignettes should cause liberal critics of Mencken to give him more credit for a sense of pathos.

In 1929, when magazines ranging from the *Saturday Evening Post* to the *New Masses* had been affected by "Americana," it seemed plausible that the department would be remembered as "one of the greatest contributions Mencken has made to American letters."[161] It was, however, merely a stroke of journalistic brilliance, a stroke that has been almost totally forgotten. The quips were usually without intrinsic literary worth. Nonetheless, a sort of native

[160] April, 1928.
[161] C. E. Shuford, "An Evaluation of the Influence of H. L. Mencken and *The American Mercury* upon American Thought," p. 106.

humor in the monthly repository aided considerably in the success of the *Mercury* between 1924 and 1928. And, as brought to perfection by the editor, "Americana" further strengthened Mencken's domination over the magazine during its early years.

5

NATHAN AS CONTRIBUTING EDITOR

"CLINICAL NOTES"

AFTER defeat in his effort as co-editor to make the *Mercury* more of a literary review, Nathan without further ado relaxed into his job as contributing editor. In July, 1925, Mencken abandoned his part of the work with the "Clinical Notes," and that department was gradually moved nearer the back of the monthly until it finally came to rest next to Nathan's "The Theatre." Thereafter until March, 1930, Nathan wrote the four or more pages of "Clinical Notes" adjacent to the five to seven pages of "The Theatre." His contributions to the magazine ranged from serious drama criticism to the lightest of quips, a range that has long confused critics. To so important a critic as Edmund Wilson, Nathan was Mencken's "satellite";[1] to others, he was a drama critic unsurpassed in American literature.

A glance at "Clinical Notes" shows that Nathan's attainments did sometimes outwardly resemble those of his Baltimore colleague. Both men were accomplished stylists, notable humorists and satirists, religious skeptics, and political conservatives. These similarities, however, cannot be stated in a less general way without becoming false; few men of letters cultivated individuality more than did Nathan.[2] The two associates, of course, shared some of the

[1] "Literary Politics," *New Republic*, LIII (Feb. 1, 1928), 289.
[2] For instance, in *The World in Falseface* (New York, 1923), is a calm yet self-conscious statement of his commitment to "art for art's sake": "I do not

same enemies, most prominently Puritanism, which Nathan
defined as "[t]he haunting fear that someone, somewhere,
may be happy,"[3] an opinion that was the basis for many
other epigrams.[4] It was not surprising to find the average
American a ridiculous fellow in the eyes of Nathan, who
was so sophisticated that he could even glibly deride "The
Smart American."[5] There were thrusts at politicians, like
the following remark elicited by President Harding's affair
with Nan Britton: "It is no longer the fashion of our Presidents to kiss babies. Babies, they have learned, sometimes
tell."[6] Nor was patriotism esteemed by Nathan, whose
aloofness from from World War I fully matched Mencken's.
A comment about advertising, "Metaphysica Americana,"
showed this disdain: "The invention of the catch-phrase,
'To Make the World Safe for Democracy,' was a masterpiece of boob-fetching. . . . The American public thinks in
terms of catch-phrases. It remembers the Maine, says it with
flowers, and needs no stropping or honing to sharpen its
gullibility."[7] Lists of silly beliefs held by Americans, beliefs
similar to those earlier assembled in *The American Credo,*

care a tinker's dam whether Germany invades Belgium or Belgium Germany,
whether Ireland is free or not free. . . . On that day during the world war
when the most critical battle was being fought I sat in my still, sunlit, cozy
library composing a chapter on aesthetics for a new book on the drama. And at
five o'clock, my day's work done, I shook and drank a half dozen excellent
aperitifs" ("Foreword," p. 11).

[3] Jan., 1925. This is assigned to Nathan on the basis of Mrs. Lohrfinck's
notes on the authorship of the "Clinical Notes," although it also has been
reprinted in *A Mencken Chrestomathy,* ed. H. L. Mencken [New York, 1956],
p. 624.

[4] Nathan's "Moral Kaleidoscope" went as follows: "The bluer the nose,
the greener the mind, the grayer the sense of beauty, the yellower the honor,
the redder the indignation, and the more lavender the sex" (Feb., 1924). In
"Latin and Anglo-Saxon" he tried to express in one sentence the essential
difference between the Latin and the Anglo-Saxon: "to the Latin, sex is an
hors d'oeuvre; to the Anglo-Saxon, sex is a barbecue" (July, 1924).

[5] "The smart American drinks St. Emilion, Graves, St. Julien and Macon,
the beverages of French peasants. He plays Mah Jong, the game of Chinese
coolies. He wears, on Sundays, a cutaway coat, the garb of English clerks.
His melodic taste is for jazz, the music of African niggers. He eats alligator
pears, the food of Costa Rican billy-goats . . ." (Sept., 1924).

[6] June, 1925.   [7] Aug., 1924.

often found their way into the "Clinical Notes,"[8] as did ridicule of New England social pretensions,[9] epigrams concerning life and love,[10] small private controversies,[11] and such minor topics as children's candy of bygone days.[12]

Nathan used "Clinical Notes" also for literary topics; indeed, once the department was wholly dedicated to an essay on George Bernard Shaw.[13] More common, however, were briefer items; when Charles Eliot, retired president of Harvard, issued his fifty-volume set of *Harvard Classics,* known popularly as "Dr. Eliot's Five-Foot Shelf of Books," Nathan impishly countered with "The Five-Inch Shelf": "I am always skeptical of the honesty of a man's culture if his library shelves fail to reveal at least a few grotesquely unintelligible volumes. In the heart of every genuinely cultivated man there is a peculiar fondness for certain books that, though perhaps trashy and empty to some of us, are for one reason or another close to his secret fancy."[14] In another essay he surveyed English authors to determine why Americans refused to see visiting English literati as writers rather than as social characters, and Nathan waggishly deplored, in the case of G. K. Chesterton, his "embarrassing habit of fingering a certain unmentionable portion of his habiliments while being interviewed." This habit, according to Nathan,

[8] E.g., "Beliefs of Children" (Aug., 1929). (As shown by a piece of juvenilia printed on pages 253-261 of *The Theater of George Jean Nathan,* he had begun his lists of foolish assumptions held by his countrymen when he was sixteen years old.)

[9] E.g., "Thumbnail Impression of the Composite American Aristocracy after a Perusal of a Certain Society Journal" (July, 1924).

[10] In "No. 3652" the epigrammatist declared that "[w]omen, as they grow older, rely more and more on cosmetics. Men, as they grow older, rely more and more on a sense of humor" (July, 1925); in "Number One," he stated that much "sentimental mush is written about a man's first sweetheart. Take, for example, your own case. Try, if you will, to think of her name! A man's first sweetheart is generally less a subject for the poets than for Havelock Ellis" (March, 1925).

[11] One such controversy was whether or not Nathan had the right to call Negroes by such names as "Sambo," "Licorice," "Chocolate," "Ethiops," and "Coons," as in Dec., 1929.

[12] Feb., 1929.

[13] July, 1929. A long attack on "The Young Intellectuals" was directed against the avant-garde in Sept., 1928.

[14] May, 1925.

was spoken of widely, distracting people from considering
Chesterton "as an essayist."[15] Nathan also attacked The
National Institute of Arts and Letters, mentioning, as
one of the reasons self-respecting writers would decline
election to that body, that "they could not quite fathom the
nature of an honor which would make them the aesthetic
equals of gentlemen whose contributions to the world of
aesthetics consisted chiefly in cheap magazine sex serials...,
books telling boys how to catch fish in Maine," etc.[16] In a
more slapstick mood, he weighed the threat of a possible
Ministry of Fine Arts in Washington, D. C. After reviewing
the potential membership, he imagined the annual banquet:
"Harry Hansen would get stewed and bite off William
Lyon Phelps' ear, and Phelps, in turn, would spill his *potage
Créole* on Amy Lowell's cigar." Dreiser, Lewis, Cabell and
"the rest of such dismal failures," concluded the cynical
Nathan, "would despairfully foregather in the back room
of some Union Hill, N. J., pot-house and see who could hit
the spittoon oftenest."[17] Other discussions of literary matters
drew upon the past, e.g., a survey of the drinking habits of
eminent authors,[18] or asserted the dignity of the profession
of drama criticism, as in "Creative Writing": "Criticism,
according to the definition, does not come under the head of
creation and, as a consequence, such things as Dryden's
'Essay of Dramatic Poesy' are not creative writing whereas
such things as Zane Grey's novels presumably are."[19]

In his remarks about philosophy and religion Nathan
clearly showed noteworthy differences from Mencken.
Nathan's skepticism was in some ways more far-reaching
than that of his colleague. Mencken believed stoutly in the
ability of science to determine and "prove" the truth,[20] but
Nathan was less sanguine: "The pursuit of truth consists
simply in running away from a swiftly pursuing pack of

---

[15] May., 1924.   [16] Aug., 1926.   [17] May, 1925.
[18] July, 1926.   [19] Dec., 1929.
[20] In "Veritas" Mencken pointed out that he could "believe unreservedly
only in what may be demonstrated scientifically. All the rest is pure speculation,

lies, with the latter gaining ground constantly."[21] (Other significant statements outside the "Clinical Notes" showed a skepticism regarding human nature.)[22] Less anticlerical than Mencken, Nathan repeatedly offered the opinion in the "Clinical Notes" that devout young ladies in some sacramental church were more charming than mannish flappers, and he claimed that atheists, for unknown reasons, prefer their sweethearts to believe in God. The Bible was usually mentioned with politeness, and his unpleasant experiences in church were reported with a minimum of indignation:

This last Christmas Eve I found myself, at the solicitation of a fair companion apparently concerned over my religious welfare, at midnight mass in St. Patricks's. Exactly eleven times during the relatively short service a basket was abruptly thrust under my companion's and my own nose by a gentleman taking up collections. The basket was piled high with notes of various denominations, together with a quart or two of coins. It seemed that every time I tried to get a look at the altar I was vouchsafed instead a view of William McKinley . . . Lewis and Clark . . . Andrew Jackson, George Washington . . . and Abraham Lincoln. So I think I'll spend next Christmas Eve developing my lamentably latent religious instinct either at the New York Historical Society or the Union Dime Savings Bank.[23]

In view of such attitudes, his eventual conversion to the Roman Catholic Church should have startled few of his acquaintances.

---

and, only too often, pure bosh. It may, at times, be beautiful, but it is never important. That Shakespeare was a great poet is not a fact; it is only an opinion. It may be abandoned during the next century, as the doctrine that the Bible was written by God has been abandoned since 1850. But the fact that the blood circulates in the arteries and veins will never be abandoned. It is true now, and it will be true forever" (June, 1925).

[21] June, 1925.

[22] Of importance is his theory announced in "The Theatre" of July, 1927: ". . . the rank and file of the people must be kept in line by the police, whether mundane or celestial. A people that didn't believe in an Almighty God might constitute an intelligent nation, but it would prove a very tough customer to handle. At least one policeman would be needed to look after every single citizen, and the jails would have to be enlarged daily. The pseudo-holy plays and moving pictures are gradually converting former believers into skeptics, and skeptics, by a recognizably natural process, into criminals of one sort or another."

[23] March, 1929.

Another strand of Nathan's thought shown in the "Clinical Notes" was his defense of imagination, a strand notable because imagination was a quality not highly considered in other parts of the magazine. In "Experience and Imagination," for instance, he observed that "[a]ctual experience is often the foe and vanquisher of imagination. What soldier has written of battle as Stephen Crane wrote? What Negro or other Southerner has composed a song of the Southland like Stephen Foster's? What god has ever fashioned an angel as beautiful as one of Raphael's?"[24] At other times Nathan sprang to defend Manhattan life when it was charged with "artificiality," and his counterattacks seemed plausible because he stressed the importance of artificiality and illusion to man's existence and because he could confront indignant rustics with as amusing panoramas of rural America as ever Mencken created. Such topics gave him a pleasant opportunity to embroider for his public an image of himself as the "quintessentialized New Yorker."[25]

According to several accounts, Nathan was paid very little for his contributions, but, because he was far more independent financially than the average author, he was not dissatisfied.[26] He clearly enjoyed his work for the "Clinical Notes" department, and the regularity of the monthly deadlines served as a convenient stimulant to compose material he knew would probably be republished in book form. His "Clinical Notes" offered a supply of witty epigrams and other entertainments light enough to offset Mencken's heavier editorial contributions.

[24] March, 1925.
[25] Goldberg, *The Theatre of George Jean Nathan*, p. 7.
[26] James M. Cain to Singleton, Feb. 1, 1959. (Others of Nathan's acquaintances concur in this appraisal.)

"THE THEATRE" AS HUMOR

IT should be pointed out that Nathan's drama criticism in the *Mercury*, limited as it was to a scrutiny of the New York City area, performed a reviewing service only for that fraction of readers who could attend plays on Manhattan Island. This meant that "The Theatre" would be a little-read part of the magazine unless it was entertaining as well as competent in judgment, and Nathan made certain that it was read by folk far distant from Broadway. His success in this respect soon earned him the reputation of having "brought laughter into our dramatic criticism."[27] A survey of his conduct of "The Theatre" should first show the adaptation of the department to the over-all attitudes characteristic of the *Mercury*. And a look at the purely entertaining qualities of the drama reviews also introduces the critical methods of Nathan.

First in importance was the matter of his prose. Nathan was recognized by Burton Rascoe as "the only stylist among dramatic critics except Percy Hammond,"[28] but Rascoe's neglect of Walter Prichard Eaton and Joseph Wood Krutch perhaps showed a bias in favor of more journalistic prose. Nathan took almost as many liberties with the language as did Mencken, who so assiduously collected and studied Americanisms in speech and writing. For example, dramatic phenomena which annoyed Nathan were described by colorful epithets like "machine-made tear-squeezer, 1890 model," "fetches the yokels," "jouncing the boobletariat," "a crook hickpricker," "thunders of boob applause," "hornswoggle the box office" and language such as that used to condemn an illogical ending of a play by Arthur Richman:

For no clearly intelligible reason, save it be financial, he makes the girl dutifully follow hokum rule 316, clause 6, and tickle the

[27] Goldberg, *The Theatre of George Jean Nathan*, p. 30.
[28] " 'Smart Set' History," *The Smart Set Anthology*, p. xliii.

boobs by shrinking in horror from the kiss of her potential new lover, an Italian count, and hokum rule 942, clause 36B, by then taking the hand of the hero, giving him a cow-eye, and telling him lugubriously that, when he comes to her a year hence, she will be waiting for him. . . . How many yokel-massaging final curtains have descended upon that banality.[29]

When James Barrie promised to expand a one-act play into a full-length drama, Nathan stated that such a feat would be as difficult "as it would be to stretch a lady's garter into a Kelly tire."[30] When a James Joyce comedy that Nathan thought too drily literary was performed, he pointed out that "its first and last curtains are merely book covers."[31] Other dramatists were similarly handled; a bad French comedy evoked the statement that when "a Frenchman turns coy and tries to write a chaste comedy, what follows is often as unfortunate as when an American paints his blue nose red and tries to write a risque comedy."[32] O'Neill, taken to task for the relative weakness of *Welded,* was lampooned for his failure to duplicate Strindberg's successful techniques in *The Father,* "the power of which is derived not by suggestion and implication, but from the sparks which fly upward from a prodigious and deafening pounding on the anvil." According to the critic, "all one gets in O'Neill's play is the prodigious and deafening pounding. The sparks will simply not come out. Now and again one discerns something that looks vaguely like a spark, but on closer inspection it turns out to be only an imitation lightning-bug that has been cunningly concealed in the actors' sleeves."[33] Charles Vildrac was once lionized by Waldo Frank as a great new French playwright, but Nathan burlesqued the discovery: "And no sooner had the foxy M. Frank planted his banner on the beach and claimed Vildrac in the name of God and Greenwich Village than a dozen or more young associates tumbled promptly out of the Algonquin and the Mad Hatter and lifted up their voices to heaven in acquies-

[29] Nov., 1924.   [30] March, 1925.   [31] April, 1925.
[32] Feb., 1924.   [33] May, 1924.

cence."[34] Eugene Brieux, who impressed the American critic as the creator of plays that could be tendentious, was treated as follows: "Take the average Brieux play, cut out all the names of its leading characters, run the text together, borrow an ice-water pitcher, and you have a first-class lyceum bureau lecture."[35] A bad sensational play was mentioned as aimed "at such blockheads as are willing to pay out fancy prices to hear a character declare that she is a nymphomaniac and to see her lewdly demonstrate it by rushing up to an actor and kissing him on the ear."[36] Of Noel Coward, against whom Nathan waged a more or less continuous war, it was said that his plays were "so many goldfish trying heroically to swim the ocean."[37]

Nathan fell upon deficient acting with equally cruel glee. Rollo Peters' performance of Antony in *Antony and Cleopatra* led the critic to record a speech showing how Peters ran the words together:

> ". . . she's good beingawne;
> The hand could pluck her back that shov'd herron.
> I must from this enchanting queen breakoff:
> Ten thousand harms, more than thills I know,
> Midleness dothatch. Ho, Enobarbus!"

The quest for life and speed has led the producer frequently to run off the speeches as if the play were a George Cohan music show. One momentarily expects a troupe of Tiller girls to come on.[38]

Of the acting in *The New Englander,* the reviewer quipped that the "characters are less Puritan stock than Puritan stock company,"[39] and in a play called *Human Nature* he deplored the acting of the leading lady: "the heroine conveys to the audience the fact that she is with child by looking steadily at her shoes."[40] Stanley Logan's overacting in Rostand's *The Last Night of Don Juan* was damned: "Every line of Rostand's poetry became for [Logan] a signal to act

[34] May, 1925. [35] Dec., 1925. [36] April, 1926.
[37] Feb., 1927. [38] April, 1924. [39] April, 1924.
[40] Nov., 1925.

as if he had drunk a seidel of Spanish-fly; every gesture was converted into a window demonstration of a rubber exerciser."[41] As to bad acting by women, Nathan was perhaps the least gallant critic of the stage: "An actress named Clare Harris, who must weigh at least thirteen stone, has been cast for the role of the delicate sweet one whose person two of the males passionately crave, and gives an appropriate performance."[42] Another play featuring a buxom songstress moved the critic to remark that "its prima donna is of a vintage that only a Richard Wagner might cause one to be satisfactorily unconscious of."[43] His most protracted cruelty was reserved for aging actresses making attempts at comebacks by having themselves cast in the roles of ingenues.[44]

Another source of pleasantries in "The Theatre" was provided by the reviewer's belief that he was a "connoisseur of the low, the true, and the beautiful."[45] Nathan believed that vaudeville and such light diversions merited some attention, and periodically he reviewed burlesque shows and musicals. He could give informed comparisons of English, French, Austrian, and American light amusements; he once went so far as to claim that the "American music show stage is miles ahead of the American dramatic stage,"[46] and at another time he praised the plebeian sideshow as "rich and juicy in American buncombe."[47] His tributes to popular entertainment did not, however, extend to motion pictures: "I go to the movies only on very rare occasions and then usually to the species in which a comedian sits down on a pie—since that is about the only phase of the art of the cinema that seems to me to have much authenticity."[48] Often Nathan conveyed in prose something of the spirit of minor entertainments by making compendiums of stock-

---

[41] Jan., 1926.   [42] Oct., 1926.   [43] Jan., 1927.
[44] Examples of his satirical technique appear in his description of Madame Olga Petrova, Feb., 1924; Madame Bertha Kalich, July, 1924; and Mrs. Patrick Campbell, April, 1927.
[45] July, 1924.   [46] May, 1925.
[47] Sept., 1925.   [48] Aug., 1924.

response situations and ancient wheezes, thereby amusing the reader even while helping him to feel superior.

Sometimes Nathan's urge to amuse led him to fill "The Theatre" with very flimsy criticism. Whole reviews were devoted to lists of stereotypes, stock situations, comic cliches, and the *reductio ad absurdum* of already shaky or melodramatic plots. Other tours de force of reviewing might consist of long lists of play titles each followed by "is trash," with the offerings of the month thus uniformly reduced to that low estimate.[49] Occasionally Nathan gave the appearance of being outraged by the low moral state of recent plays, and would hiss disapproval of "exaggerated gum-suckings and brassiere-squeezings."[50] Such surveys of what brings censors forth from their crannies afforded entertainment under the guise of indignation.[51] Rapid-fire summaries of a theater season were sometimes apparently inspired by humor, for there was little room in such staccato lists for fair discrimination.[52] Other entire installments of "The Theatre" were devoted to attacks on the movies and their public, attacks replete with advertisements clipped from movie magazines.[53] As one might expect, the interest in being funny diluted the value of many of his reviews, and, by 1927, a forced note began to creep into his jocosity.[54]

But in general the journalistic stance of Nathan was deftly suited to the *Mercury*; he disparaged reform by sneering at what he remembered of the muckrakers' crusades,[55] he discussed tartly the outstanding marks of the "Anglo-Saxon's philosophical provincialism,"[56] and he used

[49] Nov., 1926.   [50] Sept., 1927.
[51] The July, 1927, issue provides an example of this approach.
[52] June, 1928.   [53] Aug., 1928.
[54] In a review of April, 1928, he wrote in praise of Vincent Lawrence's *A Distant Drum* that "No Frenchman, and certainly no Englishman or German, has in recent years dug down further into what sentimentalists call the female heart and fetched up more subtly brilliant manure," and in July, 1928, he flashed out at modern dress in old plays: "we thus are annually entertained by a droll procession of Hedda Gablers in knee-length skirts puffing Lucky Strikes, Falstaffs who seem to be honorary members of the W.C.T.U.," etc.
[55] "Chicago meat-packers were accused of manufacturing frankfurters out of dead babies," etc. (March, 1925).
[56] June, 1925.

some of Mencken's editorial assumptions as an anvil on which to beat out criticism: "During the pre-Easter period in the theatre there is very little to write about, including *Across the Street,* by Richard A. Purdy. Mr. Purdy is in the banking business. *Across the Street* won the three thousand dollar Chautauqua Prize. The critical syllogism is thus complete."[57] At times, indeed, Nathan wrote some very funny reviews, like one coming after a preliminary discussion of the theory that drama, unlike many other arts, is more captivating "when it is thoroughly bad than when it is partly good." After admitting that to a critic there was "something fetching about smelly drama," he began his review: "Enter then *Easy Street,* a lemon of the first water." *Easy Street,* which had been hailed in Chicago, was described as full of bromides that drew laughter from sophisticated New Yorkers. Nathan ridiculed the play, sharing his glee with the reader so artfully that it was difficult, regardless how bad one's own taste might be, not to feel a superior contempt toward the droll state of Chicago's taste.[58] The possibility that Nathan's contributions were less carefully read than the other contents of the magazine[59] was, then, hardly his fault. He deserves credit for successful comic writing.

AMERICAN PLAYWRIGHTS

NEVERTHELESS, had Nathan not also been serious about the drama, he would never have attained eminence as a drama critic. In addition to his clowning he rendered distinguished services to the American stage. Of these services, one of the most important was his championing of Eugene O'Neill. His advocacy of O'Neill was tempered by oc-

[57] May, 1924.   [58] Oct., 1924.
[59] "The Theatre is read less than any other section of the magazine," said an anonymous student at Cornell ("The American Mercury," a parody published by the staff of the *Cornell Widow* [Jan., 1927], p. 17. Nathan was an alumnus of Cornell.)

casional unfavorable reviews, but usually, from the praises accompanying *All God's Chillun Got Wings* to his last contributions in 1930, Nathan functioned as a personal critic of his friend, and the grateful playwright responded by frequently sending his work to Nathan in manuscript form before production.[60] After the critic's kind words of reassurance when *All God's Chillun Got Wings* stirred antagonism because its heroine married a Negro, he criticized O'Neill's *Welded* and a Provincetown Theatre production of *The Rime of the Ancient Mariner*.[61] He publicly lectured the playwright on the direction his career should take,[62] and gave more advice in a mixed, but generally appreciative, review of *Desire Under the Elms*.[63] In a more hostile review of *The Fountain* his remarks were tempered by memories of an earlier script of the drama that he recalled as superior to the revised play and further by reminders of O'Neill's essential merit.[64] Nathan approved of *The Great God Brown* and *Marco Millions,* demanding that an established Broadway manager accept *Marco Millions* for production.[65] (Eventually, angered by the producers' reluctance, he devoted an entire instalment of "The Theatre" to an eulogy of O'Neill as a humorist and an enticing synopsis of *Marco Millions*.)[66] Even more enthusiastically received was *Strange Interlude,* for which Nathan wrote one of his very rare "rave" notices, finding the play unsurpassed by "any that Europe has given us in recent years and certainly by none that has been produced in America."[67] A long, detailed synopsis of the play was given, and later the critic scolded the "pathetic jackasses" who questioned O'Neill's use of soliloquies and asides in the long drama.[68] Yet despite

[60] Nathan in some instances privately persuaded his producer friends to undertake O'Neill plays.

[61] May, 1924; June, 1924.

[62] Sept., 1924.

[63] Jan., 1925.

[64] Feb., 1926; O'Neill was declared "the first dramatist of high position that this country has produced."

[65] April, 1926; June, 1926.

[66] Aug., 1926.

[67] Aug., 1927.

[68] April, 1928.

these praises of O'Neill—praises often accompanied by quotations from letters and conversations with the dramatist—
reservations were frankly stated whenever a specific play
was found unworthy; perhaps one of the harshest reviews
Nathan ever wrote included his listing, in double column
for nearly four pages, the frantic stage directions of the
first act of *Dynamo*. The unusual review was so devastating
that O'Neill's wife pleaded with him to have nothing more
to do with Nathan.[69] The incident proved, at any rate, that
Nathan was justified in denying the legend that his "close
friendship with and personal affection" for O'Neill had induced "a critical astigmatism as to his defects as a dramatist."[70]

Although no other American dramatist earned the
sympathetic attention shown O'Neill, Nathan responded to
individual plays with notices sufficiently enthusiastic to show
that he was not simply a chronic dissenter. This fact was
demonstrated by his comments regarding *The Miracle*.[71]
A panegyric was also inspired by *What Price Glory?*: "it is
infinitely the superior of every other play born of the late
war, in whatever language."[72] Other more restrained acceptances showed his well-known ability to recognize sound
dramatists; reviews lauded work by such remembered
writers as George Kaufman, Maxwell Anderson, Vincent
Lawrence, Sidney Howard, and Laurence Stallings. Although "The Theatre" was more often concerned with
second-rate drama than with the best, the emphasis was not
Nathan's fault; he merely had enough experience to know

[69] The review, which appeared March, 1929, followed Nathan's printing
in January, 1929, of a letter from O'Neill which explained at length what he
was trying to accomplish.

[70] Nathan, "O'Neill," *Vanity Fair*, XLI (Oct., 1933), 31.

[71] The review commenced: "The fact first. In *The Miracle*, the combined
talents of Max Reinhardt, Norman Bel Geddes, and Morris Gest have brought
to the American theatre the most vividly impressive and thunderously beautiful
spiritual spectacle, not that it has ever known—for it is too easy to say that—
but, more, that it has ever dreamt of. . . . The theatre that we have known
becomes Lilliputian before such a phenomenon. The church itself becomes puny.
No sermon has been sounded from any pulpit . . ." (March, 1924).

[72] Nov., 1924.

that few seasons were graced by new masterpieces of dramatic literature, and that therefore the normal grist for a monthly review would be largely mediocre stuff. It was true, despite his aid to O'Neill, that he would not very often join other critics in crying up "promise" in budding playwrights, a refusal that was partly an aspect of his abhorrence of "constructive" criticism. Rather than praise an endless array of unproved talents, Nathan encouraged the American stage in several more negative ways. For instance, the renaissance of American drama occurring after World War I could have come only after the era of Augustus Thomas, Bronson Howard, and Clyde Fitch was ended, and Nathan was prominent among those who deflated these dramatists' reputations, even though his lashing of them may have continued somewhat longer than necessary.[73]

In "The Theatre," of course, only actual performances were judged, not manuscripts, and thus credit had to be given for effective acting just as barbs had to be directed toward bad acting. Actors and actresses who drew frequent approval included Eleonora Duse, Katherine Cornell, Alfred Lunt, Beatrice Lillie, Gertrude Lawrence, Helen Hayes, Louis Calhern, Judith Anderson, Paul Robeson, and Lynn Fontanne. Mingled with recognition of players later to become famous were human touches: "Miss Julia Hoyt's Judith would have tickled her father, the late Charley Hoyt," wrote Nathan, referring to old friends of the Nathan family in Indiana,[74] and the single reference to movie acting in "The Theatre" was a tribute to Lillian Gish, then a close personal friend of the reviewer.[75] Nor were stage sets ignored; the unorthodox sets of Norman Bel Geddes were praised, whereas Nathan made his readers accustomed to his sneers toward the sets designed by a wretch named Basil Dean.

[73] What appears to be flailing of dead horses dominates the May, 1926, review.
[74] Goldberg, *The Theatre of George Jean Nathan*, p. 48.
[75] Aug., 1924.

FOREIGN PLAYWRIGHTS

PART of Nathan's reputation as critic for the *Smart Set* was based on his ability to obtain hearings on Broadway for modern European dramas. Only gradually did his *Mercury* contributions reflect the shift toward America to which the magazine as a whole was committed. Of English dramatists, George Bernard Shaw was most cordially received in "The Theatre." Speaking of Shaw's *Candida,* for example, Nathan declared that he knew of "no better instance of intelligent sentimental writing. . . . first-grade dramatic literature,"[76] and Shaw returned something of Nathan's regard.[77] Another Irish playwright, Sean O'Casey, also found a partisan; Nathan lauded *The Plough and the Stars*[78] and pressed American producers to pay attention to others of O'Casey's plays.[79] Unfavorably reviewed was James Joyce's *Exiles*: "The typical Irish vagueness hovers over [the] play like a chill mist . . . an irritating fault."[80] Somerset Maugham, Oscar Wilde, J. M. Barrie, and H. G. Wells enjoyed somewhat more cordial treatment than did Joyce, but John Galsworthy was disparaged[81] and Arthur Pinero was criticized sharply.[82] By 1927, however, Nathan began to make "The Theatre" a mirror showing his slowly unfolding dissatisfaction with the English stage. As Paul Morand observed in 1930, the New York stage "is reproducing the anti-European attitude of the *American Mercury,* whose former dramatic critic, my friend George Jean Nathan . . . declares that London is now provincial."[83] Actually, Nathan well before 1930 had been making more

[76] Feb., 1925.
[77] Shaw, after retiring from criticism, labeled Nathan the "Intelligent Playgoer Number One" ("Introduction," *The World of George Jean Nathan,* p. xviii).
[78] Oct., 1926.   [79] June, 1929.   [80] April, 1925.
[81] July, 1925; Jan., 1928.   [82] Dec., 1924.
[83] *New York* (New York, 1930), p. 204.

pointed accusations than "provinciality" against the London theater.[84]

Of continental plays Nathan likewise had something to say. He promoted the work of Hungarian dramatists, such as Ernst Vajda, and was, in fact, addicted in his earlier writings to berating his fellow reviewers with catalogues of such exotic authors, a habit for which he had "received many a brick in the neck."[85] Among other favorites of his *Smart Set* days still mentioned with approval in the *Mercury* were H. R. Lenormand and Edmond Rostand. At times, however, he felt that his earlier pioneering for such writers, and even for Ibsen, Strindberg, and Hauptmann, had more than achieved its goal, and he deplored an uncritical celebration of them: "As is ever the case, when worms turn, they somersault."[86] Certain continental playwrights were found wanting, including Maurice Maeterlinck, Frank Wedekind, and, less vehemently, Luigi Pirandello.[87] Only tepid acknowledgment was given to the radical German dramatists of the period, such as Ernst Toller. Of Toller's *Masse-Mensch* he said that it was "in essence and execution little more than a harangue atop a soapbox,"[88] an opinion perhaps partly inspired by his disdain for the radical ideology of the play, a disdain which may well have enhanced his later hostility toward the works of Clifford Odets.

NATHAN AS CONSERVATIVE

NATHAN's political conservatism was at no time hidden; he openly lent his influence to the managers who fought for the status quo against actors trying to organize into guilds. Indeed, a group of these managers caricatured

---

[84] For instance, Oct., 1925; Oct., 1926; and, especially, Nov., 1927.
[85] Nov., 1925.   [86] June, 1925.
[87] Feb., 1924 (Maeterlinck); March, 1924; May, 1927 (Pirandello); July, 1925 (Wedekind).
[88] June, 1924.

in 1919 in the *Liberator* looks like a gallery of Nathan's best friends among the producers—men like Arthur Hopkins.[89] Repeatedly the critic flayed actors' guilds, the Actors' Equity Association, and A. F. of L. groups: "This unionization of actors has been the last and most ludicrous straw upon the camel's back. . . . Trade unions are not for artists."[90] Such remarks in the mid-twenties, after others had yielded before the inevitable trend, helped incite leftist opposition to the *Mercury*.

Many times more important than his opposition to unionization, however, was Nathan's support of Broadway's commercial theaters against the little-theater movement. A frequent compliment from Nathan to an admired author would be that he was "a hard, old-fashioned practical playwright schooled not in art theatres but in purely commercial theatres."[91] He believed firmly that the "Shuberts have actually backed more good plays than half the art-producers who are favorites of the Drama League," and later he stated that the little theatres justified his skepticism by producing "such bad and commercially unprofitable plays as *Out of Step*" while Broadway went ahead with "such good and commercially profitable plays as *What Price Glory?*."[92] Moreover, Nathan would defend Broadway theaters against charges of "commercialism" nearly as often as he denounced plays obviously intended as bids for cash at the box office.[93] It was a cardinal principle with him that few worthwhile plays were neglected by the public. One of Nathan's shortcomings as a critic during the twenties was his general refusal to acknowledge the valuable work being done by the little-theater movement during that decade.[94]

Something of this conservatism was caused by an aversion

---

[89] (Oct., 1919), p. 34. *The Liberator* article was inspired by an actors' strike in 1919.

[90] Aug., 1925.   [91] Jan., 1924.

[92] Quotations are from Sept., 1924, and March, 1925.

[93] E.g., March, 1926.

[94] A brief and half-hearted tribute did appear in July, 1925, but these were far outweighed by such scoffing as that in May, 1929.

toward avant-garde experimentation in the theater that nearly matched Mencken's attitude toward the new poetry: concerning Pirandello he wrote that it was "all very well to
argue that the Italian is trying to fashion a new type of
drama—actually he is doing nothing of the kind—but before one sets out to fashion a new type of drama one must
have known and forgotten the old."[95] Denunciations of the
avant-garde refusal to adhere to traditional stage scenery
and lighting technique were plentiful.[96] John Howard
Lawson's experimental play, *A Jazz Symphony of American
Life,* described as "an indifferent work in what may be
called hoochie-coochie form," led to a caustic survey of ex-
perimentalism which concluded that the "frantic struggle
for new forms is the most amusing of twentieth century
artistic phenomena. . . . We thus get an endless series of
paintings that are meant to suggest nudes descending staircases in terms of fully clothed geometrical professors as-
cending staircases," etc.[97] Sometimes, unfortunately, this opposition was less wittily expressed, and mere railing[98] was
added to oversimplifications thrown at Greenwich Village
enemies, whose "little theatre dramaturgic nonsense," according to the reviewer, led them to believe that "everything
south of Fourteenth street is drama; everything north of
Fourteenth street is not."[99]

Nathan's dislike of profanity on the stage might be
credited to good taste, but his curious ambiguity toward
censorship was doubtless influenced by his conservatism.
During the first few years of his conduct of "The Theatre"
he normally commended plays which handled forthrightly
forbidden topics, but in March, 1927, he launched a sincere

[95] March, 1924.
[96] E.g., Sept., 1924.
[97] March, 1925.
[98] "Europe is full of playwrights who imagine that sophistication is simply
a matter of denying what everyone has believed for three thousand years and
setting their denial in front of some bughouse scenery" (Feb., 1929). Also of
interest is his discussion of expressionistic theater (April, 1927).
[99] May, 1926. (Another center of drama activity which drew many jibes was
Baker's drama class at Yale.)

attack on *La Prisonnière,* a play dealing with lesbianism, a play he had earlier found serious in purpose and artistically sound. The indignant Nathan, after again admitting the aesthetic merits of the drama, wrote a long tirade stating that plays, "like literature, can very easily throw morals off the tracks," and that a good piece of writing might well send "ten thousand morons to perdition."[100] A significant foreshadowing of this attitude had appeared in the following remarkable theory:

. . . the accomplishment, if perhaps not always the intention, of all art is the lowering of human virtue, in the commonly accepted sense of the word, and the conversion of men from metaphysical and emotional Methodism to metaphysical and emotional Paganism. . . . [Art] has been kept alive by man's unregenerate sinfulness alone. . . . its greatest lovers and stoutest champions have ever been the men who most truly appreciated that under its pretense of divine origin there curled a red and forked tail.[101]

Thus wrote the man who favored religion for "a nation of dolts who must ever be kept in line by fear of the hereafter." In "The Theatre" during the later twenties he included urbane surveys describing how little censorship damages drama, how few good plays are actually suppressed.[102]

Relatively little was said regarding the drama of the past in Nathan's reviews. Except for Restoration comedies, Nathan apparently had little interest in plays written before the twentieth century. Shakespeare, for instance, was almost never used to cast light upon current plays.[103]

[100] The play, by Eduard Bourdet, was first approved in December, 1926. Ironically, one finds Nathan again jeering at censors of the play in the "Clinical Notes" for December, 1928.
[101] April, 1926.
[102] July, 1927. Discussions of censorship appeared in September, 1927, and July, 1928.
[103] His name was sometimes used to disparage Nathan's enemies: "This is the time of year when the New York stages rid themselves of Shakespeare, Ibsen, Strindberg, Samuel Shipman and the other old masters and go in for . . . the music show" (July, 1924).

OTHER CRITICS

WITH the exception of James Huneker and two English critics, Shaw and Arthur B. Walkley, Nathan did not have much esteem for drama criticism by others. His few references to past critics of the stage, such as Gotthold Lessing, were likely to be playful.[104] A mention of Dryden's *Essay of Dramatic Poesy,* for instance was simply juxtaposed, for purposes of ridicule, to a discussion of a dramatist whom Nathan disliked,[105] but more constructive uses of the famous essay were lacking. To be sure, William Hazlitt was often mentioned in "The Theatre," but nearly always by Nathan's habit of referring to colleagues writing for other journals as "the local hazlittry" or "hazlitts." He did apparently enjoy flipping through the works of celebrated critics of the past to glean errors, which he gleefully marshaled into long catalogues.[106] Once, when fretting about the bad taste of the current stage, Nathan checked himself by recalling "MM Collier, Cibber, and other such indignatos."[107] Aristotle was held as fallible,[108] as were those who followed his directives too strictly; writing of A. B. Walkley, Nathan was actually describing his own attitude toward theory: "He senses the ridiculousness of sweating to build up complex theories that so little as twenty or thirty years later—thus fitful, since Aristotle lifted it out of its cradle, has the drama been—will be quite empty and useless as an old tooth-powder can." Continuing his self-revealing praise of Walkley, Nathan wrote that the Englishman "appreciates that the theatre and drama are as shifting as the sands of the sea and that, in that very shifting, lies the true secret of their golden, sunlit beauty."[109] In the eulogy of Walkley, "perhaps best to be

[104] Lessing was quoted in October, 1924, but Nathan had only jested: "(as a matter of fact, Lessing said nothing of the sort. . .)."
[105] Sept., 1924.   [106] July, 1926; Oct., 1927.
[107] Sept., 1925.   [108] Oct., 1927.   [109] Aug., 1924.

described as a British James Huneker," the *Mercury* critic
identifies himself as another adherent to Huneker's impressionistic approach to art, an adherent proud of his independence.[110] Other critics functioning in America were,
of course, seen as fawning or stupid fellows,[111] and Nathan
also made clear his opposition to academic friends of drama
by disparaging such men as William Archer as "academic."[112] As for himself, he was "surely not one of those profound dolts who believes that to write for the stage successfully one must write according to the strict rules laid
down by Columbia University professors."[113] (Nathan probably had Brander Matthews in mind; if, however, he meant
among "Columbia University professors" Joel Elias Spingarn, who had earlier been on the Columbia faculty, he
should have assumed a less casual pose.)[114] Almost the only
sign of system in Nathan's otherwise impressionistic reviews was a fairly consistent respect for what he thought
was the author's intent, a respect that provided a standard
by which he judged both plays and interpretations by
actors.[115] His hundreds of epigrams on drama and criticism
were essentially the preoccupation of a mind to which theory
was interesting but by and large superfluous.[116]

[110] "I have never for a moment flattered myself that more than one-
fiftieth of my readers . . . agreed with me, or more than one-hundredth
understood accurately what I was driving at. [With] no editorial policy
bothering me and no advertising whip threatening my rear. . . . with no mother
editor. . . . with a sizable wastebasket handy in which to throw all imbecile
letters of complaint, and with an affable but healthy coon weighing 360
pounds stationed in the outer office," independence was secured (Sept., 1924).

[111] The *Mercury* critic often quoted the worst of such criticism, then sported
with it, as in the beginning of his June, 1924, review.

[112] Aug., 1924.   [113] Jan., 1924.

[114] When Mencken, before the twenties, began to trumpet about what he
called the "Croce-Spingarn-Goethe-Carlyle" theory, which Nathan halved into
the "Goethe-Carlyle" theory and which Pierre Loving halved into the "Croce-
Spingarn" theory, Spingarn decided that something had to be done. Spingarn's
"The Growth of a Literary Myth," *Freeman*, VII (May 2, 1923), 181-183, put
a stop to the confusion.

[115] Examples include Nathan's discussions of productions of Ibsen (Feb.,
1929), Hauptmann (April, 1924), and almost all plays by O'Neill.

[116] His *The Critic and the Drama* (New York, 1922) is described by Angoff
("Introduction," *The World of George Jean Nathan*, p. xv) as "profoundly
dialectical" and as "still one of the most searching works of modern dramatic
criticism in English." The work is, however, perhaps more comparable to

NATHAN'S IMPORTANCE TO THE *MERCURY*

DESPITE the fact that "The Theatre" department began to decline by 1928, Nathan's judgments on the theater of the twenties have held up to a considerable degree. This general soundness of judgment benefited the magazine. His importance to the *Mercury* was not simply that he wrote most of the contributions having to do with belles-lettres and solicited many of the more literary pieces printed in the early monthly, but also, as Dreiser observed to Nathan in 1933, he added something less tangible though equally essential:

> Fundamentally, Mencken stated the case to me in regard to you in 1926. It was that from the beginning there had been a fundamental difference between your points of view; that all you could contemplate was the frothy intellectual and social interest of the stage . . . [and the] dilettante worlds, whereas he . . . was for serious contemplation of science, medicine, education, literature and what not. The issue, as you know for yourself, proved fatal. I was a little dubious as to his stand at the time, and so said, because I always felt that opposed to his solid philosophic, economic, sociologic and historic interests, your lighter touch was important and, for general literary as well as magazine purposes, made for a more charming and, to my way of thinking, almost equally valuable publication, the old *Smart Set*. He disagreed with me and, of course, since he pursued his intellectual course so ponderously, the *Mercury* failed. . . .[117]

Dreiser might have added that Nathan was able to get along with famous established writers (an editorial trait Mencken, as will be seen, did not long choose to cultivate). Certainly the drama critic could flatter and amuse those of the "middle minority" who followed his *Mercury* writings.

Willard Huntington Wright's *The Creative Will: Studies in the Philosophy and the Syntax of Aesthetics* (New York, 1916) than to works by Spingarn.

[117] Dreiser to Nathan, Oct., 7, 1933 (*Letters of Theodore Dreiser*, II, 642-647, 643) (Dreiser was threatening to resign from his association with Nathan as editor of the *American Spectator* because Nathan would not permit an essay on physics to appear in that periodical. The resignation later occurred.)

6

OTHER CONTRIBUTORS

NEWSPAPER REPORTERS

ALTHOUGH the *Mercury* was dominated by Mencken, without the co-operation of many contributors, it would hardly have faithfully mirrored its editor's viewpoint. The writers apparently most willing to elaborate Mencken's prejudices were newspapermen. The magazine was open to their efforts because in Mencken "they had a good friend who understood them better than the august and unapproachable editors of the older quality periodicals."[1] Some newsmen were sufficiently pleased with the monthly that a "legend" arose that "every newspaper reporter carried a copy of the green-covered magazine in one pocket of his topcoat and a bottle of gin in the other."[2] When it became known that the editor was receptive to their articles, especially those written in Mencken's idiom and from his slant, the journalists responded; after the first few issues of the monthly (which had in the beginning featured more academic contributors than those of any other class), over half the contents were contributed by journalists.

There were several reasons for this development. First, newspapermen were able to imitate, sometimes with surprising success, the characteristics of the editor's prose.[3]

[1] Angoff, *Portrait*, p. 40.

[2] Burton Rascoe, *We Were Interrupted* (Garden City, N. Y., 1947), p. 198.

[3] One of the most faithful imitations of Mencken's thought and prose is T. J. Bartlett's "The Roll of Honor," a discussion of honorary degrees, printed December, 1927. Had Angoff not stated that "Mencken did not write a single article in the *Mercury* under a pseudonym" (Angoff to Singleton, May 23, 1959), the identification of Bartlett as "an Ohioan, and a former newspaper man. . . . now engaged in business in New York" would be suspect ("The American Mercury Authors," Dec., 1927).

Second, journalists were accustomed to revision of their articles, and they were proud enough to appear in the *Mercury* that tamperings with their style or point of view did not often bother them. To be sure, a more independent author, such as Henry Pringle, or a sports writer made wretched by the insertion of Greek into an article, would complain,[4] or would even refuse to allow an essay to be published,[5] but such instances were rare. Third, Mencken's cynicism, his exaggerations and oversimplifications, and his clowning were viewed with more favor by newsmen than by scholars or creative writers. Fourth, journalists were gratified by the serious regard shown in the *Mercury* for publishing and journalism in America. In "The Library" the editor frequently reviewed works dealing with journalism, he editorialized on that subject,[6] and he commissioned such essays as "Journalism below the Potomac," "The Catholic Press," "The Negro's Press," "The Tabloids," "The New York Dailies," "Journalism in Texas," "Schools of Journalism Today," "Why Men Work for Newspapers," "Newspaper Girls," "Hearst Comes to Atlanta," "The Trade of the Journalist,"[7] "The Associated Press,"[8] "American

---

[4] Angoff, *Portrait*, pp. 118, 156.

[5] Leon Whipple, "The Revolution on Quality Street, Part II," *Survey*, LVII, 427.

[6] The best-known such editorial appeared in October, 1924: "Journalists who read the *American Mercury* for October," reported *Time*, "went hot with pride, shame or anger. Editor Henry Louis Mencken had delivered himself of another diatribe. . . . 'Menckinsults' have become famous in their way . . ." (anon., "Idealist," *Time*, IV [Oct. 6, 1924], 22, 24).

[7] Gerald Johnson, Sept., 1926; William C. Murphy, Jr., Dec., 1926; Eugene Gordon, June, 1925; Richard G. De Rochemont, Oct., 1926; Hugh Kent, Nov., 1926; Chester T. Crowell, March, 1925; Nelson Antrim Crawford, Oct., 1925; Gerald Johnson, May, 1929; Catherine Brody, March, 1925; Herbert Asbury, Jan., 1926; Richard Owen Boyer, Jan., 1929.

[8] Dewey M. Owens, April, 1927. Owens' article, which was critical of the Associated Press, followed another attack by Horace J. Hubbell ("Think Stuff Unwanted") in the March, 1927, number. Commented *Time*: "Where did this bolder picture of the Associated Press appear? Where but in that kraut-liveried castigator of every U.S. folly, real and imaginary, in the *American Mercury*. [The articles] must have caused pain to Kent Cooper, present A.P. manager. . . .

"Upon no subject is the *American Mercury* better fitted or more logically inclined to inveigh than upon U.S. journalism. It depends for much of its copy upon newsgatherers and editors facile enough to catch the style, and cynical enough to enjoy the viewpoint, of Editor . . . Mencken. Six of its 14 non-fiction articles for April were by newspaper men and women" (anon., "Think Stuff," *Time*, IX [April 4, 1927], 24).

Journalism Today," "Goodbye to the Immigrant Press," "Front Page Stuff," "The Yiddish Press," "The Labor Dailies," "The St. Louis *Post-Dispatch*," "The Springfield *Republican*," "Philadelphia Acquires a Good Newspaper," "The Art of the Copy-Reader," "The Passing of the Free Editor," and "The Troubles of a Radical Editor."[9] Mencken's great interest in reminiscent articles (he had solicited "reminiscent" essays even before he learned to spell the word)[10] included journalists; for instance, there appeared "Old Days on the *World*," "The Education of a Journalist," "Hand-Press Journalist," and "Rowdy Days on Newspaper Row."[11]

In addition to newspapers, magazines received notice. Essays were published entitled "Godey's Lady's Book," "The *Appeal to Reason*," "The *Menace*," "Mann of *Town Topics*," "*Variety*," "Mr. Munsey," "Harry Thurston Peck,"[12] "The *Congressional Record*," "The Story of the *Seven Arts*," "The *Social Register*," "Them Asses," and "*transition*: an Epilogue."[13] Other essays discussed aspects of the publishing business, including "Modern First Editions," "Our Mediaeval Typography," "American Books in France," "Modern American Printing," "The Books of Dard Hunter," and "American University Presses."[14]

[9] Chester T. Crowell, June, 1924; Albert Parry, Jan., 1933; Henry Pringle, Feb., 1927; Philip Rubin, March, 1927; Earl W. Shimmons, Sept., 1928; Samuel W. Tait, Jr., April, 1931; Duncan Aikman, May, 1926; Henry Tetlow, Feb., 1933; Kittredge Wheeler, July, 1932; William Allen White, May, 1926; C. Hartley Grattan, June, 1933.

[10] A letter of Feb. 28, 1903, to a Mr. Randall (written on Baltimore *Sun* stationery) calls for a series of "reminisant" articles. Letter in Duke University Library Manuscript Collection.

[11] Walt McDougall, Jan., 1925; W. A. S. Douglas, April, 1927; H. L. Davis, April, 1930; Walt McDougall, June, 1925.

[12] Richard F. Warner, Aug., 1924; George Milburn, July, 1931, and March, 1932; Robert R. Rowe, July, 1926; Hugh Kent, Dec., 1926; Robert L. Duffus, July, 1924; Walter Guest Kellogg, Sept., 1933. Peck was a noted critic before his death in 1910. His editorship of *Bookman* lasted from 1895 until 1902.

[13] Hilton Butler, Dec., 1925; James Oppenheim, June, 1930; Gerald Holland, June, 1932; Bob Brown, Dec., 1933. (The periodical examined was *The Masses*); Eugène Jolas, June, 1931.

[14] George H. Sargent, Feb., 1924; Douglas C. McMurtie, Sept., 1927; Lewis Galantière, May, 1924; Harry Lyman Koopman, May, 1924; Nelson Antrim Crawford, Aug., 1924, and Oct., 1929.

Mencken's pride in his journalistic contributors[15] was a reflection of his long association with the Baltimore *Sun*. While editing the *Mercury,* he remained connected with the Sun-papers, and always he considered himself partly a newspaperman. The notorious editorial on William Jennings Bryan in the October, 1925, *Mercury* had earlier appeared, in substantially the same form, on the editorial page of the *Evening Sun*. Not surprisingly, many of the steadiest contributors to the monthly were also employees of the *Sun*. (The Baltimore affiliations of contributors were not always mentioned in "The American Mercury Authors" page of identification, and the full extent of the relationship must be determined elsewhere.)[16]

For better or worse, then, journalists were the most published writers in the magazine. Although they were deplored as "hammer and tongs men—insensitive, suspicious of glamor, preoccupied . . . with the external . . . the 'national,' and the drab,"[17] some of their essays retain a spark. Among the better essays were James M. Cain's satire "The Editorial Writer" and Duff Gilfond's appreciative "La-Guardia of Harlem." The newspapermen's reliable response to the editor's directives gave him the reservoir of alert authors necessary to fill a hundred and twenty-eight pages each month with acceptable lively fare. Moreover, the journalists were more evenly scattered throughout the United States than other contributors, and this distribution helped the *Mercury* become a review truly national in scope.

[15] Angoff quotes Mencken as having declared that one "usable script by a newspaperman is worth ten by a dentist, twenty-five by a preacher, and fifty by a professor" (*Portrait,* p. 41).

[16] *Sun* personnel who also contributed to the *Mercury* included Duncan Aikman, W. G. Clugston, Virginius Dabney, Gerald Johnson, Frank Kent, Raymond S. Tompkins, W. A. S. Douglas, Margaret Cobb, John Owens, Hamilton Owens, Henry M. Hyde, J. Frederick Essary, and James M. Cain (G. W. Johnson, Frank Kent, H. L. Mencken, and Hamilton Owens, *The Sunpapers of Baltimore* [New York, 1937], pp. 384-386, *passim*). Many of the *Sun* writers would, of course, have contributed to the magazine without the editor's personal encouragement.

[17] F. Scott Fitzgerald, "How to Waste Material: A Note on My Generation," *Bookman,* LXIII (May, 1926), 263.

LEARNED CONTRIBUTORS AND WRITINGS ON EDUCATIONAL MATTERS

NEWSPAPERMEN strengthened the editor's personal influence on the magazine, but other contributors enabled the *Mercury* to transcend Mencken's intellectual limitations. Essays were printed that the editor could neither have written himself nor have outlined to others, and such essays, largely by academic persons, accounted for approximately 20 per cent of the contents. These contributions were usually ignored by critics who disparaged the periodical as too narrowly circumscribed by one man's opinions.

Of the articles by learned men, most dealt with American literature. General essays, like "Call for a Literary Historian," "Teaching American Literature in American Colleges," and "Anon is Dead,"[18] were supplemented by studies of individual authors. Of the subjects of these discussions, Walt Whitman was the most popular: his career was reviewed in "Walt Whitman's Politics," "The End of a Literary Mystery," "Walt Whitman and the *Aristidean*," "Light on Whitman," "A Whitman Manuscript," "Some New Whitman Letters," "Whitman as His Own Press-Agent," "Walt Whitman in England," "Walt Whitman on His Contemporaries," "Walt Whitman on Himself," "Walt Whitman Neologisms," "Walt Whitman and Italian Music," "Whitman in Camden," and "The Father of Them All."[19] Other subjects were Herman Melville, Mark Twain, Am-

[18] Fred Lewis Pattee, June, 1924; Ferner Nuhn, March, 1928; Henry Seidel Canby, May, 1926.

[19] Clifton J. Furness, April, 1929; Frederick P. Hier, Jr., April, 1924 (Hier's essay was an effort to show what parts of *Notes on Walt Whitman as Poet and Person* [published in 1867] were by John Burroughs, whose name was given as author, and what parts were actually by Walt Whitman himself); Thomas O. Mabbott, June, 1924; Emory Holloway, Feb., 1924, Dec., 1924, Feb., 1929, Dec., 1929; Harold Blodgett, Aug., 1929; Horace Traubel, July, 1924, Oct., 1924; Louise Pound, Feb., 1925, Sept., 1925; Dane Yorke, July, 1926; Ernest Boyd, Dec., 1925. Boyd's essay was a rather frantic effort to blame Whitman for current literary excesses. His attack was apparently designed to anger Whitman partisans.

brose Bierce, Edgar Allan Poe, and Stephen Crane, all of whom, like Whitman, were favorably regarded during the twenties. The more genteel writers of the nineteenth century enjoyed little attention, with the exception of James Russell Lowell, who was thrice examined.[20] There were very few discussions of English authors.[21]

Other essays were tributes to noted scholars and teachers, tributes begun by Margaret Münsterberg's "Santayana at Harvard,"[22] and later including "Stanley Hall: A Memory,"[23] "American Anthropology and Franz Boas,"[24] "Jacques Loeb,"[25] and "Titchener at Cornell."[26] Persons qualified by experience or training in special fields published a number of essays, and among these, an emphasis on papers concerning language, in view of Mencken's interest in that field, was not surprising. George Philip Krapp, Louise Pound, and Max Eastman were among the many who wrote regarding language, and even discussed were such minor aspects as "The Russian Language in the United States," "Notes on American Yiddish," "The American Language Fights for Recognition in Moscow," and "The American Language in Mexico."[27] The social sciences were also well represented. Among Vilhjalmur Stefansson's contributions was "Every Science an Exact Science," whereas Joseph J. Spengler contributed "Social Science Becomes Exact."[28] Melville Herskovits inquired, in June, 1924, "What is Race?," then continued his discussion on a less theoretical

[20] C. Hartley Grattan, who wrote one of the essays on Lowell, was the most frequent writer on nineteenth-century American authors in the *Mercury*.

[21] The following five articles represent nearly all that treated English men of letters: Leon Kellner, "A Note on Shakespeare," Feb., 1924; Samuel C. Chew, "Byron in America," March, 1924; Barrett H. Clark, "George Moore at Work," Feb., 1925; Frank Harris, "John Ruskin," June, 1927; H. W. L. Dana, "Shaw in Moscow," March, 1932.

[22] Jan., 1924.

[23] A. E. Hamilton, July, 1924.

[24] Pliny E. Goddard, March, 1926. Franz Boas had contributed "The Question of Racial Purity" to the October, 1924, issue.

[25] Paul De Kruif, July, 1925.

[26] Grace Adams, Dec., 1931.

[27] J. B. Wells, April, 1932; George Wolfe, Aug., 1933; Eli B. Jacobson, Jan., 1931; H. E. McKinstry, March, 1930.

[28] March, 1924; June, 1930.

level in October, 1925, in "The Color Line." Jacques Malan
presented the evidence for "The Possible Origin of Religion
as a Conditioned Reflex,"[29] and Robert H. Lowie dealt with
Indian life in America. Grace Adams was prominent among
contributors on psychology, and Warren S. Thompson's
serious essays on sociology were perhaps the most outstanding contributions from students of that field.

Lewis Mumford often explored in the monthly such
topics as "Architecture and the Machine," "The American
Dwelling House," and "Origins of the American Mind."[30]
Casimir Funk (discoverer of vitamins) was co-author of
"Instinct as a Guide to Food";[31] Woodbridge Riley, in one
of the rare articles on philosophy, explained "The Critical
Realists";[32] and Bernard De Voto, in a series of essays, de-
scribed the Western American frontier. William E. Dodd,
Louis M. Hacker, and Clarence W. Alvord often handled
historical matters in the *Mercury* (two contributions by
Charles Beard were only tangentially historical).[33] Charles
F. Talman wrote of meteorological phenomena, and Morris
Fishbein, Raymond Pearl, and Arthur Cramp surveyed the
medical situation.[34] Music, which increasingly engrossed
Mencken during his editorship, was treated by Isaac Gold-
berg, W. J. Henderson, Ernest Newman, and Edward
Robinson. Of the very few articles dealing with painting
or the plastic arts, most were contributed by Thomas Craven.

In the numerous general articles by teachers and others
on educational matters, the approach was sometimes sober,
yielding such essays as "The Inquiring Mind," "Mr. Jefferson's University," "Rhodes Scholars," and "Aboriginal

[29] March, 1932.
[30] Sept., 1924; April, 1930; July, 1926.
[31] (With Benjamin Harrow), April, 1925.
[32] April, 1924.
[33] "What is a Statesman" was printed in April, 1924, and "A Bankruptcy
Fire-Sale," which concerned European war debt settlements, in July, 1927.
[34] The presence of a large number of popular medical articles (today commonplace in periodicals) again reflects Mencken's interests. He had a hy-
pochondriac's erudition regarding medical terminology, and had originally
introduced himself to Dreiser as a medical reporter (Dreiser, "Henry L.
Mencken and Myself," printed in Goldberg, *The Man Mencken*, pp. 378-379).

Education in America,"[35] essays which would, like many of the straightforward contributions by learned men, have been printed by other quality periodicals. This sobriety is also evident in such flat-footed disquisitions as "School Ventilation" or "Shall We Have Cheap Labor or Good Nurses?"[36] and in the many autobiographical narratives dealing with school and university experiences, such as Olive Brossow's "With Honor."[37]

A more contentious approach toward the problems of learning appeared from time to time. Of critical articles, the most famous was "Portrait of a Rolling-Mill," published in April, 1927. The author, who signed himself "Malcolm B. Susser," exposed New York University as a mass assembly plant wherein hordes of mediocre students were rammed through courses in "Laundering" or "Clothing" to earn degrees. "Portrait of a Rolling-Mill," which expressed harsh opinions of several New York University officials, attracted wide notice, and that issue of the magazine quickly sold out in the New York City area. The administrators of the university bitterly but fruitlessly sought to discover the identity of the writer, who was intimately connected with the institution.[38] Indeed, satirical or simply irreverent treatments of educational matters were common. Mencken commissioned several lampoons of the historians and other academic figures who created some of the propaganda during the hysterically patriotic days of World War I, and far more trivial problems were also featured, like Chester T. Crowell's record of his quarrel with the "bank day" inflicted upon elementary school students in New

[35] Zechariah Chafee, Jr., July, 1924; Emily Clark, Feb., 1930; O. B. Andrews, Jr., Feb., 1927; Robert H. Lowie, Oct., 1928.

[36] Ernest Steel, Oct., 1929; Martha Dreiblatt, April, 1931.

[37] "With Honor" narrative was printed in October, 1929, together with Samuel Lipshutz's "Dim Joys; Cloudy Sorrows." Both essays were winners in a contest sponsored by the *Mercury* for undergraduates. Brossow discussed with candor the meaning of her graduation earlier in 1929 from a midwestern college. As *Time* observed, her narrative was more "drab, and more acidly Mercuric than Lipshutz's" (anon., "Contest," *Time*, XIV [Oct. 7, 1929], 46).

[38] "The professor who did the NYU article is still teaching there. . . . his real name had better be kept secret" (Angoff to Singleton, May 23, 1959).

Jersey.[39] Such academic types as college presidents and deans were favorite subjects for caricature,[40] and two of the most effective satires in the early years of the magazine were Karl Andrist's "The Dean of Music" and James M. Cain's "Pedagogue: Old Style."[41] Nor did other institutions of learning escape the discomfiture of New York University; among them, Duke University especially was a target for editorial barbs and full-scale attacks by contributors.[42] Much lighter in tone were Clarence Darrow's witty clowning with a sociological cliché,[43] Richard Dye's "Saving the Sophomore," Lillian Barrett's "College Elms and Chorus Girls," and Margaret Cobb's "Public School Mamas."[44] The *Mercury's* publication of serious, occasionally learned, essays beside diverse ridicule of pedantry and foolish college administrators seemed to many, as will be shown, a fundamentally healthy policy.

CONTRIBUTORS OF BELLES-LETTRES

BARELY 10 per cent of the contents of the *Mercury* were written by established, or even serious, creative writers. The relative paucity of fiction and verse in the periodical, caused by the editor's growing disdain for such writing, and an emphasis on literature that fulfilled the editor's own narrow theories, nearly prevented the literary offerings in the magazine from surpassing Menck-

[39] The pupils were obliged to bring money for regular deposit in the local bank (May, 1930).

[40] Examples are Nelson Antrim Crawford, "Lady Cops in Cap and Gown," Oct., 1933, and H. Carter Davidson, "The Making of a College President," April, 1931.

[41] April, 1928; May, 1924. (Cain's father was president of Washington College in Maryland, and therefore Cain had had ample opportunity to study elderly professors).

[42] The sharpest condemnation appeared in W. J. Cash, "Buck Duke's University," Sept., 1933.

[43] In "The Edwardses and the Jukeses," Darrow came to the defense of the common and shiftless Jukeses, deciding that they would have made much more congenial neighbors than had the puritanical Edwards dynasty (Oct., 1925).

[44] Nov., 1926; Aug., 1927; April, 1929.

en's shortcomings. Nevertheless, in the realm of poetry, ballads occasionally found their reign challenged. In the same number in which the editorial extolled musical Romantic and Victorian verse (of Swinburne: "[t]here is here a sweet soothing, a healing reassurance, a divine booziness—in brief, all the stuff of a No. 1 poetry") appeared Robinson Jeffers' "Preface," with *vers libre* form and caustic theme:

> . . . the ocean hearted
> With sacred quietness from here to Asia
> Make me ashamed to speak of the active little bodies, the
>   coupling bodies, the misty brainfuls
> Of perplexed passion. Humanity is needless.
> I said, "Humanity is the start of the race, the gate to
>   break away from, the coal to
>   kindle,
> The blind mask crying to be slit with eye-holes. . . ."[45]

Dreiser had similarly ignored the editor's preferences by his free-verse reflections on the fragility of man in a naturalistic universe:

> The little flowers of love and wonder
> That grow in the dark places
> And between the giant rocks of chance
> And the coarse winds of space. . . .[46]

It was observed that Dreiser's poem was somewhat heretical,[47] but critics rarely noticed the variety achieved in the poetry of the monthly. Some of the poems by Louis Untermeyer, Maxwell Bodenheim, Conrad Aiken, DuBose Heyward, Muna Lee, Alice Mary Kimball, Samuel Hoffenstein, and Ruth Lechlitner might well have pleased Mencken for one reason or another, but they did not conspicuously fit his dicta. These poets, though perhaps none of

[45] Dec., 1926.   [46] Jan., 1924.

[47] "[Mencken] has abandoned his valiant belief in the lyric, and admitted to this number four pieces of uninteresting prose called 'Poems,' by Theodore Dreiser" (anon., "The 'American Mercury,'" *Outlook*, CXXXVI, 90).

them were of major stature, were serious and accomplished.[48]

If the poetry in the review cannot be described entirely in terms of the editor's taste, neither can the short stories. Fortunately, despite his praises of the technique of Sinclair Lewis and Ring Lardner, Mencken the Editor was a more flexible judge of fiction than Mencken the Critic, and between 1924 and 1933 a number of stories were accepted which bore little resemblance to writings by Lewis. Among the better of these contributions were Elizabeth Madox Roberts' "On the Mountain-Side," Emily Clark's "Chocolate Sponge," Dorothy Parker's "Mr. Durant," Erskine Caldwell's "The Man Who Looked Like Himself," Julia Peterkin's "The Sorcerer," Ben Hecht's "The Sentimentalist," Josephine Herbst's "Dry Sunday in Connecticut," Idwal Jones's "A Party at Mr. K. Nagoya's," Zona Gale's "Bridal Pond," and Dorothy Thomas' "The Joybell."[49] These stories by established writers, together with fiction by now famous authors, for instance, William Faulkner's "That Evening Sun Go Down," F. Scott Fitzgerald's "Absolution," Sherwood Anderson's "Death in the Woods," and James Branch Cabell's "Above Paradise,"[50] provided relief from the many prosaic narratives and unorganized "slices of life" printed in the *Mercury*. In addition, writers whom Mencken chose less because of their fame than because of his own approval—notably James T. Farrell, but also Thyra Winslow, John Fante, Ruth Suckow, George Milburn, Sara Haardt, Winifred Sanford, and perhaps even Jim Tully—were competent stylists and craftsmen who added breadth to the fiction in the magazine.

In addition to verse and fiction, three kinds of essays of importance to belles-lettres were published. First, and least significant, were the essays written by prominent

[48] Their work was better than the "Five Poems" by the better-known Sherwood Anderson in the May, 1927, issue.

[49] Aug., 1927; June, 1925; Sept., 1924; May, 1933; April, 1925; Oct., 1924; July, 1926; Aug., 1932; Feb., 1928; Nov., 1932.

[50] March, 1931; June, 1924; Sept., 1926; Feb., 1925.

Mercury contributors on each other; for example, James Branch Cabell's "A Note on Sinclair Lewis," Joseph Hergesheimer's "James Branch Cabell," Sara Haardt's "Jim Tully," and Edgar Lee Masters' "The Tragedy of Vachel Lindsay."[51] Second, there were essays on belletristic matters by various writers, including Albert Guérard and John McClure on literary theory,[52] Albert Parry and Maxwell Bodenheim on coteries,[53] tributes to little-known authors,[54] provocative literary criticism,[55] and discussions of past experiences by Edgar Lee Masters and Sherwood Anderson.[56] Several of these essays, especially Anderson's account of his early literary friendships, are important documents.

Third, and equally valuable, were essays with unusual literary merit. Among contributions deserving recognition for reasons of style were Upton Sinclair's "MacDowell," Thomas Beer's "Hypocrisy," Hendrik Willem Van Loon's "Bread," Carl Van Vechten's "A Note on Tights," Joseph Hergesheimer's "Lillian Gish," Joseph Warren Beach's "Cyprian Hymn," J. Frank Dobie's "The Pacing White Mustang," and Walter Prichard Eaton's "In Defense of the Puritan."[57] Most of these prose compositions did not reflect the editor's point of view—especially Eaton's "In Defense of the Puritan"—and none of them was influenced by Mencken's style. Others nearly as remarkable were G. D. Eaton's "Harriet Beecher Stowe," Samuel Chew's dialogue "Mr. Moore and Mr. Chew," Waldo Frank's "Mid-America Revisited," Carl Van Doren's "The Comic Patriot,"

[51] Aug., 1930; Jan., 1928; May, 1928; July, 1933.

[52] Guérard's essay was "Fixed and Floating Literature" (Dec., 1932), and McClure's studies were cast in the form of dialogues between "Scamander" and "Polycrates," as in "Art" (June, 1928).

[53] "Belles Lettres among the Russian Émigrés" (July, 1933); "On Literary Groups" (Oct., 1924).

[54] E.g., Tomás Blanco's "A Porto Rican Poet: Luis Palés Matos" (Sept., 1930).

[55] E.g., Joseph Wood Krutch's "The Strange Case of Poe" (Nov., 1925).

[56] Masters contributed "The Poetry Revival of 1914" (July, 1932) and "The Genesis of Spoon River" (Jan., 1933). Anderson's article was "They Come Bearing Gifts" (Oct., 1930).

[57] Jan., 1926; Jan., 1927; Jan., 1926; Aug., 1924; April, 1924; Jan., 1927; Dec., 1927; April, 1924.

Elmer Davis' "The Mortician," and Gregory Mason's "This Ain't the Waldorf."[58] Anthologists seeking essays of merit should not neglect these examples in favor of the more characteristic, more showy, and, frequently, more "dated" satirical essays.

There were in the *Mercury,* then, several established creators of belles-lettres whose independent work retains worth. Perhaps the most curious fact was that great numbers of the more famous and talented writers were published only once. (The reasons for this and the increasing dearth of "big-name" authors will later be explored.) But, despite the editor's occasional acceptance of literature in disagreement with his personal theories, and despite the presence of serious belletristic matter in the magazine, Mencken's central policy remained unshaken: the *Mercury* was a review for a "middle minority" to whom "beautiful letters" were simply another aspect of American culture— like medicine, education, or politics. This policy, as will be shown, angered avant-gardists and others, but it was suitable for a balanced general magazine.

MISCELLANEOUS CONTRIBUTORS

ABOUT one-fifth of the contents of the periodical before 1928, and a slightly higher proportion thereafter, were contributed by amateurs, "discoveries," and writers belonging to one or another minority grouping. The other quality monthlies did not choose to rely so extensively on a rather motley assortment of tradesmen, panhandlers, retired military men, convicts, radicals, "old timers," proletarians, social workers, and Negroes. Mencken took special pride in his ability to wring manuscripts from persons who had no more than perhaps one or two printable narratives in them. After his editorship had ended, Mencken

[58] April, 1927; Jan., 1924; July, 1926; Feb., 1924; May, 1927; May, 1925.

was credited with the following reflection: "I remember [the minor] things a damn sight better than the clever pieces by Tom Beer and Cabell or the other names. And I think . . . history will remember them better. It's these birds of passage that make a magazine, that stamp an editor . . . ."[59] His judgment was possibly inspired by recollections of the very sympathetic editing he had lavished on manuscripts by "birds of passage," but some of the results were indeed memorable.

One of the best of such contributions came from an obscure Texas nurse, Hermine Kane, whose essay, "The End," described death as she had seen it come to various kinds of hospital patients.[60] This matter-of-fact yet sensitive essay, one of the *Mercury*'s minor masterpieces, heads a long list of articles by professional medical persons. In addition to the many contributions by Morris Fishbein, J. Arthur Cramp, and Raymond Pearl were essays by other physicians, biologists, and technicians covering many aspects of medicine, ranging from rather irresponsible debunking, like Logan Clendening's attack on periodic health check-ups,[61] to more specialized topics: "Sodium Amytal as an Anesthetic," "Skin Grafting," "The New Surgical Treatment of Tuberculosis of the Lungs,"[62] etc. These brief articles, often commissioned by Mencken from friends on the faculty of the Johns Hopkins Medical School, were usually printed in the "Arts and Sciences" department. Sometimes a mildly sensational essay would be intended to titillate the medical profession, such as "Lewis G. Arrowsmith's" reports on the "Lodge Doctor" and "The Young Doctor in New York."[63] Generally, however, the magazine showed respect and even cordiality toward the hallowed canons of the American Medical Association.

[59] Angoff, *Portrait*, p. 120.   [60] April, 1930.
[61] "Health Audits" (Oct., 1928).
[62] J. S. Sweeney, Aug., 1931; H. E. Hullsiek, Aug., 1929; J. M. Gibson, Sept., 1932.
[63] Dec., 1930, and Jan., 1931.

Another profession represented in the *Mercury* was law; the chief expounders of legal arcana were H. H. Sawyer, Anthony Turano, William Seagle, and Carl Meyer. But more numerous were the professional musicians who helped such musicologists as Ernest Newman and Edward Robinson review the art. Virgil Thomson, Winthrop Parkhurst, Harry Smith, and D. W. Sinclair wrote on more general subjects, while others examined special problems: "On Learning to Play the 'Cello," "Absolute Pitch," "The Woodwind," "The Harpsichord,"[64] etc. These articles were occasionally accompanied by entire pages of printed music or were adorned by simple graphs, which constituted, together with a few maps, the only illustrations in the periodical.

Of the maps appearing in the monthly, most supplemented battle descriptions by active and retired military personnel. The best of the contributions from military men was K. C. McIntosh's "The Campaign of B.C. 588-86," the story of Zedekiah's futile resistance against the wiles of Jeremiah and the armies of Nebuchadnezzer. McIntosh, a lieutenant-commander in the navy, based his narrative of Zedekiah's struggle on the Book of Jeremiah.[65] "The Campaign of B.C. 588-86" was nearly unparalleled in the *Mercury* in that it pretended no connection whatever with the American scene. A less remote slice of military history was prepared by Captain Henry Swindler (army), whose "The So-Called Lost Battalion" was a respectful account of a World War I episode.[66] Nor were America's Indian wars forgotten; "The Art of Fighting Indians" was by James H. Cook, and "Custer and Rain In The Face" was by General Eli L. Huggins.[67] Some discussions of military history and of the art of war were penned by officers who chose to

[64] Doris Stevens, May, 1926; Nicolas Slonimsky, Oct., 1930; John Redfield, Jan., 1928; Grace Overmyer, April, 1927.

[65] May, 1924. In this number was also army Major Emer Yeager, who wrote concerning "Airplane Observation."

[66] Nov., 1928.

[67] June, 1931; Nov., 1926. (Huggins had retired from active service in 1903).

conceal their identity, but others, like Arlington Conway, Elbridge Colby, and G. A. Moore, signed their names to articles dealing with warfare as an inevitable phenomenon.

Enough studies of architectural matters were published to show some slight interest; treatises entitled "Radio City —and After," "Symbolic Architecture," "Native Architecture in Southern California," "Skyscrapers for Art Museums," "Churches in the Moronic Mode," and "Is the Architect an Outsider?,"[68] together with several reports on landscape architecture by Elbert Peets, suggest the scope of contributions from that profession. With architecture, little serious editorial concern was shown.[69]

Fully half of the narratives by businessmen had to do with one aspect or another of the production and sale of alcoholic beverages, an emphasis caused by the editor's desire to keep memories of that industry alive throughout the Prohibition era. Businesses more legal were reviewed by persons suitably experienced; for instance, Carl Werner wrote on the tobacco industry, Frances Allen on clothing and fashion, W. L. Wanlass on business conditions, and, most frequently, Henry Tetlow on a variety of mercantile topics. None of these essays, of course, challenged the profit system; for all its criticisms of Babbittry, any reservations about capitalism in the early *Mercury* were left implicit. Occasional flip studies of men prominently associated with capital, like "J. P. the Younger" in the June, 1927, issue,[70] did not do much to qualify the basic economic conservatism of the periodical.

[68] Ralph Adams Cram, July, 1931; Lewis Mumford, June, 1926; P. E. Murphy, April, 1928; Lee Simonson, Aug., 1927; F. R. Webber, Nov., 1927; W. E. Willner, March, 1932.

[69] Mencken's only intercession on behalf of good architecture in the *Mercury* was a frivolous gesture; in "The Library" for the May, 1928, issue, he advocated hanging architects whose work was "intolerably bad": "Let each city select its worst once a year (say by vote of all the practising architects of the place . . . or that of the local subscribers to *The American Mercury,* or the *Atlantic Monthly,* or the *New Republic,* or *House and Garden* . . .) then let the nominee be seized by the police, given twenty or thirty strokes of the bastinado, and hanged in front of his masterpiece."

[70] W. M. Walker, the author of the piece, was immediately fired from the

Nevertheless, "liberal expression," as observed by Frederick J. Hoffman, worked, during the twenties, "in an uneasy partnership with the Marxists, the aesthetic radicals, and the readers of Mr. Mencken's *Mercury*."[71] This temporary truce can be traced, to some degree, within the pages of the *Mercury* itself. Mencken was hospitable toward liberal contributors, and was certainly more hospitable toward political radicals than toward aesthetic ones. Essays by radicals appeared in the monthly even before the Depression, not so much because of the editor's belief in freedom of speech, but because of his agreement with certain small areas of leftist thought—notably in the anticlericalism shared by both parties—and because such contributors were apparently willing to tone down the worst of their didacticism and militancy for a chance to appear in the magazine. It is important to examine this strange alliance, because leftist criticism, as much as any other single factor, was to determine the outcome of Mencken's editorship.

Some of the radicals were represented by autobiographical sketches. Of such contributions, Emma Goldman's contributions, including "The Voyage of the *Buford*" and "The Assassination of McKinley,"[72] were perhaps the most significant. Ironically enough, Michael Gold, who, as editor of the *New Masses,* was one of the most vitriolic critics of the *Mercury,* willingly allowed both autobiographical pieces and fiction to be printed in the green-backed monthly, as did Louis Adamic. Adamic, born in Yugoslavia, had been a manual worker on the West Coast before being discovered by Mencken. One of Adamic's experiences as a member of the I.W.W., as reported in "The 'Assassin' of Wilson,"[73] nearly ranks in importance with Emma Goldman's autobiographical documents. Another kind of leftist

---

staff of the New York *Herald-Tribune* for his effort ("The American Mercury Authors," Sept., 1927).

[71] *The Twenties* (New York, [1955]), p. 338.
[72] July, 1931; Sept., 1931.
[73] Oct., 1930.

contribution was the sympathetic portraits of radicals; for example, Emma Goldman's "Johann Most," Harbor Allen's "The Flynn," and Traverse Clement's "Mooney."[74] In such articles the human-interest slant was emphasized.

Other leftist contributors were Granville Hicks and James T. Farrell, both of whom were destined to become prominent Marxian critics during the thirties. Hicks, however, attacked no subject younger than World War I, focusing on such bygone creampuffs as Hamilton Wright Mabie.[75] Farrell restricted his contributions to fiction, as did Daniel Hennessey.[76] James Rorty, who frequently contributed to the *New Masses,* was represented only by verse. James Oneal, the socialist who contributed "The Communist Hoax" to the January, 1924, number, wrote several allied studies for the monthly. One of the more outspoken articles in the first years of the *Mercury,* from a leftist point of view, was "Cossacks," an account of brutality by mounted company police perpetrated against some Pennsylvania strikers.[77] Although "Cossacks" was not as militant as Margaret Sanger's "The War against Birth Control,"[78] her crusades had begun to take on a certain respectability by the middle twenties.

[74] June, 1926; Dec., 1926; May, 1929.

[75] "A Christian Literatus" (Oct., 1928).

[76] Hennessey, whose contributions to the monthly were signed "Robert Jeans," received a note in "The American Mercury Authors" (Aug., 1931) that illustrates the unreliability of identifications in that department: "Robert Jeans is twenty-five years old. He comes of a theatrical family and is by training and inclination a dramatic actor. Between seasons he has bummed around the country and worked at odd jobs that brought him into contact with the prize-ring, carnivals, race tracks, and other rackets."

This announcement should be compared to Louis Adamic, *My America: 1928-1938* (New York, [1938]), pp. 68-71 for a less romantic portrait. The proletarian radicals were rough, impetuous men; Owen Francis, who had been published in the monthly, once left two manuscripts in the *Mercury* office: "[Francis] did not meet Mencken, who was in Baltimore, but talked with his assistant, Charles Angoff, who he did not like . . . perhaps because Angoff, who I knew slightly, was so clearly an intellectual. The *Mercury* rejected the stories with a little green slip reading 'Thank you,' and for an hour Hal was like a kicked dog. . . . Then he raged. . . ." Francis, according to Adamic, was barely restrained from returning to the office to "beat up Angoff" (*ibid.,* pp. 53-54).

[77] W. L. Nunn and Frederick Woltman, Dec., 1928.

[78] June, 1924.

In addition to Louis Adamic and the one-time lumber-man James Stevens, other proletarians were published. Among such workaday and non-political narratives were "The Work of the Bricklayer," by a bricklayer; "Boyhood in a Coal Town," by a coal miner; "Dockwallopers," by a longshoreman; and "Happy Ending," by a taxi driver.[79] This seeming partiality toward labor did not often extend to labor organizations.[80] Another policy unusual for a quality monthly was that of printing work by panhandlers. Henri Tascheraud's "The Art of Bumming a Meal" and Thomas F. Healy's "The Hobo Hits the Highroad"[81] were samples of the better writing by such itinerants. Jim Tully also contributed accounts of hoboes, accounts occasionally far below the *Mercury*'s standard.[82] The presence of such materials led one humorous magazine, according to John Rosser, to present a cartoon of a park bum "saying to his ragged fellow sprawled on a bench: 'I liked that thing of yours in the current *Mercury*.' "[83]

Another unlikely source of contributors was prisons. Convicts whose works were accepted included Robert Blake, Ernest Booth, Robert Joyce Tasker, David Purroy, Victor Folke Nelson, and Lawrence Maynard. Writings by prison inmates ranged from informative essays like Ernest Booth's "The Language of the Underworld" to the pulp sensationalism of David Purroy's "On the Lam."[84] On the

[79] Charles Powers, Nov., 1931; Jack Conroy, May, 1931; Paul Peters, May, 1929; Patrick O'Mara, Dec., 1932.

[80] An exception was E. A. Wieck's praise of an old labor organizer in "General Alexander Bradley" (May, 1926). (Wieck was, incidentally, a coal miner.) More characteristic discussions were D. W. Ryder's "The Unions Lose San Francisco" (April, 1926) and E. W. Shimmons' "The Twilight of the A.F. of L." (March, 1929).

[81] June, 1925; July, 1926.

[82] An example is "Thieves and Vagabonds" (May, 1928), which ends as frantic melodrama. Tully once wrote to Nathan: "I have beaten the writing racket mainly because I am a barroom smart" (Tully to Nathan, n.d., printed in *Intimate Notebooks*, pp. 70-73, p. 71).

[83] "H. L. Mencken," *Real America* (Chicago, 1933), n.p. In "Articles about H. L. Mencken: Clippings: 1919-1933," E.P.M.C. I am unable to find this drawing.

[84] May, 1928; Aug., 1928.

whole, the experiment proved to be, as the editor admitted, unsatisfactory.[85]

In contrast to the relative failure to draw memorable work from convicts was the consistently sound work by and about Negroes. Mencken once wrote that "[e]very colored author in America sends me everything he writes. Most of it is bad, but now and then I strike something that is really good, and I always yield to the temptation to print it."[86] Although this statement conveys a somewhat exaggerated notion of the participation of Negro authors in the magazine, nearly a score were represented. The better-known Negro writers whose work was published were Eugene Gordon, Walter White, W. E. B. DuBois, Langston Hughes, Louis Dublin, James Weldon Johnson, Countee Cullen, and George S. Schuyler. Among other Negro contributors were Albon L. Holsey, Kelly Miller, H. Nathaniel Hall, Randolph Fisher, and J. A. Rogers. Contributions by these men dealt with the social difficulties confronting colored people, cultural problems, and a wide variety of other topics, including Eugene Gordon's "The Negro's Inhibitions" and George S. Schuyler's autobiographical "Memoirs of a Pearl Diver."[87] Equally noteworthy were informed essays by white contributors about Negro life (especially essays by L. M. Hussey, Howard Odum, and Eleanor Wembridge) and the memorable Negro characters created by Eugene O'Neill, Emily Clark, and Julia Peterkin. The lack of cant in both white and Negro contributions would make an anthology of *Mercury* writings about colored America feasible.

It is not surprising that nearly all the contributors were

[85] Of his convict "discoveries," the editor wrote in 1932 that "[O]ne of them, arrested in New Jersey for burglary, tried to make it appear that he was driven into crime by the failure of some unnamed magazine to pay him promptly, and the inference was that it was The American Mercury. . . . [A]nother sweet gentleman came out of San Quentin and announced that I had hailed him as the greatest author ever heard of. I began to believe that it is unwise to fool with such babies" (HLM to Jim Tully, Aug. 3, 1932. Copy in P.M.C.).

[86] HLM to Bob Brown, November 12, 1932. Letter in N.Y.M.C.

[87] Feb., 1928; April, 1931. (A "pearl-diver" refers to a restaurant dishwasher).

Americans; only a handful of foreigners were qualified
to write for so national a review. This situation, however,
was not defined until after the first invitations to writers
had been sent out by the editors. Aldous Huxley, one of
the few Englishmen on the first list of potential contributors, was prodded into sending a manuscript, but it
was only an off-color poem that had been elsewhere rejected
and which was likewise turned down by the *Mercury*.[88]
A story by W. L. George, an essay by the English drama
critic Arthur Bingham Walkley, along with Frank Harris' article on Ruskin, were all published, significantly
enough, in the spring of 1924. W. J. Turner was one of
the two editors of the *London Mercury* to have essays
printed.[89] Other English authors were William Orton,
Theodore Maynard, and Major Greenwood.[90] Even fewer
Frenchmen were printed, among those few being Jean-
Jacques Brousson and Albert Leon Guérard. Better represented among foreigners were Latin Americans: Ernesto
Montenegro, Juan Gómez, Jorge J. Blanco, Roberto Piña,
Tomás Blanco, Luis Muñoz Marin, and José Miguel Peterson. These authors were assisted by William McFee, Carleton Beals, Muna Lee, and other American-born sojourners
in describing Latin America and the Caribbean. The standard attitude toward countries south of the United States
was one of marked cordiality, a cordiality largely denied to
Canada and Europe. This impression was heightened by
several writers like Owen P. White in the United States,
who characteristically showed Spanish-Americans as more
agreeable than Anglo-Saxons as citizens and neighbors.

Of the contributors who fit no ready classification, yet
who helped the *Mercury* attain its journalistic goals, perhaps the most noteworthy were those who discussed religion. One article, for instance, with a point of view that

[88] Kemler, *Mr. Mencken*, p. 169.
[89] Milton Waldman, although an editor of the *London Mercury*, was an
American.
[90] Greenwood, whose "Speculations on Hatred" were printed in March,
1925, supported his thesis with footnotes—an unusual procedure for the
magazine.

little resembled Mencken's truculent materialism was written by Charles Fiske, a Bishop of the Episcopal Church. Others whose approach was more finely tempered than that of the many critics of Baptists and Methodists were Mortimer Smith and Eugene Pharo, who wrote, respectively, "The Unitarians" and "On Being a Quaker."[91] Mencken also recognized, it seems, that inside reports on Mormonism had made unfailingly good copy for over ninety years and that ex-Catholic priests had made news for over four centuries.[92] And always, in the background, were the stark sketches like "A Pastor's Daughter" and "Preacher's Wife" coming out of obscure regions of America.[93]

Although the contributors to the *Mercury* achieved, during the twenties, considerable diversity, the monthly did not lack an air of distinct individuality, nor did the editor appear to be a fawning eclectic. The *Atlantic* or *Scribner's* would possibly have printed a chess player's reflections on the game,[94] or urbane essays on insects,[95] or articles by such popular intellectuals of the day as Margaret Mead, but they would probably not have accepted Hugh Bradley's study of an old baseball umpire, or a sober survey of the literature of suicide notes,[96] or the miscellany of writings by convicts and proletarians. Mencken even strove to give a "show of fairness"[97] to Villagers, exiles, and such folk, who, like the despised farmers, remained largely unrepresented in the magazine. Like most editors, however currently well-received their own prejudices, Mencken accepted a wide variety of well-written and interesting material when it came to hand.

[91] Oct., 1929; Nov., 1932.
[92] Examples of the *Mercury*'s writings concerning Mormonism are L. W. Larsen's "Mormon Polygamy: The Last Phase" (July, 1933) and N. B. Musser's "A Mormon Boyhood" (Jan., 1930). E. Boyd Barrett was an apostate Jesuit.
[93] "A Pastor's Daughter," by Ethel Brown, appeared in Aug., 1928; Merritt Wimberly's "Preacher's Wife" was printed in Sept., 1928.
[94] "Chess Reclaims a Devotee" (Aug., 1930). Alfred Kreymborg, the author, was also a poet and playwright of some note.
[95] H. M. Parshley wrote most of the *Mercury*'s treatments of insect life.
[96] Howard Wolfe, "Suicide Notes" (Nov., 1931).
[97] Angoff, *Portrait*, p. 195.

7

THE ACCEPTANCE OF THE *MERCURY* 1924-1928

THE READERS

IN May, 1924, Mencken wrote that the monthly was doing sufficiently well that he felt justified in hoping "to run all Summer,"[1] a cautious enough attitude. By 1925, despite an average circulation of over 50,000 copies per month, it was still not known whether the enterprise would enjoy a lasting success; a poet caught the spirit of the venture in a poem which began:

> *Mencken, Nathan, and Knopf one night*
> *Sailed off in a silver bowl,*
> *Sailed off from a city of dazzling light*
> *Out to an unknown goal. . . .*[2]

It was not until 1926 that both the "editor and publisher were . . . reasonably sure that the first two years' growth had not been an unnatural and impermanent thing,"[3] a confidence based on a circulation in 1926 of approximately 70,000 copies each month. In 1927 the average monthly sales approached 80,000, with a peak reached early in 1928, when the circulation nearly reached 84,000 copies.[4] Such a circulation in a magazine costing fifty cents, without any pictorial illustrations, and with its contents concealed behind the cover, represented a solid achievement.

[1] HLM to Goodman, May 2, 1924. "Letters to Philip Goodman," I.
[2] Louise G. Humphrey, "The Three Wise Men (With Apologies to Eugene Field . . .)" (n.p., 1925), "Pamphlets on H. L. Mencken: 1917-30," E.P.M.C.
[3] *Three years*, p. 13.
[4] Interview with Charles Angoff, New York City, N.Y., Dec. 27, 1958.

The audience of the *Mercury* can be defined more accurately than that of most other periodicals of the day; people were self-conscious about being readers of the magazine. The class of readers most often mentioned were the college students, who followed the monthly with enthusiasm. According to Edmund Wilson (writing of the twenties), "when the college magazines do not sound like Mencken's *Mercury,* they sound like Eliot's *Criterion*.[5] Certainly the collegians were fond of parodying the *Mercury,* and many parodies with such features as the publisher's name changed to "Alfred A. Knock" and a "Synical Notes" department were issued by the staffs of college humor magazines.[6] (Sometimes these imitations led to disciplinary measures against the offending students.)[7] Some undergraduates carried the magazine to class to irritate their teachers,[8] and this habit caused unpopular or stodgy lecturers to be confronted with green-backed magazines waved before them by rebellious students.[9] This situation led one elderly professor at the University of Chicago to cry in despair: "the one thing that makes me fear for the future is the number of our students who read the *American Mercury;* on the campus you see it under every arm; they absorb everything in it."[10] On one occasion when direct action was taken by a college faculty against the monthly, the students protested.[11] A

[5] "Literary Politics," *New Republic,* LIII (Feb. 1, 1928), 289.

[6] Several of these parodies are bound in "The American Mercury: Miscellanea: 1923-1933," E.P.M.C.

[7] John E. Drewry, "Mencken and the Mercury: Magazine Still Reflects the Molding Hand and Policies of Its Initial Editor," *Quill,* XXVI (March, 1938), 11. Students at Northwestern who "imitated the *Mercury* in their campus magazine" were threatened with expulsion, then "let off with the lame warning to 'behave next time,'" but "the English faculty heard the disturbing sound of snickers from the back of its classrooms" (Manchester, *Mencken,* p. 212).

[8] Cleaton, *Books & Battles,* p. 184.

[9] "The Reverend John Roach Straton, addressing four hundred students at Harvard, compared Bryan to Gladstone and opened an attack on Mencken. He was heckled to a halt by boys waving green-backed magazines" (Manchester, *Mencken,* p. 158).

[10] Mark Sullivan, *Our Times,* p. 413.

[11] Undergraduates at Marshall College in West Virginia protested the withdrawal of the monthly from their library by holding "a mock funeral

report by James T. Farrell written as late as 1954 suggests something of the undergraduate response: ". . . those of us who were young in the twenties remember. How eagerly we waited for that green-covered magazine. . . . How avidly we read [Mencken]! To us he was a spokesman, a liberator, a voice speaking out in the name of truth, honesty, and sincerity."[12] Seniors at Columbia University repeatedly voted the *Mercury* their favorite magazine;[13] it was said to have been in conspicuous attendance at football games in the Yale Bowl;[14] and it had followers at Harvard, too.[15] John Farrar wrote in 1926 that an "observing traveler on Philadelphia trains or a sojourner in the Pennsylvania Station at vacation time will readily testify to the numbers of copies of a bright green magazine tucked under voluminous sleeves of Princeton-bound coonskin coats," but Farrar slyly hinted that the monthly in some cases might have been "carried for purposes of decoration only."[16] A certain callowness was identified with some of the young followers; "Fledgling intellectuals were denounced by each other as readers of *The Mercury*,"[17] and others old enough to know better were found to have embraced the magazine awkwardly.[18] *Time* suggested, in 1927, that the monthly was read at least as much by "sheepish culture-hunters" as "by serious people." In fairness, however, the reporter admitted that the "half-baked phrase-snatcher on whose lips 'babbitt' and 'moron' are now most often heard must infuriate Mr. Mencken. . . ."[19]

by torchlight, wearing crepe on their arms and carrying the latest copy on a stretcher across the campus" (Manchester, *Mencken*, p. 157).

[12] *Reflections at Fifty and Other Essays*, p. 44.

[13] Anon., [advertisement], *Publishers' Weekly*, CXVI (May 18, 1929), 2311.

[14] Whipple, "The Revolution on Quality Street, Part II," *Survey*, LVII, 428.

[15] Kemler, *Mr. Mencken*, pp. 204-206.

[16] "College Reading," *Bookman*, LXIII (April, 1926), 131.

[17] Cleaton, *Books & Battles*, p. 184.

[18] Thomas Wolfe, writing on Oct. 4, 1928, to Aline Bernstein from Europe, was harrassed to desperation by some tourists "full of quotations from the American Mercury . . . . I was nauseated by them" (*Letters of Thomas Wolfe*, p. 144).

[19] Anon., "Think Stuff," *Time*, IX, 24.

The young ladies of the period found the magazine suited to their purposes: "coeds who considered themselves sophisticated carried copies on the campus with the cover prominently displayed in order that their advanced ideas might not go unnoticed."[20] One commentator claimed that even women beyond their college years flaunted "the green cover in place of the familiar buff of the *Atlantic,* and with the reverse meaning: 'To hell with chaperones!' "[21] Moral critics who noticed such use of the periodical deplored its aphrodisiacal function,[22] a function that might have been useful to men readers also; one lusty "young widow," advertising in a California newspaper for a housekeeper position, specified that her employer be a "single gentleman of simple tastes. Subscriber to *American Mercury* preferred."[23]

Even high school students chose sides, and prim, disapproving high school parodies[24] balanced wild approval from less austere quarters.[25] Young people from the South[26] and the far West[27] found the periodical to their liking, and there is even a claim that some of the creative avant-

---

[20] Burton Rascoe, *We Were Interrupted,* p. 198.

[21] Whipple, "The Revolution on Quality Street, Part II," *Survey,* LVII, 428.

[22] Hazleton Spencer, "Thunder in the Index," *Saturday Review of Literature,* III (May 28, 1927), 858.

[23] Cleaton, *Books & Battles,* pp. 184-185.

[24] An example was named *El-Del-ator,* and was printed in an Elkins Park, Pennsylvania, secondary school ("The American Mercury: Miscellanea: 1923-1933," E.P.M.C.).

[25] "[J]azz was only a musical version of the hard-cutting broadsides that two foxy studs named Mencken and Nathan were beginning to shoot at Joe Public in the pages of the *American Mercury* . . . . That *Mercury* really got to be the Austin High Gang's Bible. It looked to us like Mencken was yelling the same message . . . his words were practically lyrics to our hot jazz" (Milton Mezzrow and Bernard Wolfe, *Really the Blues* [New York, 1946], pp. 103, 109).

[26] W. J. Cash, *The Mind of the South* (Garden City, N.Y., 1951), p. 376, explains the role of the magazine in the lives of "young Southerners of literary and intellectual pretensions."

[27] Louis Adamic described the West Coast scene: "I seldom missed an issue, although in justice to myself I should add that I was not one of the young men, in Los Angeles and elsewhere in the United States, who strolled around with copies of the . . . review under their arms, in token of their being 'civilized' and of their intellectual superiority to the general run of the inhabitants of America" (*Laughing in the Jungle* [New York, 1932], p. 262).

garde youth had their noses pressed wistfully against the glass: "for all their assumed indifference, [they] hoped for a friendly nod from the inner sanctum of the *American Mercury,* dominated by . . . Henry L. Mencken."[28] The staff of the monthly were proud of the youth of their readers, and elaborately statistical brochures were drawn up showing how young were their subscribers.[29]

In addition to collegians and other youths were college teachers, who Mencken had thought in 1923 would provide a share of the readers.[30] Although exaggerated claims have been advanced regarding followers teaching in the universities,[31] it was true that in the very first years of the monthly it enjoyed respect from many professors. Not only did its sedate cover make it look reassuringly "like a scholarly monthly,"[32] but also it contained serious, informative articles like those dealing with Walt Whitman. Ironically enough, even while the magazine was being banned on some campuses by hostile administrators, Grant C. Knight in 1926 edited *Readings from the American Mercury* expressly for college students, as his preface made clear: "The present aim in writing and speech has come to involve clearness rather than turgidity, simple emphasis rather than rhetoric. To make this plain to the student and to encourage him to think more independently and to write with less self-consciousness, this volume of selections from an open-eyed periodical has been prepared."[33] And academic approval, even after the greatest triumphs of the magazine

[28] Harvey Wish, *Contemporary America: The National Scene since 1900* (New York, 1945), p. 339.

[29] These brochures are in "The American Mercury: Miscellanea: 1923-1933," E.P.M.C.; one stated that about four-fifths of all readers were "under fifty years of age."

[30] HLM to Carl Van Doren, Aug. 20, 1923. Copy in P.M.C.

[31] Manchester (*Mencken,* p. 150) stated of "college towns" that "circulation seemed to approximate population."

[32] Wood, *Magazines in the United States,* p. 195.

[33] "Preface," *Readings from the American Mercury* (New York, 1926), p. vi. Knight included a dig at the Victorians: "It is no longer believed necessary to intimidate the undergraduate by requiring him to pore over Macaulay and Pater, Hazlitt and Stevenson, and to assume that worthy models of English prose ceased with them and their fellows" (*ibid.,* p. v).

were over, could be as extravagantly phrased as any of the attacks: "If Mr. Mencken had died at forty there would never have been an *American Mercury,* nor any of the post-World-War writing[!]. . . . For years the undergraduate has worshipped at his shrine. The result has been that the public has made some mental effort, and has learned to be respectful to critical thinking."[34]

Other readers included business executives and members of the professions. Some of the many pamphlets emanating from the *Mercury* office openly boasted that their readers tended "to be somewhat well-to-do,"[35] an assertion supported by lists of "typical" readers. These lists now appear silly[36] or even snobbish, [37] and there were indications by about 1927 that the magazine had ceased to court the "civilized minority" with the assiduity with which it sought frankly middlebrow subscribers.[38] During the first years of the monthly, however, it was often referred to as the "Bible of the sophisticates."[39] "Intelligentsia" was another frequent label applied to readers, but sometimes critics felt obliged to explain what they meant by the term. Leon Whipple especially tried to analyze the journal's readers. First mentioned were "disillusioned long-term Americans" who recalled a golden age during which hardy, freethinking, individualistic, and libertarian Americans flourished. This class of readers deplored the Babbittry and

[34] Percy H. Boynton, *The Challenge of Modern Criticism,* pp. 37, 40.

[35] "The Editor Reviews His Magazine," ([New York], n.d.), [p. 1] ("The American Mercury: Miscellanea: 1923-1933," E.P.M.C.).

[36] It was claimed that through "tactful questioning" on the Twentieth Century Limited train in 1924, a reader compiled the following list of those perusing the monthly: "An internationally known surgeon; A beautiful actress; A successful novelist; An old lady; A banker, New York's Maecenas; The Mother Superior of a select Indiana Convent; A captain in the U.S. Army; and An Episcopalian Clergyman" (*Three Years,* pp. 6-8).

[37] An example was a booklet entitled "The American Mercury's Directory of Directors for New York City," a list of very wealthy and influential New Yorkers who were paid subscribers in 1925-1926; proudly listed was Nicholas Murray Butler, president of Columbia University, together with socialites, philanthropists, and others, all of whom were duly labeled with whatever honorary degrees, etc., they might have accumulated.

[38] The phrase "civilized minority" became conspicuously absent in all circulars and advertisements concerning the *Mercury* after the first two years.

[39] Foster Rhea Dulles, *Twentieth Century America* (Boston, 1945), p. 284.

reformers and Puritans, as did the second class identified by Whipple; readers who were "Continental-minded, by birth or in spirit, who care naught for—do not even know —the tradition behind *Scribner's* or *The Atlantic.*" These "newer alien strains," claimed Whipple, "sceptic in mind and esthetic in feeling," were usually located in large metropolitan areas. The *Mercury* was itself considered in no way "foreign," but still was held as having arisen from "a ferment in our life different from that of the old quality group—a yeast that has produced *The Dial* and *The Masses.*"[40] Certainly the disregard shown to Anglo-Saxons in the review, together with the sympathy shown most minorities, would have accounted for the editor's following statement: "The figures show that the magazine is by no means confined to the so-called intelligentsia. My belief is that it reaches the minorities of all the larger national groups. In every such group there are men and women who were disgusted by the prevailing blather. The central aim of [the *Mercury*] is to provide consolation and entertainment for such persons."[41] It would probably be a mistake, however, to assume that lower-class immigrant stock followed the periodical.[42]

Of readers abroad, the English naturally were the most numerous, and most of the two thousand or so *Mercury's* that were shipped monthly to Europe, during the most prosperous years before the depression, stayed in England.[43] That the magazine was occasionally reported in odd corners of the world was probably accounted for by copies

[40] "The Revolution on Quality Street, Part II," *Survey,* LVII, 427-428.

[41] HLM to Leon Whipple, n.d., printed in "The Revolution on Quality Street, Part II," *Survey,* LVII, 427.

[42] Adamic recorded the following interview with some Slavic longshoremen in New York City: "Had I succeeded in getting anything printed yet? Yes, in the *American Mercury,* etc. They had not heard of any of the magazines I mentioned. I said the *Mercury* came in green covers. 'Oh yes, *bogati!*' exclaimed one of the older men, half in English, half in [Croatian], 'I seen it! Yeah! But that's a high-class book—no?' . . . [A] younger man said, 'It's one way to make a living.'—'Little *you* know!' I cried" (*My America,* p. 107).

[43] Interview with Charles Angoff, New York City, Dec. 27, 1958. The periodical could be purchased in such European cities as Berlin and Paris.

left behind by expatriated or merely traveling Americans; except perhaps to well-educated Mexicans, and possibly some Canadians, the review could have had little international appeal.

From a religious point of view, most of the subscribers were, of course, liberal in persuasion. Although the editor once flatly stated that "all our readers are outside the tabernacle and on their way to hell,"[44] there were doubtless many amiable Episcopalians and assorted modernists scattered among the following. Village atheists were said to have doted on the publication.[45] Dixon Wecter tried to define, though not wholly accurately, another unexpected set of readers; discussing the rise of Kiwanis, Lions, and Rotary after World War I, he observed that the "hornets of satire were not far behind, and stung with such pungence that for several years Elks and Rotarians came to be the most enthusiastic followers of *The American Mercury*,"[46] but such an opinion is perhaps less sound than, say, Burton Rascoe's affirmation of the popularity of the review with newspaper reporters.[47] Generally, then, readers of the periodical were members of a self-consciously young, urban, modern set; mostly upper-middle class in economic status (often recently so) though with followers from ethnic minorities, college communities, some literati, and a few scattered "old timers." As revealed in their letters to the "Notes and Queries" department (added to the monthly for a time in the mid-twenties), the most articulate of the readers appeared as genial, irreverent, and sometimes serious folk. And some of them did indeed look on the *Mercury* "as a religion rather than a magazine."[48]

[44] Quoted in anon., "Contributors to This Number of the Journal," *Journal of Social Forces*, III (Nov., 1924), 4.
[45] Kemler, *Mr. Mencken*, p. 174.
[46] *The Saga of American Society: A Record of Social Aspiration 1607-1937* (New York, 1937), p. 111.
[47] *We Were Interrupted*, p. 198.
[48] Wood, *Magazines in the United States*, p. 195.

A FINANCIAL SUCCESS

WHOEVER the readers, they soon helped the new month-ly achieve economic health. Alfred Knopf reports that "the magazine was an almost immediate commercial success,"[49] a happy condition indirectly reflected by a series of awed comments in the *Publishers' Weekly*.[50] Advertising, which had been little sought in 1924, played an increasingly important part in the unfolding success. The business associates in 1925 turned their attention more seriously toward that source of revenue, and soon they drew advertisers ranging from the Huntley & Palmer biscuit firm in England (which monopolized the back of the green cover for several years) to steamship lines and American publishing houses—most especially the latter, because of exchange advertisements with the house of Knopf and because of the literate readers. When in 1926 businessmen continued to regard the *Mercury* as a desirable advertising medium reaching a discriminating minority, Earle Bachman and Louis Brockway, experienced in obtaining advertising copy for quality magazines, were hired to further develop that source of income. The two new employees launched a campaign directed especially toward book publishers, a campaign strengthened by Mencken's creation of a "Check List of New Books" in the end-papers of the monthly, wherein he published numerous one-paragraph reviews.[51] The increase in the appeal of the magazine to advertisers was, however, simply that it reached nearly 70,-000 readers each month in 1926, readers who spent approximately $32,000 every month buying current issues and an

[49] Knopf to Singleton, July 28, 1959.
[50] As in CVII (May 30, 1925), 1827, and "Periodical Notes," CIX (Feb. 6, 1926), 457.
[51] For instance, one announcement by Louis Brockway ("Books in Magazines," *Publishers' Weekly*, CXII [Dec. 10, 1927], 2118) read as follows: ". . . during 1927 the *American Mercury* reviewed in "The Check List of New Books" and "The Library" 709 books. This is an average of 59 each month. Both these departments are regular features. . . ."

undetermined amount buying back numbers to complete their files.[52] In 1927 there were scores of pages of advertising in the front and back sections (such matter was never assembled other than in the front and back parts, an arrangement to enable binders to clip extraneous matter neatly out when bound volumes were desired). Advertising revenue, together with income from the many purchasers, made the commercial position in 1927 seem almost "miraculous"; "[The *Mercury*] has become," gloated the staff, "the rival in circulation, amount of advertising, and prestige, of magazines established in an age when it was not generally known that ladies had legs."[53]

Nor was the admittedly attractive five-dollar-per-year edition sufficient for all; a special ten-dollar subscription, with single copies costing one dollar each on the newsstand, was available for connoisseurs who wanted their issues printed on deluxe rag paper.

The exact profits of the magazine during its heyday cannot be determined in this study; as Mr. Knopf points out, very shortly "profits by the *Mercury* would be reflected in profits made by AAK, Inc.,"[54] and therefore it would take a skilled accountant to unravel the connections between the two corporations. It is, however, unlikely that the periodical made very large sums for its stockholders much before 1926; Mencken reported of that year that the review had a surplus of about $25,000 available in April to fight the Boston suppression,[55] an amount that probably represented most of the accumulated profits by that date in view of high printing costs.[56] Nevertheless,

[52] Thousands of extra copies were printed each month; in Sept. 1925, 52,377 copies were sold, but 59,807 copies were printed; in Sept., 1926, the trend became even more marked: 75,996 copies were sold and 90,000 printed. Despite the *Mercury*'s needed for advertisers' copies, etc., the discrepancy suggests the need for a supply of back numbers. (The monthly, of course, advertised bound back volumes.)

[53] *Three Years,* p. 29.

[54] Knopf to Singleton, July 28, 1959.

[55] "The 'Hatrack' Case," I, 149.

[56] In 1926, for example, the Haddon printers in Camden, N.J., charged nearly fifteen cents for each copy.

a claim by Leon Whipple that neither Mencken nor Knopf had, before the first part of 1927, "taken a cent from their investment"[57] ignored not only the policy of returning part of the profits into the strengthening of the monthly, but also the increasing prosperity of Alfred A. Knopf, Inc.[58] After the review had demonstrated its ability to survive, Alfred and Samuel Knopf (who owned most of the stock)[59] began to arrange an exchange of the editors' stock in The American Mercury, Inc. for stock in the larger publishing venture, an exchange that was nearly complete by 1930.[60]

Before the Depression, the business associates appeared half-hearted in their solicitations for subscribers; instead, they often cited the preponderance of newsstand purchasers (over two-thirds of all copies sold were handled by news-stands)[61] as an advantage. To advertisers they pointed out that every single issue drew buyers to remember it and deliberately purchase it twelve times each year.[62] This reliance on newsstand sales was partly, of course, an established pattern of metropolitan periodical selling, but some editors, like Ellery Sedgwick of the *Atlantic,* found the pattern undesirable.[63]

By 1928 prosperity buoyed the monthly to great heights; in that year the *Mercury* had to reject advertisers because the Post Office would not deliver second-class items with

---

[57] "The Revolution on Quality Street, Part II," *Survey,* LVII, 427.

[58] This prosperity was mirrored in the *Publishers' Weekly* by chronicles of the travels of Blanche and Samuel Knopf across the Atlantic to oversee the expansion of Alfred A. Knopf, Inc. (anon., "Personal Notes," CXII [Oct. 22, 1927], 1577). In the March 17, 1928 number (CXIII, 1282-1283) was an illustrated description of the new three story brick London offices of A. A. Knopf, Inc.; Guy Chapman headed that office.

[59] Knopf to Singleton, July 28, 1959.

[60] Not all American Mercury, Inc. stock was exchanged, even by 1933.

[61] One early brochure announced that "69% of circulation . . . is news-stand sale" ("The American Mercury: Miscellanea: 1923-1933," E.P.M.C.).

[62] *Three Years,* p. 29.

[63] Sedgwick "did not aim at a huge audience of newsstand buyers; he aimed at a small audience of intelligent men and women who would subscribe in advance and keep on subscribing year after year. . . ." Nor did Sedgwick knowingly order more copies to be printed than would likely be sold: "a sold-out edition is always a good advertisement" (Allen, "Sedgwick and the Atlantic," *Outlook and Independent,* Dec. 26, 1928, p. 1406).

too high a proportion of advertising matter.[64] The editor, celebrating the fifth year of publication in an editorial for December, 1928, was able to counter recent Methodist assertions that the hated monthly was languishing into insolvency by citing its debt-free and profitable condition.

THE "HATRACK" CONTROVERSY

THE most notorious episode in the history of the *Mercury* was triggered by "Hatrack," Herbert Asbury's account of a small-town prostitute. Asbury's April, 1926, article began a conflict that was for a short time nearly as widely reported as the Scopes "Monkey Trial" of 1925. The effects of the "Hatrack" crisis on the popular concept of the monthly, together with the legal and editorial problems created, make a brief narrative of the controversy necessary.

Censors were, in many places, well established during the twenties. A clash between them and Mencken became very likely; he conducted his review with increasingly ribald glee after 1924, an attitude best mirrored in his editorial correspondence.[65] In fact, the periodical had already, before April, 1926, been banned now and then from sale in communities of the rural South, and such features as "Americana" had led to frequent calls from the religious press and assorted individuals for more extensive suppression. Emotions that had been building up across the country for over two years found a gaudy outlet when Boston censors struck.

[64] Interview with Charles Angoff, New York City, N.Y., Dec. 27, 1958.

[65] To Ernest Boyd he sent a 1925 copy with the following comment: "Perhaps you may have some use for this extra proof. I look for a roar when the magazine reaches the stands" (HLM to Boyd, Nov. 19, 1925. Letter in P.M.C.). Later, rejecting a contribution by Boyd, he pointed out that "Nobody is insulted. There is no violation of the immemorial decencies of Anglo-Saxon men. I like the idea, but I long for the hot flush, the hostile snort, the defiant fart" (HLM to Boyd, Jan. 28, [1926]. Letter in P.M.C.).

That the first noteworthy attack should have been launched in Boston surprised neither the Reverend J. Franklin Chase, secretary of the Watch and Ward Society of Boston, nor the *Mercury* editor. Mencken had commissioned articles scoring Chase in the strongest terms,[66] and Chase had apparently promised revenge.[67] The terror of booksellers in Boston and nearby areas of Massachusetts, Chase had over the years perfected a technique for selecting the reading matter for the former "Athens of America," a technique that had drawn the admiration of old Anthony Comstock himself, and his promise of revenge was tantamount to revenge. A threat from him, or even a hint, set booksellers, news vendors, district attorneys, and police captains scrambling to obey.[68] When he examined the April, 1926, number of the *Mercury* late in March, and put his well-oiled machine into movement, there was not much doubt that his grudge against the monthly was going to be satisfied.[69] His animus led him to show that his ruling had teeth in it by having one vendor on Harvard Square arrested, and though the fellow showed spirit it was known that conviction would be virtually automatic.[70] And when Chase,

[66] Especially irritating to Chase was "Keeping the Puritans Pure," which had been printed in the September, 1925, number. The author, A. L. S. Wood, a reporter for the Springfield, Mass., *Union,* had been commissioned to write the exposé of Chase, and Mencken had made Wood prepare several revisions until satisfaction was achieved.

[67] Kemler, *Mr. Mencken,* p. 193.

[68] For the article "Keeping the Puritans Pure," Mencken had to choose a reporter from Springfield because no reporter in Boston dared criticize Chase; John Macy had done so over a decade before, and had been turned out of his job for his pains (Kemler, *Mr. Mencken,* p. 192). No Boston newspaper would advertise or in any way give note to a book after Chase had indicated his disapproval.

[69] The magazine had been delivered to newsstands by the American News Company on March 25. On March 28 J. J. Crowley, a Boston magazine promotion agent, warned the *Mercury* staff that Chase was preparing to suppress the April issue. On March 27, however, Chase had already written to John Tracey of the "Massachusetts Magazine Committee" that distribution of the April number "would constitute a violation of chapter 272, section 28" of the Massachusetts obscenity laws. Copies of this warning letter were sent to other Massachusetts towns, including Fall River, Worcester, Springfield, and New Bedford. On March 30 Chase gave out his press releases describing "Hatrack" as "filthy," "degrading," "immoral," etc. ("The 'Hatrack' Case," E.P.M.C., I, 7-9).

[70] Said the arrested vendor, named Felix Caragianes: "I got a shoe-shine

the self-appointed Methodist guardian of Boston, heard that Mencken actually wanted to venture into Boston to challenge Chase's sway there personally, the reformer was not disturbed.

Chase knew that Mencken, however wickedly he might carry on his editorship in New York City, could be jailed as quickly as any newsstand vendor, possibly with a long sentence, if he tried to sell a copy of the *Mercury* in Boston. This was Boston of the mid-twenties, a city run by Irish Catholic politicians who were reported anxious to "fix" any jury that might be called to try *Mercury* offenders.[71] The judiciary and police force had implemented Chase's will with zealous righteousness for many years, and the press, as Chase knew it would, began denunciations of "Hatrack" that reached a bitter crescendo in early April.

At the beginning Mencken would have been as surprised as Chase had he known that the routine-appearing suppression would develop into a bitter showdown. Indeed, when a reporter called him in Baltimore to tell of the ban and ask his opinion, Mencken simply unloaded a few epithets on Chase and then hung up the telephone, inclined to say and do no more. Although he had been a little uneasy about printing "Hatrack," a chapter from Asbury's forthcoming autobiography *Up from Methodism,* it had been printed, and he was not going to lose any sleep over it—he thought. The piece began innocuously enough: "When I

---

stand, and shoe-mending; and I clean hats and sell luggage. I always work hard. I never was in a police-station before" (from an article by Mary E. Prim, originally printed in the Boston *Transcript* for April 8, 1926, "The 'Hatrack' Case," I, 55). Another excerpt from Caragianes' statement to Mary Prim was as follows: "I honestly think from my heart . . . that it is a good magazine. Fine people buy it—professors from the college. I have been here sixteen years and never had any trouble. . . . I will sell the *Mercury* again, tho, if I can" ("The Case of the April *Mercury*," *Publishers' Weekly*, CIX [April 17, 1926], 1334).

[71] The spite from this quarter had been most aroused by Charles Angoff's "Boston Twilight," in the December, 1925, issue. Angoff's bitter attack on the dismal cultural state of the once great Boston stressed the intellectual wretchedness of the Irish element in accounting for the cultural debacle of the city. The threat to pack any jury against Mencken was attributed to the district attorney himself, one Thomas O'Brien (Manchester, *Mencken*, p. 194).

was a boy in Farmington, Missouri. . . ." There followed a discussion of small town harlotry with the emphasis on the role of the hypocritical, evangelistic ministry in shaping the thinking of isolated communities on the subject of prostitution. After a division indicated by a roman numeral was another discourse concerning the lurid imaginations fostered by revivals, the inability of hamlets to support other than a part-time whore, and a fallen wench named "Box Car Molly" who allegedly had eked out a living near Farmington. It was only then that Hatrack, so named because of her angular figure, was introduced. Hatrack during weekdays was a domestic servant, but Sunday, "irregardless of weather," she attended church, fervently desiring, the reader was asked to believe, acceptance and forgiveness by the preacher and his flock. Asbury tried to engage the reader's sympathy by sentimental writing: "I have seen her sit alone and miserably unhappy while the preacher bellowed a sermon about forgiveness. . . . But for Hatrack there was no forgiveness. Mary Magdalene was a saint in heaven, but Hatrack remained a harlot in Farmington." After being rebuffed by the congregation, Hatrack worked her trade on Sunday evening, using the local cemetery as her trysting place: "As each man accosted her in turn Hatrack inquired whether he was a Protestant or a Catholic. If he was a Protestant she took him into the Catholic cemetery; if he was a Catholic they went into the Masonic cemetery." The story closed: "To a stranger who offered her a dollar she said: 'You know damned well I haven't got any change.'" The tale, without artistic merit whether considered as fiction or as reminiscence, was one of the cheapest and most sensational pieces ever printed in the *Mercury*. It was unfortunate that its most famous contribution had to be such a contrived and unworthy item. But it was made to order for Chase, who felt no need to be troubled by scruples about literary merit. Furthermore, it had blasphemous touches in its cemetery setting and in Hatrack's gentle insult toward her Catholic and Masonic clients; the reformer knew the weight of the press, and public opinion would be firmly on his side.

The more Mencken began to consider Chase's ban, however, the more irritated he became. He went to New York City to consult with the Knopfs, and it was decided that Arthur Garfield Hays should be retained as attorney. (Hays, nearly as well-known as Clarence Darrow, had met Mencken at the Scopes Trial, where Hays had been a counsel for the defense.) By the time Knopf and Mencken reached the lawyer's office, the editor had worked himself into a rage, and he burst out to Hays: "Those dogs in Boston have banned *The American Mercury*. The Swine don't read it. They read 'Hot Dog.' And these wowsers aren't even in the cow country."[72] After Hays learned the situation from a calmer Mencken, he suggested that the editor travel to Boston, sell a *Mercury,* and submit to arrest. Hays advanced the idea only because he thought that after the probable conviction, an appeal could be won. If the appeal failed, a two-year prison sentence was likely.

The arrangements for the Boston sale were suitably dramatic: Mencken was to sell a copy of the banned issue to Chase himself, and if the vice-hunter failed to appear, a general sale of the magazine would be commenced on Boston Common. Chase agreed to participate, and the encounter was set on Brimstone Corner (so named because early Puritan Divines had supposedly scattered glowing brimstone over the area to illustrate the texture of Hell). Prior to the occasion both principals kept the reporters happy with outspoken press releases: Mencken charged Chase with spite in the suppression and Chase lingered over the prurient nature of "Hatrack." At two P.M. on April 5, Mencken and his friends arrived at Brimstone Corner, where a crowd of thousands, largely Harvard students who were

[72] Arthur Garfield Hays, *Let Freedom Ring* (new and rev. edition; New York, 1937), pp. 160-161. Warmth is also reflected in HLM to Ernest Boyd, March 31, 1926, in his admission that the monthly had been raided "as an obscene magazine." Letter in P.M.C.

Mencken fans, clamored for copies of the forbidden review at "almost any price. People were wildly waving one, five and ten dollar bills." At the last minute Chase sent an assistant to buy a *Mercury,* but Mencken sent him away, and at last Chase appeared and paid fifty cents for a copy. Mencken, as if to test the coin, bit it.[73] He was then seized by Captain Patterson, chief of the Boston vice squad, and a plainclothesman, and marched to a nearby police station. There he was charged with violating Chapter 272, Section 28, of the Massachusetts Public General Laws, forbidding the possession and sale of obscene literature. After the booking was completed and a judge was found, the editor pleaded not guilty to both charges. Trial was arranged for ten o'clock on the morning of the next day, and the prisoner was released under heavy bond.[74]

The following morning a more troubled Mencken returned to court; John J. Mullen, a book agent for Knopf and a native Bostonian, had spent part of the evening detailing to the Maryland interloper his jeopardy, and this new view of his predicament was taken along to the hearing. His distress was not mitigated when, on the morning of April 6, his two lawyers (Hays was assisted by Herbert B. Ehrmann of Boston) failed to appear. Moreover, the judge named to the case was well known as the secular arm of the Watch and Ward. It was fortunate that the delay caused by the absence of Hays and Ehrmann forced the reassignment of the case to the calendar of one Judge James Parmenter; and at eleven A.M. the trial was begun under the new judge. Because the evidence was considered as possibly obscene, Judge Parmenter moved the hearing over to a corner, and both defense and prosecution testimony was conducted in a whisper. Chase's lawyer, John W. Rorke, began by outlining a whispered charge of Mencken's cor-

---

[73] Anon., "Mr. Mencken is Acquitted," *Publishers' Weekly,* CIX (April 10, 1926), 1277. (The information concerning the crowd is from Hays, *Let Freedom Ring,* p. 160).

[74] I am indebted to Manchester, *Mencken,* pp. 191-193, *passim,* for most of the details of the Boston controversy.

ruption of youth. Hays countered by putting Mencken on the stand as editor of the *Mercury,* and Mencken pointed out the dignity and excellence of the magazine (here, of course, the purchase price of fifty cents, the contributors who were Senators or bishops, and the staid cover were dwelt upon), and he concluded by asserting that the monthly never printed obscene work and by stating that his only reason for challenging Chase was that the reformer's techniques were unfair and threatened his property and reputation. The defense then called other witnesses, who also, to the disappointment of the crowded courtroom, testified *sotto voce.*[75] Hays concluded his defense by an invocation of the freedom of the press, while Rorke replied by charges that liberty is not license. To crown his indictment, Rorke brought up one of Nathan's "Clinical Notes" as conclusive evidence that the April number was vile. To all this testimony Judge Parmenter had submitted without much intervention, and he closed the hearing by observing that the problem was simple: all he had to do was adjourn for a day, read the April issue, and decide whether or not "Hatrack" or other contributions were obscene. He would announce the verdict the following morning. The participants then dispersed.

Mencken spent another uneasy night, even though he was the dinner guest of the exclusive Harvard St. Botolph Club and had received some congratulatory telegrams and telephone calls for his defiant stand.

As for the April number, Judge Parmenter first found an article by Henry Osborne Osgood on "The Anatomy of Jazz," with pages full of musical annotation. Next was a tribute by Fielding H. Garrison to a great American surgeon and teacher, William Halstead, which was followed by some ballads by Stanley Vestal. Howard MacGrath con-

[75] Manchester, *Mencken*, pp. 194-195. The witnesses included Herbert Asbury, who testified that "Hatrack" actually portrayed a real person, and that the story was therefore purely factual.

tributed a light essay on wines, while David Ryder sup-
plied "The Unions Lose San Francisco." Mencken's editorial dealing with college education was conservative
enough, but Angoff's "The Methodists"[76] was an outright
assault on that faith—and disparaged, among other things,
the Reverend J. Franklin Chase. Following the "Americana"
department came S. W. Tait's essay "Indiana," Isaac Goldberg's "Literary Ladies of the South," and E. S. Pickering's
discussion of "The Cancer Problem." John McClure's dialogue dealing with "Sentimentality" preceded James
Stevens' short story "Horses," Josephine Herbst's "Iowa
Takes to Literature," Chester T. Crowell's "Journalism in
Texas," Herbert Asbury's "Hatrack," and L. M. Hussey's
fictional "The Liberator." Nathan's "Clinical Notes" were
dominated by the long note entitled "The New View of
Sex" (the note Rorke had challenged),[77] and "The Theatre,"
ironically, showed the critic in a moralistic mood. Menck-
en's book reviews were less ribald than at other times. As
a whole, the April number, thrown into such a crisis, was
not ill-suited to represent the review's achievement—with
the exception of "Hatrack."

Calling the court to order on the morning of April 6,
Parmenter disposed swiftly of Chase's charges by refuting
each in turn. He concluded by admitting that he could not
understand Osgood's essay on jazz and by making the following verdict:

I cannot imagine anyone reading the article in question and
finding himself or herself attracted toward vice. . . . The
article in question was printed in the *American Mercury,* which
appears to be a magazine interested in the discussion of serious
subjects. There is nothing in its appearance or make-up which
would suggest that it is anything but a serious magazine. . . .
My attention was also called to an article called "Clinical Notes"
in the same issue. . . . The gist of this article is merely that

[76] Angoff assumed the pseudonym "James D. Bernard."
[77] The "note," over two and a half pages long, only casually mentioned sex,
and even then in a slighting way.

sex is not nearly so important a matter in life as it is often assumed to be.[78]

Armed with this favorable verdict, Mencken immediately began his counterattack. In the inevitable press conference, hinting at libel suits and making elaborate inquiries into Chase's property holdings, the editor sought to alarm the Watch and Ward.[79] After his interview, he left the reporters for a luncheon engagement as a guest of the Harvard Union. Escorted to Cambridge by a committee of collegians, he arrived at the packed dining hall to greet the students assembled to encourage him. When Felix Frankfurter made the announcement of the wholly unexpected acquittal, the Harvard students, nearly two thousand strong, roared their approval. After Mencken made a speech praising Harvard as far different from "cow colleges," and after the students thrice sounded the Harvard cheer, the editor presented a flag (rushed by friends from Baltimore to the embattled Mencken) of the Free State of Maryland to the Union, where it was dutifully hung.

Meanwhile, J. Franklin Chase carried the war to new fronts, and on April 7 Mencken learned that the Post Office Department had banned the April *Mercury* from the mails. Chase had traveled to New York and persuaded New York Postmaster John J. Kiely that "Hatrack" deserved banning from the mails. Kiely forwarded his unfavorable opinion of the April issue to Horace J. Donnelly, solicitor to the Postmaster-General in Washington. The Postmaster-General, Harry S. New, received on the morning of April 7 a request from the Farmington, Missouri, Chamber of Commerce asking for a federal ban, and at 4:40 P.M. the ban was granted. Thus Mencken was engaged on two fronts—Boston and Washington, D. C.—and the latter of these was by far the more important. Two successive such bans would

---

[78] Parmenter's statement is printed in "The Case of the April *Mercury*," *Publishers' Weekly*, CIX, 1333.

[79] Mencken especially asked about the wealth of Charles W. Eliot, the former president of Harvard, who was an official in the Society (Manchester, *Mencken*, p. 197).

justify revoking the second-class mailing privilege, thereby ruining the *Mercury*.

Mencken won handily over Chase in Boston. First, an injunction application was granted by Judge George A. Anderson, who remarked that he would not allow interference with Mencken's right to "raise hell."[80] The important injunction hearing itself was held before Judge James Morton, Jr. in the Federal Court at Boston. Judge Morton heard Hays and the Watch and Ward's counsel Edmund A. Whitman argue the case. Hays put Chase on the stand and had him outline his autocratic methods of suppression.[81] Hays identified the *Mercury*'s position as prompted by a dislike of "the insidious, covert and suggestive method that might ruin a publication, while those involved assumed no responsibility."[82] Fortunately for Hays, Whitman suggested that the *Mercury* could avoid future interference by the Watch and Ward if Knopf would have each issue sent in advance to the Society so that it could be determined whether or not a given issue violated the sensibilities of that unofficial censorship body. This suggestion was a mistake, and Hays lost no time in seizing upon it; his resulting explosion was so vehement that Judge Morton made no effort to hide his own amusement.[83] An injunction against the Watch and Ward was granted. Judge Morton found its coercive, authoritarian technique "clearly illegal." More important, the Watch and Ward was forbidden for two years from threatening *Mercury* dealers, and if during that interval the Society did so interfere, it was open to a suit for damages by the *Mercury* for $50,000. This constituted a stunning blow to the Boston organization, which began to make Chase its scapegoat in an effort to avoid such a suit. The police commissioner announced that thereafter there would be no further automatic or routine enforcement of the Watch and Ward's literary opinions. When the *Mercury* paid the $100.00

[80] Hays, *Let Freedom Ring*, p. 170.   [81] *Ibid.*, pp. 173-176.
[82] *Ibid.*, p. 176.   [83] Manchester, *Mencken*, p. 200.

fine imposed upon the Greek newsstand operator, public sympathy was apparently with the inoffensive pawn. The conviction of Caragianes was, however, Chase's only Boston victory, and Chase himself died on November 3, 1926. Said Mencken: "We killed him."[84]

In addition to these Massachusetts legal triumphs, Mencken's effort to secure justice regarding the Post Office ban began auspiciously. Although a hearing with Solicitor Donnelly was fruitless, as everyone knew it would be,[85] a successful request for an injunction against the Post Office was carried through the Federal District Court in New York. On April 28 Judge Julian W. Mack heard the evidence and granted an injunction against Kiely, the New York Postmaster.[86] The Post Office, as expected, appealed the injunction.

To the casual observer, then, Mencken's bearding of the Watch and Ward Society had been quite victorious, but there were wounds that the newspapers did not chronicle. To begin with, the case cost the *Mercury* twenty thousand dollars in cash,[87] which was, as the editor complained, "a great deal of money."[88] There were few canceled subscriptions, but enough advertisers withdrew to cause substantial, if temporary, losses in that quarter.[89] Also damaging was the press coverage; the *Mercury* was often described in lurid and unfair ways, while Mencken was showered with such vitriol that even so thick-skinned a man threatened libel

[84] Kemler, *Mr. Mencken*, p. 214.
[85] The hearing was a farce; Donnelly was being asked by Mencken to reverse his earlier judgment against the *Mercury*, and if Donnelly chose to decide against himself, the editor would have been in a good position to press a damage suit home. Donnelly's conduct of the hearing, however, was revelatory of the dislike with which the Coolidge administration viewed the periodical (Manchester, *Mencken*, pp. 201-202).
[86] Said Judge Mack: "What is this all about? I have read *The American Mercury*; I am familiar with the article 'Hatrack.' No one but a moron could be affected by it" (Hays, *Let Freedom Ring*, p. 182). (Another part of Judge Mack's statement is printed in "'American Mercury' Wins Injunction," *Publishers' Weekly*, CIX [May 29, 1926], 1795).
[87] "The 'Hatrack' Case," I, 149.
[88] HLM to Ernest Boyd, April 24, 1926. Letter in P.M.C.
[89] "The 'Hatrack' Case," I, 120.

suits against one Boston paper. Indeed, the more important wounds were all suffered in Mencken's psyche. He forgot very quickly in the controversy that he was fighting for a principle over a very shoddy piece of goods: "Hatrack" was in bad taste. He became very sensitive toward real and imagined abandonment by his friends and the literati.[90] He considered himself a champion of the freedom of the press, and took to lingering bitterly over the treatment he had been accorded in the public prints. He did not recognize that even his best friends had difficulty in knowing how seriously he took his role as martyr, nor did he realize how Barnum-like such incidents as the coin-biting on Brimstone Corner must have seemed.

Efforts to show others how seriously he took the "Hatrack" crisis met with very limited success. He drew up a very chaste document trying to convert the hostile press.[91] He strictly and absolutely refused, despite the beseeching staff, to profit from the demand for more copies of the sensational April number, a demand reported as reaching one million copies.[92] Few newspaper editors, however, were swayed. Mencken seemingly forgot that he had damned American journalism repeatedly and that almost all of the thousands of "Americana" items were drawn from one periodical or another, and that the cumulative effect of these extracts, over more than two years, would be a reservoir of venom. Of course the liberal weeklies, such as the *Nation* and the *New Republic,* and such trade journals as the *Publishers' Weekly* did their duty in defending Mencken's stand, even though the *Nation* hinted that "Hatrack" was in poor taste.[93] The few newspapers such as the *New York*

---

[90] *Ibid.,* I, 87.

[91] "To the Friends of The American Mercury" (New York, April 16, 1926), n.p. The subtitle of the pamphlet was "Concerning the article 'Keeping the Puritans Pure,' an attack on the Watch and Ward Society in Boston." Copies of this were sent to most major Eastern newspapers, as were copies of a mimeographed brief statement outlining his motives in going to Boston.

[92] Manchester, *Mencken,* p. 200.

[93] [Oswald G. Villard], "Editorial Paragraphs," *Nation,* CXXII (April 28, 1926), 464-465; [Oswald G. Villard], "Editorial Paragraphs," *Nation,* CXXII

Times that saw the higher principles at stake were far outbalanced by other publications; one weekly news magazine's account of the Brimstone Corner challenge was typically unfavorable to Mencken: "And everybody stared unfavorably at the untidy man with the magazines. He had just committed an illicit act. Dozens of policemen, thousands of witnesses, had seen him do it; he too knew that he was guilty. He had broken an edict relating to decency. No escape was possible," etc.[94]

Another blow came when Hays warned the editor that an article entitled "Sex and the Co-ed," by Bernard De-Voto,[95] in the May, 1926, *Mercury*, might well draw a second Post Office ban, thereby allowing suspension of second-class mailing privileges because the monthly had missed two successive issues and hence was not in "continuous publication"—a device that had been used to ruin several radical magazines during the preceding decade. Despite the provocative title, "Sex and the Coed" was harmless stuff; in fact, DeVoto simply denied that the coed was as promiscuous as the popular conception held. He sketched a generally chaste and morally conventional coed whose attitude toward marriage was as dully sentimental as that of her less well-educated sisters. As for truly wild flappers, such persons were held to be very rare.[96] Although the *Mercury* could have fought a far more persuasive fight for "Sex and the Coed" than for "Hatrack," the presses printing the May number were stopped, and, at a cost of $8,000, a harmless essay "On Learning to Play the Cello," by Doris Stevens, was substituted. Although Mencken's friends and biographers have cited the substitution as a clever move, it might also be considered as a victory for the Comstocks; after all, they had induced a certain "cleaning up" of the magazine.

(May 26, 1926), 569; and anon., "The Week," *New Republic,* XLVII (May 26, 1926), 4.

[94] Anon., "Hatrack," *Time,* VII (April 19, 1926), 24, 26.

[95] DeVoto signed his article with the pseudonym "John August."

[96] A copy of the suppressed May, 1926, issue appears in "The 'Hatrack' Case," VI, Appendix II, n.p. "Sex and the Coed" was the lead article.

The censorship fight, which had begun so gloriously, soon began to trickle out into many little rivulets; a tawdry attempt to capitalize on the sensational aspect of "Hatrack" was threatened by a projected dramatization,[97] a disreputable California publication plagiarized the article,[98] and efforts by Mencken's friends in Congress to take away the censorship powers of the Post Office were defeated.[99] Many little local suppressions of the *Mercury* that were inconvenient to challenge were perpetrated by sincere or publicity-seeking officials,[100] and a Canadian ban was narrowly averted.[101] Most important, in May, 1927, Judge Mack's injunction against the Post Office was ordered vacated by three judges of the United States Circuit Court of Appeals, Second Circuit, the judges taking the position that the whole question of damage by the Post Office by banning the April, 1926, issue was "academic," for there was no lasting injury.[102] Mencken was thereby denied recompense for alleged damages caused by the federal ban; the long fight was over.

Still, many admired the editor's very real courage in going to Brimstone Corner, and the circulation of the *Mercury* continued to climb after the controversy. As for his defeat in wringing damages from the Post Office, Mencken saw the issue clearly. To Upton Sinclair he wrote: "The government brings my magazine to you only un-

[97] Anon., "Plan a Stage 'Hatrack': Musical Comedy Liberettist Takes up a Story Barred from the Mails," *New York Times,* April 30, 1926, p. 17, cols. 4-7. (The comedy was apparently not produced.)

[98] Manchester, *Mencken,* p. 201. (The name of the periodical is not given.)

[99] Not surprisingly, Senator James A. Reed of Missouri authored one of the bills to change the Post Office's censorship powers; moreover, Senator Reed offered his services as counsel to Mencken without charge. Mencken declined the offer.

[100] Some of these bans are listed in Kemler, *Mr. Mencken,* pp. 208-209.

[101] The occasion for the Canadian threat has been discussed on page 94 of this study. Commented Mencken on the outburst elicited by his editorial on England: "I can only say that the *American Mercury* acknowledges no allegiance to King George V, and that it is interested in definitions of treasons framed by Canadian politicians only as it is interested in other amusing imbecilities" (Kemler, *Mr. Mencken,* p. 209).

[102] Hays, *Let Freedom Ring,* p. 184; "The 'Hatrack' Case," VI, Appendix IX, n.p.

willingly. It tried to ruin my business, and failed by only an inch."[103]

THE *MERCURY* AS AN INFLUENCE ON OTHER MAGAZINES

Not only was the *Mercury* frequently copied on the campuses, but also more professional publishing circles were affected by its popularity. Asked Leon Whipple: "Have you heard of the revolution on Quality Street where the serious magazines live? . . . The *American Mercury*'s winged heels have raced from nothing to over 60,000 in two years." After contrasting the declining circulations of the *Century, Scribner's,* and *Harper's* with the quick rise in the *Mercury*'s subscription and newsstand sales, Whipple observed that these contrasting circulation trends were "index numbers for something in our intellectual life" and that editors "heard the thunder of the changing tides. They had to go up or go under."[104] Two years later, Harry Hanson, literary editor of the *New York World,* saw no reason to contradict Whipple's opinion of the trend.[105] Nor was there any disagreement that some kind of upheaval in the magazine world commenced about 1924. The only dispute, rather, has been whether it was the *Atlantic* or the *Mercury*—Sedgwick or Mencken—that was more responsible for the changes in the mid-twenties. Most commentators have awarded the laurels to the *Mercury,* and some have carried their speculations to great lengths: one critic identified, to his satisfaction, *Mercury* influences on Henry Luce's *Life.*[106] Such sweeping claims are hard to prove or disprove; only a few indications of the *Mercury*'s impact can be traced.

[103] HLM to Sinclair, Sept. 9, [1926?]. Copy in P.M.C.
[104] "The Revolution on Quality Street, Part I," *Survey,* LVII (Nov. 1, 1926), 119.
[105] Quoted by John Drewry, "American Magazines Today," *Sewanee Review,* XXXVI (July, 1928), 349.
[106] Lloyd Morris, *Postscript to Yesterday* (New York, 1947), p. 144.

The most frequently made assertion is that, because of its bounce and vitality, other reviews more stodgy or dull were goaded into brightening their formats, covers, and editorial policies.[107] For example, a discussion of the refurbished *Bookman* under Burton Rascoe's editorship accounted for the new gay cover and sprightlier contents by pointing out that "(like *Harper's,* the *Atlantic Monthly,* etc.) the *Bookman* is feeling the sharp spur of the *American Mercury* in the sluggish sides of thoughtful periodical publishing in the U. S."[108] After *Harper's* appeared with a new cover and format in September, 1925, several writers stated that the *Mercury* was responsible.[109] It has also been asserted that *Harper's* helped resurrect itself by stealing writers away from the *Mercury.*[110] Several "borrowings" have been charged to Harold Ross of the *New Yorker:* according to Angoff, the famous New Yorker "profile" was "born in the office of the *Mercury.*"[111] It is more possible that the *New Yorker's* amusing excerpts from the press were suggested by the "Americana" idea. In addition, Mencken had occasion to become bitter when such of his carefully trained authors as James M. Cain abandoned the *Mercury* for the *New Yorker.*[112] The hoary old *North American Review* was also said to have responded to the threat posed by the upstart review.[113] Other monthlies strove less successfully to match its buoyant and challenging tone; the failures of the *Century* and the *Forum* were frankly considered as caused by an inability to adapt the

---

[107] As in Adamic, *Laughing in the Jungle,* p. 262.

[108] Anon., "Magazine Changes," *Time,* X (Sept. 5, 1927), 20. In the *Time* discussion a Jewish monthly, *Reflex,* established in 1927, is also mentioned as possibly influenced by the *Mercury.* I have been unable to obtain a copy of *Reflex* to determine whether or not such an influence existed.

[109] Drewry, "American Magazines Today," *Sewanee Review,* XXXVI, 350.

[110] H. I. Brock, *Meddlers* (New York, 1931), p. 297.

[111] "The Inside View of Mencken's Mercury," *New Republic,* CXXXI, 19.

[112] "Whether [Cain will] be happy on the *New Yorker* remains to be seen. My impression is that it is a somewhat Broadwayish sheet, manned mainly by shrewd go-getters" (HLM to Goodman, March 6, 1931. "Letters to Philip Goodman," III).

[113] John Drewry, "The American Mercury . . . ," *Contemporary American Magazines* (2nd ed.; Athens, Ga., 1938), p. 13.

Mercury formula to their special purposes.[114] (The *Century* had become a monthly instead of a quarterly in 1925, and so continued until 1929, when it joined with the *Forum* to make the *Forum and Century*.)[115] Altogether, it should be remembered that the spirit of the twenties would itself probably have induced some soul-searching among editors, even if unaided by the success of the *Mercury,* and the general tributes to Mencken's monthly should be viewed partly in that light.[116]

In the lesser-known and less important magazines, however, the *Mercury*'s influence can be more clearly discerned. The best of the deliberately imitative reviews was V. V. McNitt's soundly edited *McNaught's Monthly,* published from 1924 to 1927. Seeking to be intelligently pro-American, *McNaught's Monthly* featured some of the better writers who also appeared in Mencken's magazine, but it attacked the *Mercury*.[117] McNitt began a department called "Intelligentsia" which quoted absurd comments of *cognoscenti,* a department considered "opposed to Mr. Mencken's 'Americana.' "[118] Other imitations were less valuable: G. D. Eaton established *Plain Talk* in 1927, a magazine with a red cover patterned after the more celebrated green one. The contents of *Plain Talk,* although not disgraceful during its first years, exploited the debunking and exposé approach in an increasingly sensational manner before its disappearance in 1938. Two imitations of

[114] Whipple, "The Revolution on Quality Street, Part I," *Survey,* LVII, 178.

[115] A less important magazine that may well have been damaged by the success of the *Mercury* was *McClure's,* which adopted a cover looking quite like a blue *Mercury* cover before it was merged, ironically enough, into the *New Smart Set* in 1929.

[116] I can find no evidence for claims that the *Mercury* influenced *Scribner's* and the *Atlantic.* Moreover, it should be observed that Whipple argues for the pre-eminence of the *Atlantic* in leading the "revolution" ("The Revolution on Quality Street, Part I," *Survey,* LVII, 124); and it should be remembered that the circulation of the *Atlantic* was at all times at least twice that of the *Mercury.*

[117] As in K. V. Hoffman, "Mencken, Landlubber," *McNaught's Monthly,* III (March, 1925), 89. Stuart Sherman and Walter Prichard Eaton were among the better contributors to the fifteen-cent periodical.

[118] [John Farrar], "The Lurking Cap and Bells," *Bookman,* LXII (Jan., 1926), 53.

the *Mercury* were printed in the form of monthly news-sheets: Isaac Goldberg's Boston-edited *Panorama,* which lived from 1933 until 1935, and the *American Spectator,* which lasted from 1932 to 1937. (The *American Spectator,* together with *Aesthete 1925,* will be examined in detail in Chapter VIII.) There is a little evidence of an influence on the English; the London *Outlook* called for an "Anglicana" to be the English counterpart of "Americana,"[119] and at least one editor obliged: the editor of the *Week-end Review* wrote of his compilation of imbecilities in that journal: "Probably never since Domesday has a whole nation [so] collaborated. . . . I . . . salute Mr. Mencken . . . whose idea we frankly copied in the *Week-end.*"[120] (An "Americana" which appeared in the *London Mercury* probably owed nothing to its transatlantic cousin; rather it featured serious information concerning American history.)

When the *New Masses,* the most important literary publication of the American Communists, was founded in 1926, the editors repeatedly mentioned the *Mercury* as a possible model. John Dos Passos, in an editorial debate with Michael Gold, observed that "The *American Mercury* explores very ably the American field," and that the new Communist periodical, without finding the "face of Mr. Mencken mirrored in every prairie pool," would profit by tempering its attitudes with some healthy skepticism.[121] When the *New Masses* came to imitate the *Mercury,* it imitated, like so many other magazines, the "Americana" idea: "Capitaliana" first appeared in July, 1927. The first entry in an early "Capitaliana" read:

Ideal qualifications for President of a Menckenized United States, as set down in the redoubtable *Mercury*:

They are all what, for lack of a better word, is called gentleman.

---

[119] Quoted in anon., "Are We More Banal than Others?," *Literary Digest,* LXXXVIII, 29.

[120] Gerald Barry, "Introduction," *This England* (London, 1933), p. ix.

[121] "The New Masses I'd Like," *New Masses,* I (June, 1926), 20.

Also pilloried were "Pious wish of a liberal writer in the *New Republic*," "Enlightened method of handling labor unrest described in the short staccato style of *Time*," "The correct bourgeoise attitude toward sex," "How the poor working girl gets by on a low salary [as shown] between the lines of this dispatch to the *World*," etc.[122]

Another equally significant imitation of the "Americana," this one from the far right, was inaugurated by George Lorimer of the popular *Saturday Evening Post*. Lorimer, according to several accounts, took the *Mercury*'s audacity bitterly to heart. It was not simply that the *Mercury* continued the *Smart Set* habit of scoring the *Saturday Evening Post* in the bluntest kind of invective, nor could it have been that it drew away some of Lorimer's contributors.[123] Rather it was that there have been few more deeply sincere custodians of the conservative, anti-intellectual heritage of rural and small-town America; for years Lorimer's editorials rapped "knockers" in the most indignant way. In 1927 he launched his counterattack in his own "Americana," and the *Mercury* and the *Saturday Evening Post* drew alongside and fired broadside after broadside of news items at one another in one of the most comical—and apparently now forgotten—wars of modern journalism. Lorimer's principles of selection for his "Americana" clippings were bitterly and neatly antithetical to Mencken's. Paraded in the great weekly were items designed to prove how unfair were Mencken's selections of imbecilities. The terse introductions to the *Saturday Evening Post* clippings often echoed querulously, sarcastically, or triumphantly the *Mercury* rhetoric: when a man returned to a village to repay some long overdue bills, the entry was headed: "An everyday chronicle of Boobus Americanus from the York, Pennsylvania Gazette and Daily"; when a polo game was reported in Iowa, the introduction was: "Bucolic diversions of the steer stuffers

[122] Quotations from *New Masses*, III (Aug., 1927), 13-14.
[123] The latter claim is made by Brock, *Meddlers*, pp. 295-296.

of the McNary Haugen littoral revealed by the Drovers Journal, Chicago."[124] A banal instance of charity in Oklahoma was announced as "Unexplained social phenomenon observed in the remoter fastness of the Republic by the Oklahoma City Oklahoman"; a cultural victory achieved when the Perkasie, Pennsylvania, Rotary Club helped with school consolidation and economy in government was ironically presented as "More evidence of the abyss between commerce and art, as noted by the Associated Press in a dispatch from Chicago." Tear-jerking items were liberally used in Lorimer's "Americana,"[125] and other tidbits concerned Boy Scouts, park improvements, wise and kindly Rotarian groups, frugal bishops, Kansas villagers owning airplanes, efficient trolley companies, loans to students attending Methodist colleges, long-lived Victorian ladies, "Service," philanthropy, and social harmony.[126] Flappers and various evidences of modernism were ridiculed, while other items were presumably meant to embarrass such writers as Sinclair Lewis.[127] Some of the clippings aimed at the *Mercury* scored palpable hits.[128] But in general the

[124] This phraseology is largely borrowed from Mencken's "The Champion," a "Clinical Notes" contribution printed October, 1924.

[125] An "Astonishing account of one little deal by businessmen in which there was no hope of a cash dividend, as set forth in the columns of the Philadelphia Inquirer: . . . [T]he parents of the little sufferer had almost given up hope when the Memphis Kiwanis Club offered to assume all financial obligations. . . . Approximately $20,000 is said to have been spent" ("Americana," *Saturday Evening Post,* CIC [May 21, 1927], 52).

[126] For example, when it became known that two youths from the feuding Hatfield and McCoy clans were amiably living as fraternity brothers in a West Virginia college, the press item was introduced: "Outrage reported in the Roanoke, Virginia, Times, wherein American life is robbed of another illy-spared bit of color" ("Americana," *Saturday Evening Post,* CC [Sept. 10, 1927], 238).

[127] One such item began: "'What do you make of this, Watson?' items that may be taken from any newspaper from Capetown to Tientsin: "Lindbergh, Charlie, Little Falls, Minnesota, population 5500, 36 miles ENE of Sauk Center, population 3000, the original of Main Street" ("Americana," *Saturday Evening Post,* CC [Aug. 13, 1927], 35).

[128] One of the best of these ("Americana," *Saturday Evening Post,* CCI [Nov. 12, 1927], 49) was the following:

Local-boy-makes-good item celebrated by the sprightly Betty Bienville, social editor of the Mobile Register:

I will, in spite of what pops up, return to talk of our graduates and the honors that are coming to them, and I saw in a recent Birmingham

battle was one-sided, and many of Lorimer's "Americana" entries tended more to justify the *Mercury*'s sophisticated disdain than to challenge it.[129] Lorimer's testy acknowledgment of the impact of the original "Americana" on complacent folk, an acknowledgment sent out to millions of *Saturday Evening Post* readers, caused considerable glee in the *Mercury* offices; Mencken delighted in clipping items from Lorimer's "Americana" and firing them back at the *Post*.[130] At any rate, Lorimer's sincere effort to scotch the green viper helps identify the *Mercury*'s place in the cultural scene.[131]

paper the picture of a Mobile boy, the seventh son of Mrs. J. O. Railford. Julian Railford, 18, has distinguished himself as a writer by having two poems published in the *American Mercury*. . . . He has been writing only a year, attaining in that short space of time a place in Mencken's selection of Alabama poets. . . . But now I am going to tell you a little back history of this bright boy, who when a little fellow worked in the Register, stacking for the paper. He then was a junior leader of the B.Y.P.U., and now is chorister in Birmingham. Are we proud of him? I should say we are.

[129] For instance, when a French atlas that had been published in Amsterdam in 1733 came to light in an Indiana library, the fact was announced under the proud caption: "Light on the widely accepted belief that Americans are too young a people to have established any real culture, as furnished by the Associated Press in a dispatch from Madison, Indiana" ("Americana," *Saturday Evening Post*, CIC [June 25, 1927], 50).

[130] One of the *Saturday Evening Post*'s "Americana" items treated to such an indignity originally appeared in June 25, 1927 (CIC, 50):

Chicago dispatch via A.P., indicating a hitherto unsuspected community of interest between Rotary and revolution:

King Albert of Belgium and the royal family will receive Rotarians at his palace in Brussels between June 10 and 14, the International Board of Directors was informed today by Felice Seghezza of Genoa, Italy, board member for Continental Europe. Signor Seghezza also brought word that Premier Mussolini of Italy is not opposed to Rotary, as he said had been reported in this country. 'There are seventeen Rotary Clubs in Italy,' Signor Seghezza said. 'Mussolini's brother is a member of one, and four of his cabinet are members.'

In August, 1927, Mencken entered into his "Americana"
Solemn proof that this Americanism is conquering the world, from the *Saturday Evening Post*:

Signor Seghezza brought word. . . .

[131] Lorimer received a number of letters commending him for his sober defense of the Midwest's values against the "machinations of men like Mencken and Nathan . . . in their new *American Mercury*" (John Tebbel, *George Horace Lorimer and The Saturday Evening Post* [Garden City, New York, 1948], p. 229).

THE YEARS OF ACCLAIM

> . . . The Mercury made by such as these
> Is a purely American Brand.
> So shut up your eyes, Old World, and think
> Of the wonderful things to be;
> For the sea is a turbulent sea of ink,
> And the quicksilver bowl that skims the sea
> Is the bowl of the American Mercury
>   With Mencken
>   Nathan
>   and Knopf.[132]

After the flurry of approval in 1924, there arose from certain quarters an increasing hymn of tribute. George B. Logan systematically outlined the virtues of the review.[133] "Americana" items were liberally represented in an anthology of *The Best Humor of 1925*,[134] and during that year the superlatives aimed at Mencken became sweeping: Walter Long identified the editor as "America's greatest legendary hero."[135] Looking back on the period twenty years later, Maxwell Geismar characterized the *Mercury* as "almost the most enviable periodical in the field."[136]

In 1926 the critical acclaim became even more marked. It was then that the furore surrounding the "Hatrack" suppression was most hectic, and Mencken uncovered some unexpected allies. Art Young, a veteran radical who had been an editor of the old *Masses,* signified his high estimate of the *Mercury* in a cartoon occasioned by the cen-

---

[132] Louise Humphrey, "The Three Wise Men . . . ," "Pamphlets on H. L. Mencken: 1917-30," E.P.M.C.

[133] Logan conducted the "Guides to Periodical Reading" department of *The Journal of Social Forces*. His laudatory comments, chiefly dealing with sociological essays in the *Mercury,* appeared as follows: III (March, 1925), 492; III (Sept., 1925), 186-187; IV (Dec., 1925), 314-315, 383-385; IV (March, 1926), 539-542.

[134] Ed. by N. H. Dole and H. S. Dole (Boston, 1926).

[135] "Shots for Four," *Modern Quarterly,* III (Oct.-Dec., 1925), 76.

[136] *The Last of the Provincials: The American Novel, 1915-1925* (Boston, 1947), p. 32 n.

sorship of the first number of the *New Masses*.[137] This early instance of respect from the older generation of radicals showed that at least some of them agreed that, when, in 1923, "Mencken and . . . Nathan brought out the *American Mercury,* the ranks of the critics of big middle-class America were . . . solidified."[138] The liberals also approved now and then; Edmund Wilson in the *New Republic* commented with favor on aspects of the *Mercury* accomplishment,[139] and the liberal *Dial,* though somewhat nervously ("Americana is not America"), admitted that the items were "obviously genuine."[140] Burton Rascoe, soon to be editor of the *Bookman,* declared the *Mercury* in its second year to be "the most talked-about magazine of the time."[141] The approval was sometimes extravagant: J. D. Logan wrote a pamphlet to show that "In founding 'The American Mercury' Mr. Mencken's ideal was genuinely noble, his 'cause' truly and splendidly patriotic."[142] By December, 1926, Walter Lippman could hail Mencken as "the most powerful influence on this whole generation of educated people." Lippman found the editor's forceful writing to have an "extraordinarily cleansing and vitalizing effect. . . . The wounds he inflicts heal quickly. . . . He calls you a swine, and an imbecile, and he increases your will to live."[143]

From England came words of praise nearly as strongly

[137] Young's drawing depicted a vulture-like figure representing censorship. The vulture is nesting in a pile of lewd and trashy tabloid sensationalism, which it condones. The vulture is drawn reaching out its scissors-like beak to chop at the "Old Masses," "The New Masses," and "The Mercury"; the caption under the drawing is ironical: "He makes his nest out of shoddy, and tries to kill everything that looks alive" (*New Masses,* I [Aug., 1925], 14).

[138] F. C. Palm, *The Middle Classes* (New York, 1936), p. 368.

[139] Two examples are "The All-Star Literary Vaudeville," XLVIII (June 30, 1926), 158-163; and "Mencken's Democratic Man," XLIX (Dec. 15, 1926), 110-111.

[140] Anon. rev., *Dial,* LXXX (April, 1926), 342.

[141] *We Were Interrupted,* p. 198.

[142] "A Literary Chameleon: A New Estimate of Mr. H. L. Mencken" (Milwaukee, Wis., 1926), p. 22. "Pamphlets on H. L. Mencken: 1917-30," E.P.M.C.

[143] "H. L. Mencken," *Saturday Review of Literature,* III (Dec. 11, 1926), 413-414.

expressed. J. W. Drawbell, the English editor who had admitted copying "Americana" in the "So This Is England" department in his *Week-end Review,* claimed that "[e]very-thing good in American letters was flowing towards the green-covered, outspoken magazine of those wonderful days."[144] In 1927 English praise reached a peak with state-ments by Herbert Read, then conducting the "Foreign Reviews: American Periodicals" department of the *Cri-terion.* Read began calling attention to the *Mercury* in the January number of Eliot's magazine,[145] and his fascination inspired perhaps the most revealing and notable estimate of the American monthly from the English point of view. Commenting that, of the contributors, the great majority were Americans ("only four of 361 authors were living in England"), Read observed:

There is food for thought in these figures. In the first place, they are inconceivable for England. *The American Mercury* is not a popular magazine in our sense of the term: it has elements in common with the *Truth* of Labouchère, but it has a wider range . . . particularly more pretense to literature. For the *Mercury* is the product of a higher journalism than *Truth* ever commanded: there is a cool command of energy and science in its direction. It is undoubtedly an instrument of power, and within the limits of its materialistic and hedon-istic outlook, a source of enlightenment. It is also intensely national; nowhere does the American nation wear the aspect of a cohering and decisive unity as in the pages of this magazine, and this despite its denunciation of national shams.[146]

In December, 1927, Read maintained that the magazine

continues to be amazingly fresh and vital. . . . Mr. Mencken is creating a new kind of literary interest, even a new kind of culture. He studiously avoids the normal components of a magazine—taste, learning, romance, politeness, all the con-ventions—and concentrates instead upon what can only be rather lamely called human interests. . . . *The American Mercury* has the effect of making the *Dial* look like an exotic

[144] *Night and Day* (London, 1945), pp. 176-177.
[145] *Criterion,* V (Jan., 1927), 167-168.
[146] *Criterion,* V (June, 1927), 373.

bird and most of the other magazines like bazaar goods. The mystifying quality about Mr. Mencken's achievement is a certain unity, consistency and character which is maintained month after month. It is this quality which suggests a new type of culture. . . . an indigenous culture, and there is no parallel in England. . . . no parallel and no possibility of a parallel. To appreciate and understand the *American Mercury* implies an *a priori* interest in the American scene.[147]

In America in 1927 the monthly gathered laurels easily. *Time,* apparently repenting of its unsympathetic view of Mencken's stand at Brimstone Corner, one year after the episode admitted that the *Mercury* was "the most provocative review in the U. S."[148] Other periodicals lauded their competitor in 1927, some of them, like the *American Review of Reviews,* showing signs of a nervous reluctance.[149] The *Dial* continued its approval, as did those who were impressed by the editor's success against the Boston Watch and Ward Society.[150] This celebration was but another sign of the magazine's journalistic force, a force so great that it was considered "perhaps unparalleled in American magazine history."[151] By 1927 its "amazing"[152] influence on other publications was probably at its peak; "the green revolution" was the term used to describe its impact. Leon Whipple, trying to account for its success, wrote that it was "inspiringly eclectic in both subjects and authors," and added that one "may read about morons, perfumes, the Coolidge myth, the possibilities of birth-control, surgery

[147] *Criterion,* VI (Dec., 1927), 572-573.

[148] Anon., "Think Stuff," *Time,* IX (April 4, 1927), 24, 26. (A photograph of Alfred Knopf was labeled: "Publisher Knopf/*His editor oscillates*").

[149] Albert Shaw, editor of *American Review of Reviews,* stated that the *Mercury* "publishes things every month that irritate many people who are contented optimists" ("Mencken and His Aims," LXXVI [Oct., 1927], 412). Shaw invited Mencken to contribute a "Testament," which was printed *ibid.,* 413-416.

[150] Alyse Gregory, "Criticism in America," *Dial,* LXXXIII (Sept., 1927), 252; Hazleton Spencer ("Thunder in the Index," *Saturday Review of Literature,* III [May 28, 1927], 858): "Since his late jeopardy of person in the cause of freedom under the very shadow of the Park Street Church, his prophesyings . . . assume a new dignity. . . . [T]hat expedition to Brimstone Corner . . . undoubtedly resulted in a considerable increase of personal esteem for him."

[151] Cleaton, *Books & Battles,* p. 184.

[152] Wood, *Magazines in the United States,* p. 195.

. . . , and in each [essay] get a quality of realism, frontal attack and frankness that stirs the . . . brain cells. It is plain 'good stuff,' ably edited. Really, I think lots of folks read The Mercury just because they like the darn thing." Under a photograph of the editor, Whipple wrote: "Henry L. Mencken . . . , who had made the American Mercury the gadfly of a civilization. . . . A national institution at forty-six, heaven-bent for hell."[153] Others agreed that the magazine had become "a national institution" with which the doughty editor, according to Jim Tully, "taught a million thinking people the value of fundamentals."[154] To his college readers, "he became virtually a member of the faculty *in absentia,* whose printed lectures no good student ever cut."[155] The genteel Agnes Repplier, who had received her share of Mencken's *Smart Set* jibes, apparently forgave him: asked to survey "American Magazines" for the *Yale Review,* the elderly spinster became excited over the *Mercury*: "Even radicals and free-thinkers are permitted to have their say," she marveled. "When we read the pages of that very brilliant and very aggressive monthly. . . . we feel the full value of an escape from smugness, the full weight of discerning observation." Like Whipple, Miss Repplier found the contents adequately varied: "We grow tired of being edified, and we grow tired of being shocked. But after a particularly flippant article in the Mercury— let us say, on Philadelphia, or on matrimony. . . . we are just in the mood to read and enjoy its scholarly study of William James."[156]

It was in 1927 that the *Mercury* staff sent out one of the most significant—and now mercifully forgotten—documents in the history of the monthly. Their booklet, *Three Years: 1924 to 1927: The Story of a New Idea and Its*

[153] "The Revolution on Quality Street, Part II," *Survey,* LVII (Jan. 1, 1927), 427-428.
[154] Sullivan, *Our Times,* p. 413; *College Humor,* Oct., 1927, n.p. ("Articles About H. L. Mencken: Clippings: 1919-1933," E.P.M.C.).
[155] Manchester, *Mencken,* p. 211.
[156] *Yale Review,* XVI (Jan., 1927), 266-267, 270.

Successful Adaptation, was not modest. It claimed that
the magazine had completely rediscovered America, "from
flora and fauna to the inevitable Indians." The first issue
was carefully traced from its printing to the trucks of the
American News Company, which, "like so many storks,
delivered the lusty infant" to all the large cities: "In literate
homes eager fingers tore open the wrappings, over-stuffed
chairs were pushed before the fire, and the reading of the
American Mercury began. What happened is as much history as Paul Revere's ride and General Grant's whiskey."
Of their contributors the editorial staff primly pointed out
that "Even distinguished writers, who are occasionally
tempted to water cream for other magazines, are required
to deliver cream to *The American Mercury*." "The hack
writer," according to the exultant booklet, "never receives
attention." Proudly mentioned was the review's unsenti-
mental scrutiny of religion, especially "in its overlapping
the profane life of politics and the arts." In a "Postscript,"
the editor bluntly expressed his pride in the monthly: "It
is costly to produce and sells at a good round price. It is
not aimed at cheap people." In the closing pages, Allan
Nevins,[157] Arnold Bennett, F. Scott Fitzgerald, and others
hailed the publication, adding to the rhetoric that had
compared the editor to personages ranging from Diogenes,
Rabelais, Swift, Voltaire, to even the Devil himself.

As the first five years of the venture drew to a close, the
assorted tributes slackened somewhat, but the magazine
seemed to rest on a plateau of high regard. Its success, of
course, had been partly based on its policy of encouraging
the postwar cynicism and the defiant anti-Victorianism of
the twenties, and these two related attitudes did not ebb
until after the Depression set in. The monthly had sustained its editor's influence and authority so well, wrote
Lloyd Morris, "that the gay and gaudy decade came to be

---

[157] Allan Nevins, in his *American Press Opinion: Washington to Coolidge*
(Boston, [1928]), reprinted Mencken's "The Champion," from the October,
1924, "Clinical Notes" (pp. 582-584).

called by his name. It was the Age of H. L. Mencken, whose celebrity exceeded that of any previous critic of the national culture. . . . Mencken made the *Mercury* . . . a monthly national insult as withering in its effect as the sub-machine guns of gangsters."[158] By 1928 there seemed little reason to doubt that the review would long continue, "gay and latitudinarian enough to entertain the gods themselves."[159] Indeed, Mencken's fifth-year editorial was sufficiently boastful to draw sharp criticism from the editors of the *New York Times*.[160] If ever a magazine staff was guilty of hubris, and was thus destined to exchange pride for woe, it was that of the *Mercury*.

[158] *Postscript to Yesterday*, pp. 142-143.

[159] *Three Years*, p. 13.

[160] "Congratulations Are in Order," Nov. 23, 1928, p. 24, col. 5: "The American Mercury has suddenly joined its own hated *Philisterei*. It seizes the opportunity of its fifth anniversary to do a lot of bragging . . . in the finest style of Babbitt and Main Street. It has made money. It has got a big list of permanent subscribers. Advertisers are flocking in ever larger numbers to the support of the finest thing that ever appeared in American periodical journalism.

"All this cannot but surprise devoted readers and admirers. . . . When a despiser of the vulgar herd takes to imitating all the rest, what hope is left? . . . [A]s one reads the . . . Mercury's eulogium of itself, including even a pledge that . . . it is going to be Bigger, Better, and Brighter, one gets a new impression of the invincible might of that terrible American bourgeoisie in attempts to destroy which The . . . Mercury has wreaked itself. *O homo boobiens, O Americano, thou hast triumphed!*"

8

CRITICS OF THE *MERCURY* BEFORE 1930

CRITICISMS FROM THE RIGHT

THAT Oscar Wilde was denounced in perhaps nine hundred American sermons between 1895 and 1900[1] illustrates the American fascination with a literary bête noire. Wilde, however, was easily surpassed by Mencken as the featured demon in sermons; and the gentlemen of the cloth were aided, as has been seen, by laymen, including Legionnaires, critics of "Hatrack," the *Saturday Evening Post,* and those conservatives who lamented the initial appearance of the monthly. These attacks on the *Mercury* were as important as the varied praises, because they represented the opinion of most average Americans as well as many professors and some serious literary critics.

Prominent among pious critics of the periodical were men who deplored its freethinking, aggressively naturalistic attitude. The Reverend F. P. Turner, speaking before a pastor's federation in North Carolina, felt obliged to condemn Mencken as a magazine editor bent on "undermining the churches' work"; and another North Carolinian, addressing a Christian students' conference, charged that "the intellectuals of the class-room are not reading the Bible, but prefer Mencken. . . . Such reading will produce its fruit of evil."[2] It was not surprising that Methodist organs referred

[1] Thomas Beer, *The Mauve Decade* (Garden City, New York, [1926]), p. 129.

[2] Citations from "Menckeniana: A Schimpflexicon," III, n.p.; *Menckeniana: A Schimpflexicon,* p. 40.

to the review as "the Greenbacked Monster";[3] it was to Methodists above all other sects something reprehensible. "Not a few youths of the present generation," announced the Reverend Herbert Jump, "seem to think it is smart to dispose of God in a wise crack, to impale goodness on the point of an epigram. In poetry it is symbolized by Omar Khayyam, in drama by George Bernard Shaw, in fiction by Michael Arlen, in magazine literature by H. L. Mencken and his *American Mercury*." Another clergyman stated that "Mercurianity is the name of a new religion, the Bible of which is a greencovered monthly magazine," and Edwin Mims, a Southern professor who had been smartly rapped in Mencken's "The Library" concurred that the monthly had "established a new religion, Mercurianity, instead of Christianity."[4] Missionaries in China contributed vituperative comment,[5] and domestic invective was equally harsh. Said the bulletin of the Anti-Saloon League of Virginia: "H. L. Mencken, editor of the *American Mercury,* is a notorious writer, the idol of the earthly, sensual, devilish elements of our country." Others elaborated their low opinions in language more shocking than that used in the magazine itself: "His initials are H. L., meaning the first and last of the word Hell. He publishes a magazine called the *American Mercury,* and any doctor will tell you that nobody takes mercury but degenerates who have acquired the most loathsome social sexual disease known after an illicit honeymoon with some unwashed Lazar or Lazarette of the highways." Loyal Mississippians were wrathful at the editor's habit of calling "upon his store of greenish scum to besmatter Mississippi," while the Methodist Board of Temperance, Prohibition and Public Morals offered a suggestion: "drop the

[3] W. V. Kelley, "At the Sign of the Basilisk," *Methodist Review*, Aug., 1925, p. 518.

[4] Citations from "Menckeniana," I, 91; *Menckeniana*, p. 68; *ibid.*, p. 45.

[5] H. C. Connette, writing in the *North China Star,* observed that the intelligentsia "ought to know better than to read the filth [put out in the] green-covered magazine. [Its] appeal has been to the derelicts of society, who, by their very acts, have cut themselves off from decent folk and are at war with the society which will no longer tolerate them" (*Menckeniana*, p. 65).

second word from the title of the magazine." Some citizens suggested that violence was the answer to the outspoken editor who, one critic claimed, wrote most of the magazine "under pseudonyms." Mencken was seen in the backwoods as a "literary firebrand whose red light illumines the *American Mercury*."[6]

Other more plaintive and even amusing statements revealed the provincial conservatives sharing Lorimer's anguish. Mencken's vehement anti-farming and anti-ranching attitudes drew the following query from the Wyoming *Stockman-Farmer*: "What we'd like to know is who told him we were knaves, swindlers, speculators and imbeciles?" Someone on the staff of the *Idaho Statesman* was consistently alert toward the depravities of the green monthly; in an article on Mencken entitled "He Never Knew a Mother's Love," he pointed out that "There is another coyote that hunts with Mencken, named Nathan."[7] Flora Seymour, apparently agreeing with a New England verdict that the *Mercury* was "perhaps the worst magazine in the United States," observed that, "having closely followed thirty-three numbers of the *American Mercury*—we cannot but conclude that its . . . formulae of sneer and sarcasm . . . write it down unquestionably as the most monumental sham of modern life."[8] A Californian recalled that an "embittered artist once painted a picture of a vampire nobility sucking the blood of a wretched, starving world of workers," adding that there "now exists a heartless, barren aristocracy of intellect, the Mencken breed, who fly under the colors of the Green Book. They live by the labor of those they deride. Yet they add no whit of comfort, no mote of beauty, no chord of harmony to the world." A Midwesterner asked: "Who is he that he has any right to criticize any American, no matter who?"; another cried: "H. L. Mencken is rude

[6] Citations from *Menckeniana*, pp. 65-66, 69, 95, 97-98; "Menckeniana," III, 206, 207.
[7] Citations from "Menckeniana," III, 191; *ibid.*, I, n.p. (this reference to Nathan was omitted in the compilation of the published *Menckeniana*). (Another comment from the *Idaho Statesman* is printed in *Menckeniana*, p. 70.)
[8] "Menckeniana," I, 71.

and insulting. He might speak of our mental deficiencies with a more restrained tone."[9] An anti-Semitic critic, deciding that the magazine's shortcomings were grounded in Mencken's Jewish background (!) and the Jewish faith of most of the other *Mercury* associates, wrote articles, had pamphlets printed and sold, and traveled across the country making hostile speeches.[10] (Eventually a Jewish publication was deluded into listing Mencken as a Jew.) And, of course, there were scores of Rotary and Kiwanis speeches dealing briskly with the *Mercury*'s contributors, most of these speeches trying "to shout them down as knockers."[11]

One professor wrote a booklet asking "whether the ownership of a Victrola is not as culturally valuable as a subscription to the *Mercury*?" The author pointedly refused to answer his question, lest he reveal himself as "chautauqua-minded, rabble-rousing, blithering, and low." He felt it "useless to preach a gospel of relativity and . . . insist that . . . the Philistine is the true realist in a society obviously arranged more for his comfort than for that of either native or imported *Mercurys*." He further concluded that if an angel were to assume control of the monthly, "and proceed to view the libertati [*sic*] from that ivory tower he would find them about as dignified and intelligible as any dung beetles in God's pasture."[12] Professor Fred L. Pattee (later to modify his estimate) attacked the "Americana" department as "monthly rakings . . . from the entire press of America, with everything winnowed out save those scraps that tend to belittle our civilization,"[13] and K. V. Hoffman shared Pattee's low opinion.[14]

[9] Citations from *Menckeniana*, p. 67; *ibid.*, p. 51; "Menckeniana," I, 128.

[10] William Salisbury, "Mencken, the Foe of Beauty," pamphlet (New Rochelle, N.Y., 1925), rewritten from an article originally printed in *The American Parade*, ed. W. Adolphe Roberts (New York, 1926). (The pamphlet was sold for ten cents per copy.)

[11] Palm, *The Middle Classes*, p. 369.

[12] Joseph B. Harrison, *A Short View of Menckenism in Menckenese* (Seattle, Washington, 1927), pp. 21, 19.

[13] "One Mencken in a generation is positively all that we can endure" (in the *Christian Advocate*, reprinted in *Menckeniana*, p. 67).

[14] "Mencken, Landlubber," *McNaught's Monthly*, III (March, 1925), 89: "The Olympian Mr. Mencken seems to see things only on the surface. Not only

Some found fault with the review for printing so many writings by convicts, while others mistook its attacks on Coolidge as signs that it was a Communist organ. It was denounced on the floor of Congress as pro-anarchist, subversive, and "widely circulated among the Reds," while the Department of Justice was alleged to have fostered reports charging that the periodical was directly subsidized by Moscow.[15] That many sober citizens took these charges seriously, or otherwise independently arrived at the opinion that it was Communistic, is suggested by a painful experience of Fred Beal, one of the organizers of the bloody textile strike of 1929 in Gastonia, North Carolina. Writing eight years after his arrest there, Beal still showed apprehension: "to prove my radicalism, [The Gastonia *Gazette*] reported that on the night of my arrest I had with me a copy of 'Mencken's Magazine' (*The American Mercury*). This association was enough to burn anyone in the chair!"[16]

It should not be thought that all rightist shafts, however pitifully launched some of them were, were ineffective or unjustified. And by 1928, when the *Mercury*'s period of glory began to end, a battery of right-wing critics of learning and intelligence opened up on the monthly. Had the Depression not given the leftist critics a weapon with which to bludgeon the review, it is possible that the New Humanists, speaking chiefly in the *Forum* and the *Bookman,* would have inflicted great damage without much assistance. The salvo of January, 1928, included an attack by Catherine B. Ely, who ridiculed the "Menckenites" as "an esoteric band" of "barren intellect,"[17] and, more important, Paul Elmer More's judgment that "the critical ideas of the immature

that, but he sees only the scum. His 'Americana' is a collection of fanaticisms, bigotry, and inane stupidities, culled from our hastily and poorly-written press, but no fair-minded person could call it a true reflection of American life and thought."

[15] Mencken, "Memoirs of an Editor," *Vanity Fair,* XLI, 16; Manchester, *Mencken,* pp. 157, 215.

[16] *Proletarian Journey* (New York, 1937), p. 183.

[17] "The Sorrows of Mencken," *North American Review,* CCXXV (Jan., 1928), 25-26.

and ignorant are formed by brawling vulgarians like H. L. Mencken."[18] In February of 1928, the barrage intensified; Irving Babbitt found that Mencken's writing "is nearer to intellectual vaudeville than to serious criticism." Babbitt's well written article was truly challenging, and it deserved a formal reply from Mencken, a reply the editor did not deign to accord it. Babbitt found that the "effect of Mr. Mencken's writing . . . is to produce pride . . . pride ultimately based on flattery. The reader, especially the young and callow reader, identifies himself imaginatively with Mr. Mencken and conceives of himself as a sort of morose and sardonic divinity surveying from some superior altitude an immeasurable expanse of 'boobs.' " Babbitt was "reminded in particular of Flaubert, who showed a diligence in collecting bourgeoise imbecilities comparable to that displayed by Mr. Mencken in his *Americana*. Flaubert's discovery that one does not add to one's happiness in this way would no doubt be dismissed by Mr. Mencken as irrelevant." A warning by Flaubert seemed pertinent to Babbitt: " 'By dint of railing at idiots,' Flaubert reports, 'one runs the risk of becoming idiotic oneself.' " The New Humanist concluded: "It may be that the only way to escape the unduly complacent cynicism of Mr. Mencken and his school is to reaffirm once more the truths of the inner life."[19] A second attack in the same month, while not so challenging as Babbitt's, indicates fairly a trend of the day, a trend which saw the New Humanists begin to recapture some of their ground earlier lost to Mencken in the colleges and elsewhere. In "Mencken Outmoded," an anonymous writer for the conservative *Literary Digest* dismissed Mencken, "so long leader of the left wing in literature," as having ruined himself by the railings at "Rotary and revealed religion so often appearing" in the *Mercury*. Observing that if one

---

[18] "The Modern Current in American Literature," *Forum*, LXXIX (Jan., 1928), 135-136. More's charges were soon printed in *The Demon of the Absolute, New Shelburne Essays* (Princeton, New Jersey, 1928), I, 76.

[19] "The Critic and American Life," *Forum*, LXXIX (Feb., 1928), 162, 166.

"would be up to date, Menckenism isn't the line," the author pointed approvingly to the recent religious conversions in France of Jean Cocteau and Paul Morand.[20] As 1928 progressed, it continued to be affirmed in certain circles that Mencken was becoming *passé*: "We have passed Mencken," wrote Henry Flury, "who has fallen off the band-wagon and who appears to be unable to run fast enough to jump in again."[21]

But the most persistently vociferous criticisms were printed in the *Bookman,* converted by Seward Collins into a lively New Humanist organ in 1928. The *Mercury* came under well-directed sniping in 1928, and by 1929 *Bookman* contributors were more bluntly critical. Under a full-page photograph of Mencken, with the caption "Henry L. Mencken, Grub Street's George A. Custer, who rides along on his charger, *Mercury,* to the basin of the Little Big Horn," was also the question: "Who is the 'Sitting Bull' to take the scalp of 'Yellow Hair'?"[22] The *Bookman* soon began to criticize in greater earnest: Mencken was described as tired and "losing his grip": "Certainly his influence has waned appreciably; even his most devoted admirers are heard to express concern and dissatisfaction." Certain of the less wise ruminations in "The Library" were advanced as evidence of the decline.[23]

This gradually strengthening conservative opposition is significant. The fall of the *Mercury* has usually been ascribed to the advent of the great Depression, which today seems so neatly to slice the twenties from the thirties. Actually, the coming of the Depression in October, 1929, has been overrated as a cause of the declining fortunes of the monthly; the opposition, both right and left wing, had struck telling blows earlier.

[20] *Literary Digest,* XCVI (Feb. 18, 1928), 27.
[21] "More, Babbitt, and Mencken," *Forum,* LXXXIX (April, 1928), 634.
[22] Robert H. Davis, "The Literati under the Lens," *Bookman,* LXIX (Aug., 1929), 626.
[23] Anon., "Chronicle and Comment," *Bookman,* LXX (Oct., 1929), 186-187.

BARBS FROM THE LEFT

THE *Mercury* put the leftists of the twenties in a quandary. On the one hand, they could not but admire many aspects of the magazine: its dashing and effective attacks on the Republican Party, its stalwart atheism, its anti-rural and anti-Puritan bias, and its toleration of minority ethnic groups frankly pleased such radicals as Art Young, somewhat impressed John Dos Passos, and led such critics as Vernon F. Calverton to wobble considerably in their estimates of the monthly and its editor. On the other hand, the green-covered review clearly sponsored no revolutions and proposed no reforms (it pointed with cool mockery toward Prohibition as an example of utopian legislation); and, for all its flamboyance, its discussions of the status quo could be seen, by a dedicated leftist, as merely superficially critical. Some of the older radicals must have recalled Floyd Dell's prophecy of 1919;[24] at any rate, such authors as Upton Sinclair soon began to nag the editor to adopt a more positive stance. (Mencken replied to one such plea: "The news that *The American Mercury* is 'lacking in constructive points of view' is surely not news to me.")[25] The cause of the radicals' complaints regarding the monthly's disdain for reformers was that it made such inroads upon the impressionable youth of the decade. The *Mercury* was a Pied Piper drawing collegians and other young intellectuals into an aloof and mocking attitude toward their wretched countrymen. That the review fostered a sort of irresponsible disillusionment is attested by a despairing statement by the Socialist Norman Thomas: "The old reformer has become the Tired Radical and his sons and daughters drink at the fountain of the *American Mercury*. They have no illusions

[24] "Popularity," *Liberator*, Dec., 1919, p. 42.
[25] HLM to Sinclair, Dec. 10, 1924. Printed in Sinclair, *Letters*, pp. 239-240.

but one. And that is that they can live like Babbitt and think like Mencken."[26]

In the first number of the *New Masses* the cynicism and nihilism of "the modern school" were outlined in a dialogue between an "Editor" (apparently meant to suggest Mencken) and a "Contributor" (clearly a radical). The "Contributor" admitted that a magazine "even greater than the *American Mercury*" could be based on cynicism, but he warned that the only hope of the artist is "contact with the masses. These feed his soul, and give him strength. Yes, these despised morons and yokels of Mr. Mencken."[27] Throughout the remainder of 1926 the carping at the periodical continued, less and less interspersed with praise such as Art Young's. Michael Gold felt moved to score its "middle-class" popularity, stating that "futilitarianism is an easy way of evading one's social ideals. . . . This renegadism Mencken had made seem the jolliest and most sophisticated of gestures." Cartoons elaborated Gold's animadversions, as did attacks on the ultra-conservative Nathan.[28] When the Socialist James Oneal contributed to the *Mercury* several relatively objective sketches of the troubles of the labor movement, the *New Masses* snarled: "the intellectual and discerning *American Mercury* will gladly pay a hundred or so for an entertaining *scherzo* about the agonizing gropings, hither and thither, of revolutionary American labor at odds with itself—in short, [Oneal] discovered that eating two Communists for breakfast every morning pays."[29]

Vernon Calverton, editor of the leftist *Modern Quarterly*,

[26] "Where are the Pre-War Radicals? A Symposium," *Survey*, LV (Feb. 1, 1926), 563.
[27] M. H. Hedges, "The War of Cultures," I (May, 1926), 20.
[28] Gold, "America Needs a Critic," *New Masses*, I (Oct., 1926), 8-9. A cartoon, captioned "Among the Asses," pictured Mencken feeding from a bottle an infant with horn-rimmed glasses and a mortarboard. Mencken is dressed like a Madonna, with his "child" an academic youth. The caption concluded: "the immaculate conception of the American Superman" (II [Dec., 1926], 4). The criticisms of Nathan appeared in Harbor Allen, "Our Foremost Critic," II (Jan., 1927), 26.
[29] James Fuchs, "Chronicle of Confusion," III (May, 1927), 30-31.

criticized his fellow Baltimorean,[30] while Upton Sinclair began to sound the toscin in his *Money Writes!* and in various articles which charged the *Mercury*'s intimacy with Wall Street, Mencken's not inconsiderable profits in his publishing adventure, and the monthly's fundamental irresponsibility from a social angle. Of the "democratic control of industry," Sinclair held Mencken "as ignorant as any Babbitt-boob," and disaster was prophesied, despite the fact that under the capitalistic system "The American Mercury has built up a hundred thousand circulation [*sic*], and the editor is not nearly so discontented as he talks."[31] The *New Masses* maintained its insults; when Mencken observed that the majority of the population possessed the minds of eighteen-year-olds, and that movies were appropriately designed, Don Ryan concluded the syllogism: "Therefore movies will continue to be manufactured for readers of the *American Mercury*."[32]

That the Communists were so gentle surprised at least one critic; Edmund Wilson marveled, early in 1928, that the "*New Masses* has been content with an occasional jibe,"[33] but in that year the truce was renounced, and the Communists joined the resurgent New Humanists in louder opposition. In March Gold decried Mencken's middle-class efforts to reconcile "American youth to business. . . . his common sense is that of a prosperous grocer. . . . Mencken is losing his followers; they are discovering he is shallow." With the June number, when the emphatic Gold assumed editorial control of the Communist publication, the diatribe became downright silly and sometimes hysterical.[34] Mary

[30] "The American Literary Radicals," *Modern Quarterly*, III (Sept.-Dec., 1926), 252.
[31] "Mr. Mencken Calls on Me," *Bookman*, LXVI, 256.
[32] "The Movies Join the Union," III (Oct., 1927), 12.
[33] "Literary Politics," *New Republic*, LIII (Feb. 1, 1928), 289.
[34] Gold, "Hemingway—White Collar Poet," III (March, 1928), 21. The June number appeared with cheaper paper and the following editorial announcement: "The *New Masses* does not compete with the *Mercury*. . . . It is the voice of the lowbrow, the failure, the rebel . . . the men and women at the bottom. Writers for other magazines wear high hats; our writers have to panhandle their meals," etc. (IV, n.p.). Gold displayed further dissatisfaction in his

Sinclair, the wife of Upton Sinclair, purchased a full-page advertisement in the *New Masses* to berate the *Mercury* for its wrongs toward her gullible husband.[35] In the *Communist,* a more theoretical Marxist-Leninist organ, Joseph Freeman observed that the Mencken vogue "seems to be waning" because he had not been able to progress beyond his "contempt for the American Masses, for democracy, prohibition, and the Methodist church. If he has changed at all," wrote the Communist, "it is in his cynicism about university professors. The *American Mercury* . . . carries a disproportionate number of contributions by academic gentlemen."[36] Gold soon offered yet another criticism: "How sickening to read every month twenty imitators of Mencken in the *Mercury*. Eugene Jolas, the editor of *transition,* is a poet with a tragic vision." In 1929 leftist criticisms often took the form of disparagement of writers associated with the monthly. Of so gentle a man as Sherwood Anderson, it was pointed out that his humility was a sham: "Like the clerks who lean on the superman idea as diluted in the *American Mercury,* he feels that the artist is an aristocrat"; Jim Tully, cursed with "the fake literary swagger of Menckenitis," was held up as an upleasant "example of the influence of H. L. Mencken on young writers in this country."[37]

"Editorial Notes," *ibid.,* p. 2: "Ernest Booth has written a series of sketches of thieves he has known. One of them appears this month. Booth first was printed in the *New Masses,* but H. L. Mencken has since 'discovered' him for the *Mercury*." An extremely bitter poem by James Miller, entitled "Professors," arraigns professors for their interest in Mencken (IV [July, 1928], 20).

[35] "Beware My Dog! (Warning from the Wife of a Friend of Mankind)," IV (Aug., 1928), 23.

[36] "The 'Wilsonian' Liberals," VII (Aug., 1928), 516.

[37] Gold, "3 Schools of U.S. Writing," *New Masses,* IV (Sept., 1928), 14; Joseph Freeman, "Sherwood Anderson's Confusion," *New Masses,* IV (Feb., 1929), 6; Gold, "Shanty Irish," *New Masses,* IV (Feb., 1929), 26.

OTHER CRITICS

MORE important from a literary point of view than most of the opposition of consciously leftist or rightist critics were reservations expressed by serious artists and cultural critics who had been originally well disposed toward the *Mercury*. Disillusionment concerning its attitudes toward belles-lettres appeared, as seen in the response to Boyd's "Aesthete: Model 1924," in the reception accorded the very first number. Generally, to aesthetes both at home and abroad, the periodical was seen as philistine. As observed by Frederick A. Hoffman, the literary younger generation of the twenties "was taken in neither by [their] commercial fathers nor by the boisterous anti-Americanism of the Mencken-Boyd-Nathan *Mercury,* but was impressed by . . . Pound . . . Stein . . . Ford Madox Ford." In return, since Mencken was an outsider, it was natural for his review "to regard the carnivalism of revolt as simply the reverse side of the bourgeois coin."[38] Certainly the more "arty" expatriates remained unimpressed: even the Greenwich Village furore of 1923 caused them to open only one eye: *"The American Mercury* has made its appearance," yawned Kenneth Jewett in the *Transatlantic Review:* "Mr. Boyd has attacked the dilettantes, and Mr. Rascoe has replied."[39] It appears that many of the expatriates ignored the whole drama of the *Mercury* until it was over, and its adventures must have seemed futile in the thirties, when the exiles began to return to America.[40] Ford Madox Ford seemed more

[38] Citations from respectively, *The Twenties,* p. 14; *The Little Magazine,* p. 226.

[39] "And from the United States," I (April, 1924), 207. (As has been seen, Rascoe chronicled the event from the point of view of Boyd, and so his account cannot be construed as a "reply" in any sense.)

[40] Zechariah Chafee summarized for the returning exiles the *Mercury's* fight with the Watch and Ward Society by simply remarking that Mencken was "arrested on Boston Common for selling a shady short story" ("The Law," *America Now: An Inquiry into Civilization in the United States,* ed. Harold E. Stearns [New York, 1938], p. 297).

disturbed than many native Americans about the caricatures of American civilization; in both books and articles he denied Mencken's logic and accuracy, especially in the interpretations of the Midwest from a New York City perspective.[41]

Ernest Hemingway, however, was one expatriate who broke the silence concerning the monthly: his satire, *The Torrents of Spring,* devoted several pages to the *Mercury.* One of Hemingway's foolish female characters, near the conclusion of the narrative, tries to lure back her loved one by flaunting a copy of the review:

"Scripps, dear, wouldn't you like to come home?" Diana's voice quavered. "There's a new *Mercury.*" She had changed from the London *Mercury* to *The American Mercury* just to please Scripps. "It just came. I wish you felt like coming home, Scripps, there's a splendid thing in this *Mercury.* . . ." "Do come, Scripps, dear," Diana said softly, "There's a wonderful editorial in it by Mencken about chiropractors."

Scripps looked away. . . . "No," said Scripps, "I don't give a damn about Mencken any more."

Diana dropped her head. . . . This was the end. She had her answer now. She had lost him. . . . Quietly, silently, gathering her shawl around her, clutching the cage with the sleeping bird and the copy of *The Mercury* to her breast. . . . she opened the door of her beanery, and went out into the night.[42]

Meanwhile, literary figures in the United States, mostly from the avant-garde, had drawn up a reprisal for Boyd's "Aesthete: Model 1924." In January, 1925, such writers as William Carlos Williams, Hart Crane, Matthew Josephson, John Wheelwright, Slater Brown, Kenneth Burke, and Malcolm Cowley issued *Aesthete 1925.* This publication (which might have become a periodical had funds permitted) contained a saucy, but rather incoherent, harangue on the subject of the *Mercury* and its editor: "Since he has

[41] Especially important is Ford's *New York Is Not America* (London, [1927]) which challenges Mencken's stereotypes as obsolete. Also noteworthy is Ford's letter printed in the *Transatlantic Review,* II (Aug., 1924), 210-213.

[42] (New York, 126), pp. 131-133.

changed from *Smart Set* to *American Mercury* Mencken can be read without offence by women and children." If it is true, as described, that the entire polemic, except for a short story by Slater Brown, was written in a room of the Broadway Central Hotel on a Saturday night, the literary faults of *Aesthete 1925* are easily accounted for.[43]

Although there were a number of scattered protests from serious men in 1925, for instance, one by Frederick Lewis Allen,[44] by 1926 the rejection of Mencken as a cultural force by younger writers had gone to such lengths that Edmund Wilson felt justified in warning them. Wilson admitted Mencken's excessive repetition of his basically simple ideas, but recalled the editor's excellence as a stylist: ". . . I derive a certain literary satisfaction from even his editorials in the *American Mercury*." As evidence of the merits of Mencken's prose, Wilson claimed that the editor's leaflet intended to arouse sympathy in his quarrel with the Watch and Ward Society "displays most attractive eighteenth century qualities of lucidity, order and force, for lack of which the youngest literary generation, who have thrown Mencken overboard, have so far proved rather ineffective." As for the editor himself, he seemed to miss very little the supporters he had originally won by his *Smart Set* crusades; indeed, the failure of writers to flock to his support during the "Hatrack" ordeal led him to admit an odd—and significant—position for an editor conducting a magazine with some literary pretensions. Accounting for the literati's refusal to show much concern during April, 1926, Mencken wrote: "I was not popular in that quarter, partly on account of my book reviews and partly because I had given over the *American Mercury* mainly to new writers, and excluded most of the established performers."[45]

[43] I am indebted to the Princeton Library for making available their copy of *Aesthete 1925*. In the Princeton Library copy is a letter by Allen Tate dated Jan. 28, 1942, which supplies most of the information concerning the thirty-five cent magazine. The citation is from *Aesthete 1925*, p. 33.

[44] "Public Opinion," *Forum*, LXXXIV (Dec., 1925), 895.

[45] Wilson, "The All-Star Literary Vaudeville," *New Republic*, XLVII, 160; "The 'Hatrack' Case," I, 87.

Nevertheless, the writers themselves offered different reasons for their growing dissatisfaction. Most often, they alleged that the review was in a rut: "many a valiant veteran," wrote Louis Bromfield, "keeps making faces after the battle is won"; Eunice Barnard judged that, "as for our modern sport of baiting Victorianism, of which Mr. Mencken's . . . popular magazine is so consistent an exemplar, it is pantomime over a corpse. Shaw served as St. George to that dragon twenty years ago." John Farrar summed up the reservations of much of belletristic America in the following well-meant advice:

It is almost time that Mr. Mencken stopped being an irritant and turned to more useful pursuits. He has a good mind. He is an excellent editor. . . . If H. L. Mencken should take a year off in which to study the moods of literary America he might conceivably have something to say about our letters worth hearing. . . . he is bawling out the same headlines damnations in which he has indulged for years. It is time he matured. There are moments when he seems to be the hero of American youth, but he cannot continue to be that forever; in a few more generations young men will be shouting at other doors, and then what will become of him?[46]

F. Scott Fitzgerald, by 1926, felt that his earlier enthusiasm for the *Mercury* was misguided; moreover, he felt that its failure was to blame for an inability in novelists to fulfil the promise shown at the beginning of the twenties. Fitzgerald sensed the promise latent in the monthly, with an editor whose invective, "sharp as Swift's," could make "its point by the use of the most forceful prose style now written in English," and he therefore expressed dismay at the subordination of aesthetic aims to ethical aims and at the many imitative contributors who "manufactured enthusiasm when each new mass of raw data was dumped on the literary platform—mistaking incoherence for vitality, chaos for

[46] Citations from, respectively, "The Point of View," *Bookman,* LXIII (March, 1926), 2; "G. B. S.: The Father of the Flapper," *New Republic,* XLVII (July 28, 1926), 272; "Mustard Plaster Mencken," *Bookman,* LXIV (Dec., 1926), 389.

vitality." Some English novelists began to share their American colleagues' lower estimates of Mencken: Frank Swinnerton wrote a dream fantasy battle of the books which featured him entering an arena to combat a Mencken who was armed with a copy of the *Mercury*.[47]

Certainly Mencken's book reviews had an influence on the trend; he showed no great partiality to his old friends Dreiser, Lewis, and Anderson. He lectured them freely and rehearsed their shortcomings in patronizing detail. The result was that he began to alienate his most vocal and influential supporters among writers. Thirty years later the editor cast some light on what he was doing: "My hardest job in the days when I was writing book reviews was to break up the Mencken party."[48] He indeed succeeded in "breaking up" the party, but why he wanted to do so is not clear. It was true that the circulation was not hampered; his greatest journalistic triumphs came in 1927, well after many lovers of belles-lettres had ostentatiously washed their hands of the *Mercury*. But actually he was only replacing the *old* Mencken party—men of some stature—with a new party composed of such fry as Jim Tully, Ernest Booth, and James Stevens.

Mencken's break with Dreiser came in 1926 over Mencken's unfavorable review of *An American Tragedy,* a novel on which Dreiser placed great hopes. It has been popularly thought that "Mencken's *American Mercury* loudly proclaimed the worth of Dreiser's novel,"[49] but nothing could be further from the truth. Not only did the reviewer mock the length of the novel, the occasional bad writing, faults of structure, and its generally boring nature, but he also showed that he had not fully understood one of the crucial scenes. Dreiser was infuriated; after all, it seemed that even Stuart

[47] "How to Waste Material; A Note on My Generation," *Bookman,* LXIII (May, 1926), 263; "The Great Mencken Fight," *Bookman,* LXIV (Dec., 1926), 463-467.
[48] *H. L. Mencken's Notebooks: Minority Report* (New York, 1956), p. 80.
[49] Harvey Wish, *Contemporary America: The National Scene since 1900,* p. 339.

Sherman was able to write a more intelligent and understanding review of his masterpiece. Dreiser's curt note to the editor was their last communication for many years.[50]

In 1927, the *annus mirabilis* of the monthly, fewer serious critics and writers wanted to challenge it, but now and then someone would protest.[51] In the following year, however, the protests of 1926 returned, more insistent and more sweeping. At nearly the same time that he was himself being exposed by the *New Masses* as a *Mercury* disciple, Sherwood Anderson wrote Nelson A. Crawford complaining about the "whole modern Mencken, hard-boiled attitude. It takes strength to be tender, and these men haven't strength."[52] In other ways the dissatisfaction could be gauged. In his *Anthology of Magazine Verse for 1928 and Yearbook*,[53] W. Stanley Braithwaite indicated the monthly's relative standing among periodicals printing poetry by including nothing whatever from the *Mercury*.

Equally important, the review was not "discovering" enough worthwhile new writers to justify its pretensions of being the blessed haven for young talents. The *New Yorker* proved itself able to espy talent that Mencken missed. The *Mercury* had rejected such authors as James Thurber and Kay Boyle, both of whom were welcomed by the competing weekly.[54] Nor did Nathan, in his limited editorial capacity,

[50] Dreiser wrote to Mencken after the review: "As to your critical predilections, animosities, inhibitions—et cet. Tosh. Who reads you? Bums and loafers. No-goods" (printed in Kemler, *Mr. Mencken*, p. 172).

[51] An example was F. A. Kummer's "Something Must Have Happened to Henry," *Bookman*, LXV (June, 1927), 408-410. Commenting on an attack by Mencken on Poe, Kummer reflected: "Henry knows better than all this, of course. But having packed his bladder with a brick, he takes an increasing joy in using it. To bean a man of note, such as Poe, over the left ear attracts wide attention, makes a lively show." Regarding the editor's attacks on O. Henry and Bryan, Kummer pointed out that it was a "savage exhibition Henry is giving us" (pp. 408, 410).

[52] March 18, 1930. *Letters of Sherwood Anderson*, ed. Howard M. Jones and Walter B. Rideout (Boston, 1953), pp. 215-216. Anderson's private estimate of Mencken had been low for many years; on May 23, 1918 he had written to Van Wyck Brooks: "One cannot surrender to the cheaper inclination in writing, to win perhaps the secondary approval of an ass like Mencken as his reward" (*ibid.*, pp. 36-38).

[53] (New York, 1928).

[54] Information from Kramer, *Ross and The New Yorker*, p. 158; HLM to Mrs. E. B. White, Jan. 8, [1935?] (copy in P.M.C.).

always choose wisely and well: he refused the enormously successful *Gentlemen Prefer Blondes,* by Anita Loos, and later had difficulty explaining his act. It has been claimed that the *New Republic* was able to draw some of Ring Lardner's works from the *Mercury.* Whether or not this claim is true, Lardner appreciated differences between periodicals in rates of payment. For a story published in the *Delineator,* he was paid only a fraction of the price paid by the *Saturday Evening Post,* but nonetheless, the *Delineator*'s rate was still "three or four times as much as Mencken would have paid."[55] Two cents a word for prose, with an occasional bonus to such writers as Sinclair Lewis, meant that as a matter of course many of the best creative writers sought first markets elsewhere, and sent their manuscripts to the *Mercury* as a second choice. In these circumstances, the editor could hardly afford to pass by such manuscripts as those submitted by Thomas Wolfe, and that they were returned with tactful and even inspiring notes did not benefit the magazine, however eagerly such notes may have been read.[56] Another indication of Mencken's growing interest in presenting a lively show at the expense of refinement of thought and expression was a rejection note sent to Ernest Boyd: "Somehow, I have a feeling that this is a bit too refined and philosophical for the Merkur. It is excellent stuff, but it is not rowdy enough. Nobody is insulted."[57]

The explanation is simple: the editor was no longer very deeply interested in literature. He therefore guided his magazine into economic and political areas. Unfortunately, he continued to conduct "The Library" without respite,

[55] Information from Rascoe, *We were Interrupted,* p. 198; Elder, *Ring Lardner: A Biography,* pp. 284, 371.

[56] Wolfe to Madeleine Boyd, Feb. 15, 1929, expresses the novelist's thoughts upon having portions of his *Look Homeward, Angel* rejected: "I am very much pleased by Mencken's note—his praise was moderate, but I take it at its literal value: I do not believe he writes such notes as a matter of form. And of course his belief in one's work would be of tremendous value to a writer" (*Letters of Thomas Wolfe,* p. 125).

[57] HLM to Boyd, Jan. 28, [1926]. Letter in P.M.C.

and by 1929 one of his more eager partisans had to admit tactfully that as "a critic of literature, Mr. Mencken is no longer an efficient guide."[58] And though by 1929 the review could still stimulate controversy, it was using more sensational tactics, as shown in its anonymous caricature of vice-president Charles Curtis.[59] In fact, one important article was rebuked in an editorial by the *New York Times* for its irresponsibility.[60]

By 1929, then, despite occasional respect shown by economic conservatives like Ezra Pound,[61] radicals like Vernon Calverton,[62] and some of Mencken's loyal cronies, the editor's journalistic course had come into greater and greater question from intellectual circles. In addition, there was a perceptible weakening of his popular triumph. He no longer issued his series of *Prejudices* after 1927, because the demand for them began to decline even in that halcyon year of successes. That some weakening in his reputation had commenced is best seen in statements from his publisher. The sales of works like *Americana 1926* did not warrant a continuation of the project.[63] Nor can it be said that Mencken had not been warned about such a possibility; his friends had often voiced their worries concerning his intellectual development, and the handwriting had been clearly on the wall before 1925.[64]

[58] Shuford, "An Evaluation of the Influence of H. L. Mencken and *The American Mercury* Upon American Thought," p. 122.

[59] "Heap Big Chief," Aug., 1929.

[60] An editorial, "Spoken Very Sarcastic," Sept. 30, 1929, p. 24, col. 6, was concerned with W. J. Cash's "The Mind of the South," which appeared in the Oct., 1929, *Mercury*. The sarcastic editorial ended: "In the next number the same quantity of broad statements will be made. This, in callow articles, is considered the basis of sociological comment."

[61] In a letter of February, 1929, Pound advised Charles H. Ford to "attack idiocy" in reviews of poetry by a *sottisier*, as done in Mencken's "Americana" (*Letters of Ezra Pound*, pp. 223-224).

[62] Before inveighing against Mencken's limitations, Calverton, as late as 1929, felt like acknowledging him as "often an inspiring force" ("Revolt among American Intellectuals," *New Masses*, IV [April, 1929], 4).

[63] "Publisher's Royalty Statements: H. L. Mencken: 1916-1941," E.P.M.C., *passim*.

[64] As early as 1920, Burton Rascoe, in the eulogistic *H. L. Mencken*, written together with Vincent O'Sullivan and F. C. Henderson, had to admit one great defect: "As a critic of poetry he is, I think, probably the worst in the world"

Had the *Mercury* been less famous as Mencken's personal sheet, had the editor been more retiring, there would have been no ominous linkage between the destiny of the magazine and its editor. But their reputations were intertwined too closely; in fact, had the *Mercury* associates known what was threatening, it would perhaps have been too late by 1929 to avoid the mutual downward journey. In 1928, the year of the proud five-year anniversary editorial, the official circulation sagged from the 77,277 average of 1927 to 73,841. In 1929, a further drop to 67,420[65] was registered, a drop incurred, as will be seen, in the face of an intensive advertising campaign to sell the monthly. In view of the resurgent criticisms of 1928 and 1929, the noteworthy decline in circulation, and the waning popularity of the editor, the common assumption that the *Mercury* was ruined by the Depression must be modified; the glorious heyday of the green monthly was over by the time of the great economic upheaval.

([New York, 1920], p. 12). Isaac Goldberg, in the first full-length biography of the editor, was the first to diagnose one threat confronting the magazine: "Already a *Mercury* school, or rather group, begins to grow, in danger only of echoing the chieftain's themes and mannerisms" (*The Man Mencken*, p. 203). As for the editor's own development, a letter from Harrison H. Schaff to Goldberg, August, 1925, stated the following reservation: "In the last twenty years Mencken has not changed fundamentally. . . . Methodists still serve him as a symbol of social and cultural development, while the inherent ignorance and vulgarity of the masses (which is an obvious and accepted fact that long since ceased to occasion the slightest wonder or resentment on the part of those capable of sensing conditions), still serve him as [phenomena] on which to expatiate with . . . invective that becomes more . . . difficult to make effective as its intensity increases" (*ibid.*, p. 376).

[65] Figures from Ayer's *Directory*, 1928, 1929, 1930.

9

CRISIS AND DEFEAT

THE *MERCURY* DECLINE

THAT Mencken was an economic conservative should have been amply clear in the twenties. His occasional praise of tycoons—for instance, Henry Ford[1]—was but one of several indications of his allegiance to capitalism. Repeatedly he avowed that his personal interests were substantially those of the propertied class, and therefore it was not his fault if liberals overlooked his attitude on economics before the Depression. As for the *Mercury,* it drifted to the right as it entered its fifth year. In 1928 a financial column of investment advice was added to the magazine. Business success became more genially viewed.[2] That a more conservative following began to rally to the monthly was not accidental: as the number of subscriptions dropped in 1929, the business managers began to advertise their magazine in other periodicals, and these advertisements were directed toward the businessman.[3] By the early thirties, readers were

[1] In a review of Ford's *My Life and Work,* Mencken stated that he had "never read anything by George Santayana one-half so sound and important as this modest tome by the Detroit E. W. Howe" ("Confidences," *SS,* LXX [Jan., 1923], 140).

[2] An interesting contrast can be drawn between W. M. Walker's "J.P. the Younger" (June, 1927) and Max Lerner's "Jupiter in Wall Street" (July, 1930); Lerner's essay on the House of Morgan is more sober and favorable than Walker's treatment.

[3] An advertisement in the *Nation,* CXXIX (Nov. 20, 1929), 593, was addressed to "A Clubwoman," "A Minister," "A Modern Girl," "An Attorney," "A Mayor," "A Salesman," "An Executive," "A Banker," etc. An advertisement of special interest to those concerned about Mencken's reputation as a critic of literature appeared in *Publishers' Weekly,* CXVI (July 20, 1929), 246: "In 1928 The American Mercury reviewed 759 books . . . a total not even distantly approached by any other general or literary monthly. The book

often business executives; one brochure claimed that four out of ten readers enjoyed incomes of over ten thousand dollars per year.[4] Another sign that the review was becoming distinctly more conservative was approval from conservative quarters.[5]

More important, from an intellectual point of view, was the weakening shown in the magazine's contents. Nathan's theater reviews became much dimmer after 1928, and eventually they flickered out in February, 1930. The offhand composition of the thinner reviews and Clinical Notes must have depressed some of the New York City followers of his departments. Still, Nathan's work was better than what replaced it,[6] and it is likely that Nathan's exit caused some of the loss of subscribers in 1930, when 1929's average circulation of 67,420 dropped to 62,074. Verse almost disappeared from the monthly: in the twelve issues for 1930 there were but five poems printed, and in the following year, only three. Short, tightly edited essays became much rarer after 1928, and as the essays became fewer, they were often more diffuse and less meritorious. Short stories became more plentiful, and the quality tended to be lower than during the first years of the magazine.

The contributors were drawn more frequently from a clique which had mastered Mencken's formulae: Isaac Goldberg, Benjamin DeCasseres, and Idwal Jones, among others.

---

reviews . . . are in keeping with the times; concise, and to the point. They give the reader, in fewest words, a comprehensive and critical picture of the book." (The "Interesting Portraits" were placed in such newspapers as the *New York Times*, the Philadelphia *Bulletin*, and the St. Louis *Post-Dispatch* during 1929.)

[4] Information from a letter soliciting advertising from Lord, Thomas, and Logan, 247 Park Avenue, May 1, 1931 ("The American Mercury: Miscellanea: 1923-1933," E.P.M.C.).

[5] E.g., " 'Progressives' Flayed," *Time*, XIII (April 1, 1929), 14: "The leading article in the April *American Mercury* was a bitter denunciation of the 'Progressives' of the Senate written by a person who, to insure his future comfort in Washington, D.C., signed himself simply 'A Washington Correspondent.' "

[6] After Feb., 1930, a department treating music was established; phonograph records and books dealing with music were reviewed in the department. Collections of aphorisms by various hands were commissioned now and then to replace "Clinical Notes."

These writers were joined by Mencken's friends at Johns Hopkins, reporters (especially newsmen connected with the Sunpapers), and a motley band of itinerants. As for scholars, they became almost as infrequently represented as were sincere men of letters, particularly after 1930. Equally noteworthy was a weakening of the "Americana" department, a weakening that drew contemporary comment,[7] elicited a lament from Mencken,[8] and was later tacitly admitted in a *Mercury* anthology.[9] Part of the strange decline of "Americana" may have been the fault of Angoff, who did not find congenial the task of assembling clippings of absurdities. He lacked the sensitivity and zeal of Mencken in arranging his prizes, and the entries became longer and usually more commonplace; they were too often drawn from such humdrum sources as newspaper columns advertising palmistry, astrology, etc. These several trends helped account for the swelling criticisms of the magazine in 1928 and 1929.

THE DEPRESSION STRIKES

ONE of the worst mistakes of Mencken's editorial career was the choice to ignore almost completely the Depression. There was some explanation for the editor's course. He had been away in Europe when the financial crisis first began to look ominous, and, also, his mind was filled with plans for his approaching marriage to Sara Haardt. More influential, however, were his favorable recollections of his and Nathan's policy of steering the *Smart Set* strictly clear of acknowledgment of World War I. Mencken believed, as

---

[7] "The 'Americana' department," wrote Fred Lewis Pattee, "once mildly amusing, is pathetic now" (*The New American Literature, 1890-1930* [New York, (1930)], p. 431).

[8] In a discussion of the *Americana 1925,* Mencken admitted in 1932 that, of the states ridiculed in the collection, many had unfortunately changed in recent years. He blamed the loss of colorful native absurdity on standardization (HLM to Bob Brown, May 27, 1932. Letter in N.Y.M.C.).

[9] Of twenty-seven "Americana" items reprinted in Lawrence Spivak's *The Mercury Reader* of 1944, the four *latest* selections were from a 1930 issue—a clear indication of a falling off in verve and humor.

did many others, that the business crisis was only temporary, and he looked forward to seeing the Cassandras of the early thirties humiliated when economic recovery set in. Holding to these convictions, he chose to write no editorial on the Depression until 1932! Nor were more than a handful of such acknowledgments written by other hands in the *Mercury* before 1932, a year that saw the average circulation plummet from the more than 60,000 of 1931 to 42,000. Mencken's monthly seemed less and less relevant as the Depression deepened and its shadow spread over large parts of the civilized world.

Nevertheless, it has been too often held (perhaps because of Mencken's delay in publicly discussing the Depression) that the magazine lacked intelligent efforts toward rehabilitation. The editor, however little he regarded the Deflation, had not departed from his senses, and his attempts to check the loss of subscription support for the *Mercury* showed some alertness. The first change wrought by the staff was external: the reliance on newsstand purchasers, who became less free with their fifty-cent pieces after the crash, forced abandonment of the noncommittal cover. The cover of the March, 1930, number featured a square box listing some of the more notable articles. In May, 1930, a cheaper paper began to replace the hitherto imported variety.[10]

The editor began to bargain more closely with prospective contributors,[11] the *Mercury* staff was somewhat pruned, and Angoff's salary was cut.[12] Mencken reinstated the abandoned "Notes and Queries" department in the form of "The Soap-Box," which drew low-cost contributions of trivia to fill space. An interest in more than the purely

[10] Mencken once stated that the old paper had to be abandoned because it shed a fuzz that hampered printing (HLM to Raymond Pearl, Dec. 14, 1933. Copy in P.M.C.).

[11] For example, on March 12, 1930, he wrote to Madeleine Lomas that he would print her contribution if she would accept $150. His letter indicated that the price had been considerably debated (letter in Duke University Library Manuscript Collection).

[12] Angoff's salary was twice reduced: in 1930 and in 1932 (interview with Angoff, Dec. 27, 1958).

national was tenuously shown in response to the rising
world crisis.[13] Now and then a stridently leftist outburst
would appear side by side with a relatively rightist essay.[14]
(In fact, within the *Mercury* can be seen the increasing
ideological tensions of the era strain and shatter the truces
between radicals, the avant-garde, and liberal writers during
the twenties.) Yet this loss of editorial focus was partly
caused from inside: Angoff veered toward the left, and
favored contributions from that quarter, while Mencken's
conservative friends appeared more often.[15] Changes of
Mercury policies were tried: serials began to be accepted,[16]
the cover pleaded more and more importunately for attention,[17] and efforts were made to follow constructive suggestions published in "The Soap-Box"—the last of which in-
novations was perhaps the most cruelly revealing.[18] Sensible
articles of economic advice for people of moderate means
were printed. Efforts were made to lighten a periodical
that had become too heavy; not only were college essay
contests arranged, but fiction frankly intended as light entertainment was prominently featured.[19] One attempt to

[13] For instance, neither Oland Russell's "Suicide in Japan" (July, 1930),
Elizabeth Morrow's "Our Street in Cuernavaca" (Aug., 1931), nor George
Schuyler's "Uncle Sam's Black Step-Child" (June, 1933), is a national study.

[14] Contrast Harold E. West, "The Power Trust Bugaboo," with Sterline D.
Spero, "War in the Kentucky Mountains" (Feb., 1932); John N. Beffel, "Four
Radicals," with Hoffman Nickerson, "Democracy and Mass Massacre" (April,
1932); Hoffman Nickerson, "The Collapse of Parliaments," with C. Hartley
Grattan, "The Troubles of a Radical Editor" (June, 1933).

[15] In 1933 Angoff's acceptance of a liberal article dealing with the German
crisis caused Mencken to forbid him to purchase essays until approved in
Baltimore (interview with Angoff, Dec. 27, 1958). Although Angoff interprets
the action as indicative of a lack of humanitarian zeal, Mencken probably was
following his general policy of staying with American subject matter. The
Mercury was one of the very first of foreign publications suppressed in Germany
after Hitler assumed power.

[16] E.g., Harvey Fergusson's six-instalment "Rio Grande," printed in 1931.

[17] E.g., the Jan., 1932, cover stressed political analysis; among features
mentioned were "Oswald Spengler on the World Crisis," "One of Mr. Hoover's
Friends," "The Stabilization Nonsense," "A Democrat Looks at His Party," etc.

[18] Two aspects of "The Soap-Box" were pathetic: first, the requests for
revivals of earlier contributors ("what has become of . . . James M. Cain . . .
George Philip Krapp . . . Emory Holloway . . . ? All of these were in your
first two volumes. It would be pleasant to see them back" [Nov., 1932]);
second, the frequent and damaging criticisms of inaccuracies and shoddy writing
by Mencken's clique of contributors (as in Jan., 1933).

[19] One such contribution, Joel Sayre's farcical "Rackety Rax," was ad-

enliven the magazine was Mencken's and Angoff's serial
effort to determine "The Worst American State."[20] Most
important of all, during the sad years of the Depression,
the percentage of satirical and debunking essays diminished
markedly.

All this suggests that by 1930 Mencken was aware of his
monthly's loss of appeal. His private correspondence further
strengthens such an impression. To Ernest, Boyd, in 1930, he
expressed plaintive hopes to continue printing the *Mercury*
for many years, God willing.[21] The following month, he
wrote in a half-jocular tone to Philip Goodman of slow
collections. If the printer abandoned them, Mencken humorously proposed, they could turn to mimeograph.[22] In
1931, affairs did not improve, and Alfred. A. Knopf, Inc.—
as were other firms—was beginning to tighten its belt.[23]

Nevertheless, before 1932 Mencken was not altogether
aroused to the strength of the trends undercutting his position. He was less engrossed in his editorial duties; his marriage to Sara Haardt in 1930, several trips abroad during
the first years of the decade, and his wife's serious illnesses
led him to show a more and more perfunctory concern with
contemporary life. His editorials were less challenging than
before, more pleased with the status quo. Antireligious
utterances became fewer both in his editorials and in "The
Library," and nostalgia for the good old days became
stronger. He argued humorlessly and incessantly for repeal
of Prohibition, using the same arguments again and again.

---

vertised on the cover of the January, 1932, number as a "Short Novel . . .
Complete." The genuinely comic story was over forty pages long.

[20] The three-instalment survey, which featured scores of graphs and elaborately statistical analyses, was published in September, October, and November of
1931. (Mississippi was found to be the worst state.)

[21] HLM to Boyd, Oct. 24, 1930. Letter in P.M.C.

[22] HLM to Goodman, Nov. 14, 1930. "Letters to Philip Goodman," III.

[23] On March 7, 1931, Alfred Knopf announced the closing down of his
"English publishing firm, Alfred A. Knopf, Ltd." His reason was that, since
American books were finally being freely distributed, the mission of his
branch publishing house had been accomplished. London agents were, however,
retained ("Knopf and English Market," *Publishers' Weekly*, CXIX [March 7,
1931], 1164). Of interest in this connection is Mencken's editorial of October,
1930.

A thinness crept into routine editorial work which showed but little genuine excitement.[24]

His continuation after 1929 of watered-down attitudes of the twenties was not what the public wanted, but even less did it want his eventual diagnosis of America's economic troubles. When, in 1932, in his editorial (renamed "What is Going on in the World," and moved, not very prudently, to the front of the magazine) some statement concerning the Depression seemed inescapable, his remarks sounded in part like Republican party sentiments:

I have long denounced democracy as an insanity, but I have always held it to be endurable on the ground that it is sub- servient to capitalism—that the politicians, in the last analysis, must take orders from [the bankers]. But now . . . the United States [is] getting into so dreadful a mess that the bankers are forced to bellow for help to the politicians. . . . No wonder I am upset! All my natural prejudices have been outraged. Temperamentally incapable of Socialism . . . I find myself hang- ing upon a precarious branch, trying unhappily to figure out what is going to happen next.[25]

When with this statement the drop in circulation did not slow, a full-dress study of the Depression was included in his March, 1932, editorial. President Hoover was seen as a whipping boy taking "thwacks that ought to be fanning other pantaloons, including yours and mine. For we all had a hand in making the depression, and we all deserve the evils, some real and some imaginary, which now beset us. Most of us, indeed, are getting off very lightly." After bland- ly imagining a "case history" of a well-to-do person who was reduced by the Crash back to his original pre-specula- tion nest egg, Mencken continued: "Are the rest of us in the same boat? I doubt it. The boat we are in is getting some

[24] In 1930 and 1931 most of the editorials were dedicated to such things as proposals that America should always be having a war (Nov., 1930), that America should institute a monarchy so that titles could be given (Dec., 1930), that the man who invented the thermostat was praiseworthy (Jan., 1931), that contemporary architecture was wretched (Feb., 1931), that the end of the era of the steam locomotive was lamentable (Sept., 1931), that beer was a good thing (Nov., 1931).
[25] Jan., 1932.

unpleasant rocking from the foundering of the other, but it is tighter of seam and will survive. We have all lost something," admitted the editor, "but not many have really lost everything. In actual value the country is still rich, and any man who owns any honest part of it still has that part, and will see it making money for him when the clouds roll by." His conclusion assumed moderate wealth on the part of the reader: "We have all been spending too much, and we have all been succumbing to trashy and bogus values. I could live comfortably on half of what it has cost me to live since 1924, and so could you. Both of us used to do it, and were quite comfortable." Other opinions in "What is Going on in the World" came to sound more shrill. His traditionally boisterous caricature of the lowly farmer became somber: "The real issue in American politics since the turn of the century," he wrote, has been "one no politician ever mentions. It is. . . . whether the cities . . . are to have their just and lawful freedom or to continue under the hooves of a decayed and ignoble peasantry." His clientele melted steadily, and by the summer of 1932 the outcome was so apparent that he decided to limit his editorializing; he had not resolved the troubles of his magazine by discussing the current crisis.

He had been having considerable difficulty, he confessed to Goodman, composing either editorials or "The Library," inasmuch as he had no ideas.[26] More surprising for the intrepid editor were his admissions in print of his reluctance to tangle with the economic situation as an editorial subject.[27] In letters of 1932 his jests were infrequent; he seemed sincerely alarmed by the *Mercury*'s financial plight.[28]

[26] HLM to Goodman, Feb. 8, 1932. "Letters to Philip Goodman," III.

[27] The frankest admissions appeared in Jan., 1932, and Nov., 1933. A tacit admission occurs in an editorial named "Leaves from a Waste-Basket" (Aug., 1931). No editorials were printed in the following issues from 1929 to 1933: Jan., 1929; May, 1929; April, 1930; July, 1932; Aug., 1932; Sept., 1932; Oct., 1932; June, 1933; July, 1933; Aug., 1933; Sept., 1933; Oct., 1933.

[28] "The magazine is in very fair shape, considering the times. By dint of magnificent sacrifices in the cause of art we have kept the budget balanced and at the moment we actually show a small profit. But it will remain very small until there is a general turn upward. God knows if that will ever come.

His fears in 1932 and his resulting efforts to improve the review were more worthy than anyone has apparently noticed: the general contents of the magazine in 1932 were better and more varied than in the preceding year. Indeed, some of his bewilderment at the steady erosion of his audience is understandable. The *Mercury*'s decline was not absolute: many meritorious contributions were printed; there were several radical essays and many liberal ones, and a few authors were allowed to discuss unemployment, etc. Moreover, he did try to follow his reader's suggestions, and writings by Louise Pound, James M. Cain, and other authors praised in "The Soap-Box" were printed in the journal. Faulkner, Farrell, and a few other better creative writers of the day were occasionally published; some vigorous satire remained; the music world partly replaced the theater-going public alienated by Nathan's departure;[29] and the strictly American focus was somewhat broadened.[30] But these improvements were too small to offset the larger weaknesses, weaknesses that conspired to swamp a vessel beyond recovery. A good magazine had benefited when Mencken's vogue had been at its height; a fair magazine suffered when its editor's national reputation sagged.

ATTACKS BY CRITICS INTENSIFY

IN 1928, when the New Humanists made their first hurtful criticisms of Mencken, Howard Mumford Jones sprang to his defense,[31] but the champions were to grow fewer and the scoffing louder. The nihilism of the magazine was de-

I begin to believe, in fact, that we are in for a whole era of Low Living" (HLM to Goodman, May 5, 1932. "Letters to Philip Goodman," III). More blunt was a letter to Goodman of March 16, 1932 (*ibid.*, III).

[29] An indication of the magazine's popularity with musicians was Randall Thompson's 1932 composition based on *Mercury* material. The piece was performed before an approving audience by the A Capella Singers of New York.

[30] The "Americana" department began in 1930 to list foreign follies.

[31] "Professor Babbitt Cross-Examined," *New Republic*, LIV (March 21, 1928), 158-160.

plored in 1929,[32] and by 1930, the *Bookman* besieged the green-covered monthly with irreverent histories[33] and with jokes at the expense of Mencken's "new" conservatism.[34] Critics in the *New Freeman* also sounded forth: Newton Arvin suggested that the valuable part of Mencken lay in the files of the *Smart Set,*[35] and Irwin Edman sarcastically berated the *Mercury* editor for the faults of his *Treatise on the Gods,* published in 1930.[36] As the rejection of Mencken rose to a chorus, several voices were heard above the tumult, voices counseling caution: James Oppenheim,[37] Thomas Wolfe,[38] and Fred Lewis Pattee[39] each warned that Mencken

[32] Waldo Frank, *The Re-Discovery of America* (New York, 1929), p. 321.

[33] "Mencken and Nathan put over boob-bumping with a bigger bang than ever, achieving a circulation comparable to that of the muck-rakers of twenty-five years ago. . . . The *Mercury* continues, but Mencken is clearly on his way out. Already the silk-merchants, chorus girls, golf-players, radio-fans, club women . . . have fallen away. He is completing the circle of his career, and now finds his audience among those who first acclaimed him: the backgroundless, the disinherited, the pathological; first-generation immigrants, unhappy college boys, paranoiac newspaper reporters, intellectual bohemians" (anon., "Chronicle and Comment," LXX [Jan., 1930], 543-544).

[34] William Troy, "The Story of the Little Magazines: II. Making No Compromise with the Public Taste," LXX (Feb., 1930), 658.

[35] "The Passing of the Twenties," I (March 15, 1930), 21.

[36] "God Settles God," I (May 24, 1930), 260: "He enables those with a mentality just one cut above the booboisie to feel they are miles above it, and makes Rotarians in Pullman smokers delightedly thumb their pages of the *Mercury* and their noses at the rest of the world."

[37] "Thus the growing anvil chorus all the way from the Humanists to the Deweyviks. However, it is common mythology that when a god dies on Friday he is resurrected on Sunday. H. L. Mencken is an authentic American phenomenon, as authentic as Walt Whitman, and more Rabelaisian and amusing.

"I myself panned 'Treatise on the Gods.' . . . But for all that I am convinced that H. L. is of more importance to the present and future of this land than General Motors or the Humanists. While every one else of any intelligence has been running around with panaceas in an attempt to culturize [and] reform. . . . Mencken's series of explosive laughters has made the life of this land livable. Dead, eh? In a recent number of the *American Mercury* I stumbled on an editorial . . . and I was . . . overwhelmed by mirth. . . . As for his ideas. . . . Bother his ideas! What is important is that . . . he has lifted American laughter to a new level of intelligence. . . .

"This pompous interring of H. L. Mencken is an interesting spectacle, but amusing only in an inverted sense. The coffin they are lowering happens to be empty, while the supposed corpse is working like a demon on Fifty-Seventh Street . . . " ("A Man Named Mencken," *New Freedom,* I [June 4, 1930], 280-281). (After Oppenheim's counter-blast, the *New Freeman* treated Mencken with respect throughout the short life of that periodical.)

[38] Wolfe wrote bitterly, as Mencken lost his following, that his "probable successors" would turn out to be "all potential neo-Humanists—'Genteel' " (Wolfe to Henry and Natalie Volkening [letter never mailed], May 14, 1930,

was in great danger of being underrated. But, despite such sound admonitions, most literary spokesmen were satisfied that the editor of the *Mercury* was the first major victim of the new decade: "In 1930," wrote Horace Gregory, "literary criticism in America took on a self-consciously serious tone. The time had come to rebury the dead, and the first funeral was that of the nineteen-twenties. Chief among those cremated and placed within a vault was H. L. Mencken."[40] But perhaps the most painful evidence of the editor's deflated reputation was negative: when the Humanists compiled a forceful manifesto entitled *Humanism and America* in 1930, and the young liberal critics were moved to reply in *The Critique of Humanism,* Mencken, the arch-critic of the New Humanist forces, was quite ignored in the counter-attack. The anti-Humanists' lack of significant reference to him suggested that he was a liability to the young liberals in the controversy; his erstwhile disciples were clearly ashamed of him.

By 1931, as might be expected, Michael Gold's wrath at the *Mercury* had become almost apocalyptic. Next to a drawing of a hideous skull meant to represent, not a capitalist, but so inoffensive a person as Lincoln Steffens, Gold denounced Steffens as the "founding father of the scrambled ideology one finds today in the . . . *American Mercury.*"[41] Some of Gold's outcries were little more than incoherent shrieks.[42] Joseph North, railing at the antics of middle-class professors, lashed out at the alienation of proletarian youth

Letters of Thomas Wolfe, p. 227). (Wolfe continued to send MSS to the *Mercury,* but without success until 1934).

[39] *The New American Literature, 1890-1930,* p. 430: "One must not overlook the courage of the man."

[40] "Our Writers and the Democratic Myth," *Bookman,* LXXV (Aug., 1932), 377-378.

[41] "Mr. Steffens Liked Everybody," *New Masses,* VII (June, 1931), 5.

[42] "[An Open Letter to] H. L. Mencken, Editor of the American Mercury," *New Masses,* VII (Sept., 1931), 3: "Rare Sam Johnson of our time: Farewell! Good-bye! Everything is finished between us. Your thunders do not awe us any longer. . . . [Y]our work is ended, and it would be better to retire. . . .

"For you have uncovered a phobia. You are a Tory who hates the Soviet Union. Worse than that, you are a white Nordic chauvinist who fears and hates the yellow races, and preaches war against the Soviet Union, because it is forging the brotherhood of all races. . . . "

who got into colleges: "Before they knew it, these sons of
the proletariat began bearing green-covered magazines un-
der-arm," and began dismissing political concerns.[43] North's
indignation showed how keenly radicals felt about their
lack of appeal to the youth of the nation during the twenties.
In the early thirties, as the esteem for the *Mercury* diminished in the colleges,[44] the young turned to the New
Humanists or to the left wing for light and leading. Yet
it was proof of the artificiality of some of the opposition
that more impartial critics, even in 1931, could still state
that "Bourgeois America . . . is admirably represented both
by *Harper's* and *The American Mercury*. One can probably
get nearer to what goes on in the mind of the educated
American by reading these magazines than in any other
way."[45]

In 1932 dismissal of the periodical became the order of
the day; even the *Criterion* abandoned it to domestic
critics.[46] The magazine was still seen as nihilistic,[47] and
sincere liberals—one-time allies of Mencken—took turns rejecting him: "Today his latest articles in the *American
Mercury*," wrote Mortimer Smith, "arouse about as much
controversy as the daily reports of the weather man."[48]
Possibly the most startling blow to the editor in 1932 was
the establishment of the *American Spectator* by Nathan,
Boyd, Dreiser, Cabell, and O'Neill. The opening editorial
of the new competing journal contained thinly veiled

[43] "Communism Comes to College," *New Masses*, VII (Nov., 1931), 16. See
also Joseph Freeman, "Social Trends in American Literature," *Communist*, IX
(July, 1930), 641.

[44] Manchester, *Mencken*, p. 258.

[45] B[onamy] D[obrée], "Foreign Periodicals: American Periodicals," *Criterion*, X (July, 1931), 782. Earlier in 1931, Dobrée, after commenting that
too many English writers were in the *Yale Review*, had written that "Mr.
Mencken's *The American Mercury*, however, is loyal to its country, and continues to be interesting, and sometimes scathing" ("Foreign Periodicals: American
Periodicals," *Criterion*, X [April, 1931], 587).

[46] H[ugh] S[ykes] D[avies], "Foreign Periodicals: American Periodicals,"
Criterion, XI (Jan., 1932), 362.

[47] Ludwig Lewisohn, *The Story of American Literature* (New York, [1932]),
p. 417.

[48] Essay in *Unity*, Jan. 4, 1932 ("Articles About H. L. Mencken: Clippings:
1919-1933," E.P.M.C.).

reference to the difficulties of the beleagured monthly.[49]
The *American Spectator* was clearly meant to recapture
some of the belletristic glory of the *Smart Set* and the first
years of the *Mercury*.[50] The abandonment by members of
his own generation and his original circle nettled Mencken,
and he growled about the new venture to some of his correspondents,[51] despite a politeness shown to others.[52]

From a wider perspective, however, this turbulence in
the "Middle Generation" of American authors was a tem-
pest in a teapot; the trend of the period was away from the
entire group. The *American Spectator* was ably criticized in
the *Bookman* as a hopeless effort to "revive the dear dead
days of 1915-1925: the days of Mencken, the *Smart Set*,
defiant bohemianism, pseudo-sophistication, anti-Puritanism,
belated aestheticism, and Huxleyism."[53] And even a friendly
review concluded (in an article ironically entitled "Sophisticate, 1933"): "Among the current Americans, Hemingway,
Faulkner, and Dos Passos are holding up well. The old
guard—Cabell, Dreiser, Mencken, Nathan (in fact the whole
staff of the *American Spectator*)—is now regarded as somewhat pathetic."[54] In 1933, writing for the then vigorous left,

[49] Anon., "Editorial," *American Spectator*, I (Nov., 1932), 1: "The essential
editorial problem of the better and more ambitious type of monthly magazine
is that it is much too large. Any man who has ever served as an editor of such
a magazine knows—and, if caught partly *inter pocula*, will sadly admit—that
it is impossible to get enough good copy each month to fill his magazine. He
is only too happy, indeed, if he can get even so many as two things that
really please him. . . . Another defect of the average magazine is that its
editor often permits himself to remain in harness long after his imaginative
oats have given out and the magazine thereafter continues simply as a matter
of habit."

[50] *Mercury* departments adapted to the *American Spectator* format included
"The Library" ("Boyd Digests the Books"), "The Theatre" ("Nathan Digests
the Theatre"), and "Americana." Some authors who contributed to the new
periodical were Ring Lardner, Louis Untermeyer, Clarence Darrow, Lincoln
Steffens, Frank Swinnerton, Sherwood Anderson, John Dos Passos, and, of
course, the five editors. (One article in the first [Nov., 1932] number,
"Aesthete's Progress," by Ernest Boyd, was his *n*th reworking of his original
"Aesthete: Model 1924" triumph in the Jan., 1924 *Mercury*.)

[51] HLM to Raymond Pearl, July 29, 1932. Copy in P.M.C. Mencken also
sulked about the new venture in letters to Goodman (Feb. 23, 1933; Feb. 24,
1933. "Letters to Philip Goodman," III).

[52] HLM to Ernest Boyd, May 5, (1933?). Letter in P.M.C.

[53] Anon., "The American Spectator," *Bookman*, LXXV (Dec., 1932), 830

[54] Richard Sherman, *Vanity Fair*, XLI (Feb., 1934), 27.

Granville Hicks was able to describe the plight of Mencken with perhaps more tenderness than one might have expected.[55] But by 1933 the editor and his periodical had so little currency that a certain charity began to appear in the comments of the few who thought the matter worthy of attention.

MENCKEN'S RESIGNATION

As the Depression brooded over the publishing world, and as the *Mercury*'s circulation and advertising revenues dwindled, Mencken wrung some scant satisfaction from the notion that his dilemma was widely shared.[56] Now and then he even stated that his monthly was better off than most others,[57] but circulation figures show that his review was harder hit than certain other quality magazines.[58] Knopf found momentary relief because of a windfall in 1932: the American Tobacco Company signed a large advertising contract. Mencken was then enabled to write that 1932 saw the review make a slight profit.[59] The good news led Alfred Knopf to reassure the public concerning the *Mercury*'s health.[60] But no one was sanguine about the

---

[55] *The Great Tradition: An Interpretation of American Literature since the Civil War* (New York, 1933), pp. 212, 249, 257.

[56] HLM to Goodman, July 8, 1932; Dec. 24, 1932. "Letters to Philip Goodman," III.

[57] HLM to Raymond Pearl, Sept. 30, 1932. Copy in P.M.C. (According to Peterson, *Magazines in the Twentieth Century*, p. 63, the number of periodical establishments varied from a "high of 2,925 in 1929 to a low of 2,002 in 1933.")

[58] The following figures (Ayer's *Directory*, 1931, 1933, 1935) show that, while the *Atlantic* and *Harper's* were somewhat hurt by the Depression, they fared far better than did the *Mercury*. The circulation of the *New Yorker* shows that certain magazines actually enjoyed swift growth throughout the early Thirties:

	1930	1932	1934
Atlantic	129,798	107,544	103,028
Harper's	120,947	107,668	103,202
American Mercury	62,074	42,007	31,023
New Yorker	98,960	114,018	121,032

[59] HLM to Goodman, Dec. 8, 1932. "Letters to Philip Goodman," III.

[60] Knopf took several of the closing pages of the Jan., 1933, number, to stress the solvency of the periodical.

coming year; the monthly would, observed the editor, make little if any profit in 1933, but it would hardly lose much money either. By the end of the spring of 1933, the distress flags were privately run up by the editor, who wrote to Goodman of the general crisis in magazine and book publishing and who begged for an article from Goodman.[61] Goodman, however, chose only to write letters to "The Soap-Box" criticizing mistakes in *Mercury* essays; he never did anything else for the review.[62]

That the monthly was making heavy weather of it financially was no secret after 1932. In that year Samuel Knopf died, and curious outsiders were granted a glimpse of the magazine's predicament because of the publication of information concerning his estate.[63] Alfred Knopf has agreed that after his father's death, "the *Mercury* was not an asset, for it was losing money. . . ."[64] As the magazine sank further into the red (the circulation hovered near 30,000 by the summer of 1933, and was still dropping), Knopf became annoyed.

Mencken's few editorial contributions in 1933 were very

[61] Information from HLM to Goodman, Jan. 15, 1933; May 1, 1933, "Letters to Philip Goodman," III.

[62] Goodman and Mencken, according to Angoff, ended their friendship by 1933 because of a difference of opinion over the Hitler question: Goodman evidently felt that the editor condoned the Nazi persecution of the Jews. Goodman's statements, as recalled by Angoff, show him concerned about the decline of the *Mercury*. Some of Goodman's remarks are presented in *Portrait*, pp. 208-209, 211, 226.

[63] "Samuel Knopf Estate $240,974," *New York Times*, June 14, 1933, p. 19, col. 1: "No value was given to 125 shares of the capital stock of the American Mercury, Inc., publisher of the American Mercury Magazine, among securities held by Mr. Knopf" (statement from a "transfer tax appraisal" filed June 13, 1933). As Alfred Knopf has pointed out, one should remember that because of estate taxes, an attorney representing any estate does his best to establish the lowest possible value on any properties. Mr. Knopf has further explained why no value was given to the stock: ". . . because $149,250 carried as a good will asset in the balance sheet of the magazine company, was eliminated and held to be worth nothing" (Knopf to Singleton, July 28, 1959). Of great interest was an affidavit filed by J. C. Lesser, comptroller at A. A. Knopf, Inc., who stated that the *Mercury* was especially hard hit by the Depression because it depended wholly on the "activity, ingenuity, and popularity" of H. L. Mencken. Lesser explained carefully that the *Mercury* could not effectively be rehabilitated because it was a "one-man magazine catering to a very selective class of readers who are followers of its editor" (information and quotations from Manchester, *Mencken*, p. 266).

[64] Knopf to Singleton, July 28, 1959.

weak. When the public did not recognize the actual improvements made in the 1932 contents, he seemingly isolated
himself from areas of the contemporary American scene.
Even "The Library" was sometimes wholly devoted to conservative fulminations having nothing to do with books.[65]
In January, 1933, his "What is Going on in the World" was
concerned with the United States Senate, but the commentary was chiefly persiflage. In February he denounced the
public schools of the nation; their excessive costs and cur-
ricular pretensions were soberly pilloried. He praised greatly private schools, which were seen as suffering unfair
competition from overelaborate schemes of public schools.
Public education was told to confine itself "to the teaching
of the three R's to the children of persons unable to provide
that instruction at their own expense," and the extension of
free schooling beyond that modest goal was damned in
arguments drawing upon fears of high taxes and upon
references to the social philosophy of Nietzsche. Next casti-
gated were public departments of health, which were revealed as basically socialistic arrangements designed to
tamper with the professional privileges of doctors.[66] From
the point of view of old subscribers, Mencken perhaps
reached his nadir as an editorialist in April, 1933, when a
revaluation of Coolidge found him a better sort of President
than had been thought; this opinion overturned assumptions
on which the editor of 1924 had based his magazine. After
April, Mencken was quiet until November, when his first
forthrightly anti-New Deal essay appeared. Among the
targets of the diatribe were the farmers, who were seen as
getting rich at the expense of their urban betters: "It is an
almost ideal existence that they lead, for if they plow
and reap they are well paid for it, and if they plow
without reaping they are paid even better." That this
truculent view of the farm situation of 1933 was not
very apt perhaps bothered lingering readers less than

[65] E.g., Sept., 1933.   [66] March, 1933.

the tone of hopelessness and despair that darkened the editorials. Even though Prohibition had died on April 6, 1933, taking away one of the last issues that truly lent itself to Mencken's pen, he remained stern even in his triumph.[67]

Another noteworthy change was the editor's decision to widen the appeal of his magazine by courting Catholic readers; Catholic writers became more prominent in 1932, and in May, 1933, *Mercury* readers found a Brother Cajetan explaining monastic life in "They Call Me a Monk." On the other hand, George Seibel ridiculed militant atheists in an essay entitled "Atheism Succumbs to Doubt."[68] By 1933 political radicals were almost unrepresented; as in 1931 Mencken seemed determined to hew closely to a line of political orthodoxy.[69] As for literature, the state of the 1933 *Mercury* can most clearly be seen by a contrast with one of the best of the literary monthlies—*Scribner's*. The contributors to *Scribner's* were generally more serious and accomplished than those whose writings appeared in the *Mercury*.[70] Mencken had lapsed too far into nostalgia to be receptive to contemporary literature even had it been written according to his standards. Writing to Louis Untermeyer about the bad poetry of 1932, he recalled that poetry of a decade past was markedly better than the offerings of 1932.[71] His opinions about the fiction of the day were even more disdainful,[72] and none of these views, however they

[67] M. B. Hamilton was commissioned to write an indignant article entitled "Lest We Forget" for the May, 1933, number. Hamilton presented graphs showing the voting record of congressmen on the question of Repeal.

[68] Dec., 1933.

[69] Of interest is the editor's patriotic letter to Upton Sinclair, April 12, [1931?]. Copy in P.M.C.).

[70] In 1933, *Scribner's* was publishing the work of such writers as Edmund Wilson, Thomas Wolfe, André Maurois, Caroline Gordon, Ernest Hemingway, and Malcolm Cowley—none of whom contributed to the *Mercury* of 1933. The *Mercury* found it very difficult to find good manuscripts in the early thirties, according to Angoff (interview, Dec. 27, 1958).

[71] Nov. 9, 1932. Copy in P.M.C.

[72] Anon., "Book News," *News-Week*, II (Sept. 16, 1933), 38: "Mr. Mencken is discouraged. He told the Associated Press last week that the 'gaudy eruption of novelists,' observed from 1919 to 1921, was but a flash in the pan. According to Mr. Mencken, American writers still continue to 'labor in the literary doldrums.' "

may have been justified by the literary output of the day, was likely to arouse a literary following for the monthly. So, despite a feeling that the *Mercury* could possibly continue with a loyal band of perhaps 20,000 readers,[73] and despite his good health (he was only fifty-three years old in 1933), Mencken saw that it was time to withdraw.

Earlier in 1933 he had hinted to friends that retirement was a possibility,[74] and so some of them should have been prepared for his decision to resign from the *Mercury*. The December, 1933, circulation was probably not much more than 23,000;[75] hence it is likely that the editor sensed his publisher's reluctance to put up with affairs as they then were going. The decision to resign was apparently made at the beginning of October. By October 3 the editor was sending out confidential announcements of his retirement.[76] From these scores of letters, Mencken's expressed reasons for his departure can be pieced together. To Dr. A. G. Keller, he stated that he had for a year been trying to get away, and that his resignation as editor did not affect his status as a director in Alfred A. Knopf, Inc.[77] To Robert C. Pooley, he gave as one of his reasons for retiring that he needed time to revise *The American Language*,[78] and to Eugene F. Saxton he broadened this stand into a declaration that he considered himself primarily an author, not an editor.[79] To his colleague Ellery Sedgwick, he wrote that he would have left sooner, but the Depression and Samuel Knopf's death postponed his decision.[80] The explanation to Monsignor J. B. Dudek seemed more searching: Mencken admitted that the magazine would likely be improved by his departure; the editor wrote that he had not

---

[73] "Ten Years," (Dec., 1933).
[74] HLM to Harry Leon Wilson, Feb. 9, 1933. Copy in P.M.C. HLM to A.E. McDannald, Sept. 19, 1933. Copy in P.M.C.
[75] Angoff, *Portrait,* p. 228.
[76] HLM to Hoffman Nickerson, Oct. 3, 1933. Copy in P.M.C.
[77] Oct. 4, 1933. Copy in P.M.C.   [78] Oct. 6, 1933. Copy in P.M.C.
[79] Oct. 9, 1933. Copy in P.M.C.   [80] Oct. 9, 1933. Copy in P.M.C.

been working quite as hard in recent years as he should have.[81] He also wrote gracious notes to the veteran contributors, telling many of them that their work was among the best printed in the review.[82] But in none of these letters, however candid they might have seemed at the time, did he identify the central factor in the timing of his departure— his tremendous decline in national popularity.

The public was apprised of his resignation in a release to the *New York Times* on October 6, a release which sounds rather evasive.[83] All public statements stressed that there had been no strain in the friendship between the editor and his publisher.[84] Mencken was allowed to name his editorial successor: Henry Hazlitt, a stalwart conservative on economic matters.

Most of the press comments caused by his departure were charitable, but no one felt the step premature. One editorialist paid a mellow tribute, but pointed out that "To the young intellectuals he is now an old fogy."[85] This sentiment was widely echoed: "His chief reason for abandoning his editor's chair now is that in the past ten years most of his enemies have disappeared, leaving him in the role of shadow boxer."[86] Concluded a *Time* writer: "The *Mercury*['s] crusading became sufficiently successful to seem a little antiquated and unnecessary. To his admirers, Editor Mencken's retirement . . . seemed unmistakable if regrettable evidence of his skill and judgement."[87] Even

---

[81] Oct. 21, 1933. Copy in P.M.C.

[82] For example, HLM to Bob Brown, Oct. 9, 1933. Letter in N.Y.M.C.

[83] " 'As a matter of fact,' he said, 'my retirement had been pretty well agreed upon some time ago, about the time the depression came along. But . . . we were having tough going. . . . I want to make it plain that there has been no break of any kind between Mr. Knopf and myself. . . . Frankly, my reason for retiring is that I've been editor long enough. . . . I don't feel stale, or anything, but I think that some one else will be able to fill the job with [more] zest" ("Mencken Retires as Mercury Editor," *New York Times*, Oct. 6, 1933, p. 15, col. 3).

[84] E.g., anon., "Mencken Retires as *Mercury* Editor," *Publishers' Weekly*, CXXIV (Oct. 14, 1933), 1330.

[85] "Mr. Mencken on His Own," *New York Times*, Oct. 7, 1933, p. 14, col. 4.

[86] Anon., "Mercury: Mencken Retires as Editor of Critical Monthly," *News-Week*, II (Oct. 14, 1933), 28.

[87] Anon., "Hazlitt for Mencken," *Time*, XXII (Oct. 16, 1933), 43.

some of the leftist magazines condescended to pay some sort of tribute.[88] As for Mencken's parting editorial in the December, 1933, number, it dwelt most explicitly on the need for time to attend to the making of books, and it suggested that ten years' service, first to the *Smart Set,* and then to the *Mercury,* were enough. In his last contribution to "The Library," he reviewed several books treating the rise of Hitler, a review that brought down upon him suspicions of being anti-Semitic and emotionally callous.[89]

THE BITTER DREGS

IN February, 1934, Mencken published in *Vanity Fair* a brief account of his ten years with the *Mercury.* He good-naturedly recalled personal experiences during his editorship. His concluding sentences were, in the light of his own rejection, rather sad: "the only thing asked of [editors] is that they get their magazines out on time, and fill them with stuff that is generally endurable, and thrilling now and then. . . . And if they incline toward retirement they may have their wish just as readily, for no man whose name is so constantly before the public is so thoroughly obscure as a magazine editor, or so little missed when the time comes to let go his hold."[90] Still, as a summary of his *Mercury* accomplishment, his "Memoirs of an Editor" were, as one bibliographer expressed it, "[e]ditorial recollections of no great significance."[91]

[88] Anon., "H. L. Mencken—Farewell and Hail!," *Panorama: A Monthly Survey of People and Ideas,* Oct., 1933, p. 4: "Radical thinking and writing in America today need a Mencken." (*Panorama,* edited by Isaac Goldberg, was an imitation of the *Mercury* born in Boston in October, 1933.)

[89] Angoff, *Portrait,* pp. 226-227. Angoff's charges, however, seem to this writer hardly justified by the issue of "The Library" under question. Moreover, the December, 1933, book reviews must be studied with earlier and more adverse statements about anti-Semitism in order to reach a balanced view of Mencken on that subject. For instance, "The Library" of May, 1932, helps clarify the editor's attitude toward the Jews of America.

[90] "Memoirs of an Editor," XLI, 54.

[91] Ralph D. Casey, "An Annotated Bibliography of Journalism Subjects in American Magazines," *Journalism Quarterly,* XI (June, 1934), 208.

Mencken showed himself sensitive to the several hostile remarks occasioned by his resignation. To Louise Pound he wrote thanks for her kind thoughts upon hearing of his leaving. He added that other comments were so severe as to lead him to contemplate a new edition of his Schimpf-lexicon.[92] But much of the resilience and practical-joking of 1928 were gone; it was less fun being dismissed "airily as a back number."[93] The result of his pain caused by abandonment was an almost uninterrupted silence concerning the *Mercury*. Although his most exciting and famous decade had been spent in its editing, after 1933 his very few observations on his *Mercury* career were largely embittered. The magazine is simply not discussed in his three-volume autobiography.[94] His concern with quality journalism after 1933 shifted to the *New Yorker*.[95] The most significant statements about his monthly made after his resignation were elicited by a rather petty quarrel with Upton Sinclair[96] and by his work in assembling the eight volumes of "Hatrack" material for the Enoch Pratt collection.[97] His attitudes late in his life toward his editorship and toward writers were jarringly told in his *Minority Report: H. L. Mencken's Notebooks*, which was written in 1948 and published in 1956. Some of his remarks underscore his dissatisfaction with writers as a group:

The so-called intellectuals of the country are simply weather-vanes blown constantly by foreign winds, usually but not always English. . . . The New Deal fetched them by brigades

[92] Oct. 31, 1933. Letter in Louise Pound Collection, Duke University Library Manuscript Collection.

[93] Frederick Lewis Allen, *Since Yesterday: The Nineteen-Thirties in America* (New York, 1940), p. 159.

[94] *Happy Days* (New York, 1940); *Newspaper Days* (New York, 1941); *Heathen Days* (New York, 1943).

[95] His voluminous correspondence with prominent members of the staff of the weekly can be seen in the P.M.C. on microfilm. His autobiography was published serially in the *New Yorker*. His rare mentions of his old monthly were indirect and nostalgic, as in HLM to A. G. Keller, Oct. 4, 1933. Copy in P.M.C.

[96] HLM to Sinclair, May 2, 1936; May 26, 1936. Copies in P.M.C. HLM, "The Open Forum," *American Mercury*, XXXVIII (June, 1936), 4-5.

[97] "Introduction," "The 'Hatrack' Case," I, 1-155.

. . . . They were all ripe, in 1930, for any sort of revelation, however bogus. The post-war disillusion of the 1920's was simply too much for them to bear. . . .

Historians will be diverted but certainly not edified by the bellowing of the American intelligentsia in the years following 1932. It would be flattery to say that they followed the Communist party line, though they undoubtedly made some effort to do so. . . . Their imbecilities reveal dramatically the intellectual bankruptcy of the United States.

Of specific movements in literature, the aged Mencken was very critical: "The so-called regionalists of the South, who made a great pother in the 1930 era, were simply a gang of eighth-rate poets who fought to give their maundering some dignity by ascribing to it a profound political purpose. The same thing was true of . . . the so-called proletarians." When he referred to his earlier editorship, his lack of sympathy with authors was further borne out:

. . . I came into contact with a large number of professional writers of a presumably higher grade—producers of short stories, poetry, articles, etc. Nine-tenths of them needed some help; indeed, many of them needed so much help that my struggles with their manuscripts spread the legend that I was trying to make all contributors to the *American Mercury* write alike. I had no desire to make them write alike, but my own way of writing was the only way I knew, and when theirs turned out to be impossible I had to substitute mine.[98]

Of these sour reflections, the last is most easily defended;[99] the others show loss of perspective. If the general silence maintained by the former editor seems excessive, it can be partly accounted for by the rough handling he received after 1933. In 1934 his former friend Burton Rascoe claimed that, after the removal of Nathan from the *Mercury,* it had "degenerated into a tiresome sort of yokel baiting. . . . Brave aims, even long pursued and long sustained, have a distressing habit of tiring out the way *The Smart Set*

[98] *Minority Report* (New York, 1956), pp. 28, 30, 80, 240.
[99] Many of the manuscripts edited by Mencken survive in the N.Y.M.C.; often they needed to be thoroughly rewritten, and the editing appears generally sensible.

curled up and went to Hearst." More forceful excoriations
were penned by Malcolm Cowley, who scored "the pious
God-and-Pierpont Morgan-fearing Mencken of these depression years."[100] Vernon Calverton, after a withering survey of Mencken's work, concluded that "the gods that
Mr. Mencken bludgeoned into oblivion in the twenties
seem now to have never lived."[101] The low point was perhaps reached on December 8, 1934, when Mencken was
present at a large Press banquet attended by President
Roosevelt, senators, cabinet members, governors, industrial-
ists, and prominent publishers. Roosevelt was harrassed
during the early part of the evening by satirical Republican
skits. Mencken gave a brief speech attacking the New
Deal. Eventually, when Roosevelt stood to reply, he referred amiably to "my old friend, Henry Mencken," and
then proceeded to a slashing indictment of the reactionary
press. It was only gradually that the audience realized that
Roosevelt was reading from one of Mencken's own essays of 1924.[102] The effect was humiliating to the former
iconoclast; nearly "eight hundred eyes peered through the
smoky hall at Mencken's face, now coloring like an autumn
leaf."[103] Mencken as spokesman for the conservative anti-
New-Deal forces was being arraigned by an old *Mercury*
editorial read by the President himself, and the former
editor was enraged.[104] Mencken's acute shame is worth
brief comment. He had become ashamed of his writings for
the *Smart Set;* and he likewise became embarrassed by
certain of his *Mercury* writings. Presumably, when he was
one of the foremost anti-Roosevelt polemicists during the
later thirties, writing a well-paid column for William Randolph Hearst, he discovered something to do with his pen

[100] Citations from " 'Smart Set' History," p. xliii; "Former Fugleman,"
New Republic, LXXXI (Nov. 21, 1934), 51.
[101] "Sinclair Lewis, The Last of the Literary Liberals," *Modern Monthly,*
VIII (March, 1934), 77.
[102] The *Mercury* editorial (Oct., 1924) eventually appeared as "Journalism
in America," *Prejudices: Sixth Series* (New York, 1927).
[103] Kemler, *Mr. Mencken,* p. 271.   [104] *Ibid.,* p. 271.

that would keep up his self-respect in his declining years. But in his later polemical writings most of his former disciples saw confirmation of their belief that he was always at heart a reactionary.

THE LATER *MERCURY*

MENCKEN partisans have gone so far as to claim that the *Mercury* died in 1933 with its founder's resignation,[105] an obvious untruth. Yet it certainly has been agreed that, after the resignation of Mencken, the monthly was unable to approach its glory of the middle twenties. Henry Hazlitt, a former associate of the *Nation,* chosen by Mencken as editor partly because of his conservative economic opinions and partly because of his tolerable critical abilities, was not the sort of man to embark on any dazzling course. However laudably sound his thinking, Hazlitt was perhaps one of the dullest writers of the period, and few readers returned to the foundering periodical. Therefore, despite a new breadth of contents and an adjusted course,[106] after four months Knopf secured Hazlitt's resignation. Angoff continued producing the magazine after Hazlitt left, and was named editor in August, 1934.

As managing editor under Mencken, Angoff, who was of very liberal persuasion, had smarted under his employer's conservative behests. His policies, when he assumed the editorship, were politically liberal: "Angoff," wrote Mencken, "took [the *Mercury*] far to the Left, and became a hero to all the New York Reds, who regarded the conquest of

[105] Jane Wilhelm, "H. L. Mencken" (pamphlet), Enoch Pratt Free Library, n.p., n.d.

[106] Knopf announced in 1934 that the review had "abandoned completely its pre-occupation wholly with the American scene" and would "treat foreign topics with the same uncompromising realism with which it for ten years dealt with purely American themes and personalities. . . . [It] will, on the whole, probably bear a closer resemblance to Mencken's *Mercury* than to any other periodical" (quoted by John E. Drewry, "Mencken and the Mercury: Magazine Still Reflects the Molding Hand and Policies of Its Initial Editor," *Quill,* XXVI, 11, 23.

the *American Mercury,* with plenty of reason, as a notable feat."[107] This summary was supported by at least one event: when Angoff commissioned John L. Spivak, allegedly a Communist,[108] to write a sweeping exposé of the Red Cross for the November, 1934, number, a considerable stir resulted. There was emphatic approval in radical quarters.[109] Nevertheless, Knopf became alarmed at Angoff's militancy and discouraged by the continued low circulation.[110] Knopf had long wanted to sell his worrisome magazine, and when Paul Palmer, who had been associated with Mencken on the Baltimore Sunpapers,[111] made an offer, Knopf promptly accepted and left for Europe. The *Mercury* sale price was remarkably low—$25,000.[112]

Radical circles sorely lamented the transaction. They claimed that Angoff, who was not directly told of the sale until January 19, 1935, had not been fairly treated.[113] More disturbing, it was apparent from the outset that Palmer meant to mold the *Mercury* into a conservative organ.[114] Angoff hotly turned down Palmer's offer to work as managing editor, despite a trip by Mencken from Baltimore to help persuade him to remain.[115] It should not be imag-

[107] "The 'Hatrack' Case," p. 101 n.

[108] Anon., "John L. Spivak," *Panorama,* Nov., 1934, p. 4.

[109] "John L. Spivak," *ibid.,* p. 4: ". . . the *American Mercury* . . . has found new vitality under its former sub-editor, Charles Angoff. It has become, indeed, the most outspoken, the most forward looking, of the quality group, and this overnight. . . . At one time it looked as if Angoff [were conservative]. . . . If so, that time is gone. The *American Mercury* may still sport a green cover; inside it is becoming a healthy . . . red. . . . I hereby dub . . . Angoff as one of the most important of the new American editors, and the rejuvenated *American Mercury* as compulsory for the new type of reader as it was, under Mencken, for the old."

[110] Official average circulation during 1934 was 31,023 (Ayer's *Directory,* [1935]).

[111] Johnson, *et al., The Sunpapers of Baltimore,* p. 386 n.

[112] Kemler, *Mr. Mencken,* p. 266.

[113] George Simpson, "Mr. Knopf Makes a Sale," *New Masses,* XIV (Feb. 5, 1935), 20. Simpson's extraordinary article, which seems well informed about Angoff's editorial troubles, is an important statement about the post-Mencken *Mercury.*

[114] Anon., "The Week," *New Republic,* LXXXI (Feb. 6, 1935), 346: "We admit freely that we preferred Mr. Angoff's *Mercury* to that of Mr. Mencken; but we feel quite certain that we shall like the new incarnation less than we did that of the Bad Boy of Baltimore."

[115] Simpson, "Mr. Knopf Makes a Sale," *New Masses,* XIV, 20.

ined, however, that Palmer's editorship was incompetent; he encouraged a variety of contributors that had not hitherto appeared in the magazine, and he conducted a worthy journal of conservative opinion.[116] The circulation slowly began to climb.

In September, 1936, however, the era of the *Mercury* as a quality magazine ended; after that issue it was reduced by Palmer to digest size: the articles were condensed and the price was lowered to twenty-five cents. The circulation further increased after this revolution, and by 1939 Palmer sold the monthly and took a position on the staff of the *Reader's Digest*. The new owner of the changed *Mercury* was Lawrence E. Spivak, who had become business manager in 1933, and who, during Palmer's editorship, was publisher.[117] After himself editing the March, 1939, number, Spivak named Eugene Lyons editor, a move, it was popularly thought, that would shift the allegiance of the monthly to the New Deal.[118] Instead, it followed a rather middle-of-the-road policy. Although the magazine made little money for its successive owners, Spivak, according to Angoff, kept it for tax-reducing purposes as one of his publishing enterprises.[119]

After eleven years ownership, Spivak sold the *Mercury* to Clendenin J. Ryan, a wealthy investment banker who promptly shifted the review toward the right. Ryan's editor, William Bradford Huie, guided it from December, 1950, until August, 1952. During Huie's editorship the legend "founded by Henry L. Mencken" was placed under the

---

[116] Some of the better known writers who appeared in Palmer's *Mercury* were Ford Madox Ford, Pearl S. Buck, William Faulkner, G. B. Shaw, Robert Frost, G. K. Chesterton, George Santayana, Bertrand Russell, Agnes Repplier, Stephen Leacock, Thomas Wolfe, and John Dos Passos.

[117] "L. E. Spivak Buys . . . Magazine from Paul Palmer," *New York Times,* Jan. 11, 1939, n.p. (N.Y.M.C.).

[118] Carl H. Mote, *The New Deal Goose Step* (New York, 1939), p. 112: "The *American Mercury* has kept its relatively few readers well advised of New Deal vulgarities. . . . Walter [Winchell announced] on January 31, 1939, that 'the American Merk's new set-up will embrace F.D.R. and other liberal American tendencies with the April issue' [with] Eugene Lyons, a Russian Jew . . . editor."

[119] Interview, Dec. 27, 1958.

magazine's name. The tone of the contents was uniformly one of indignant conservatism.

In August, 1952, the journal was sold to J. Russell Maguire, who had garnered a fortune in brokerage transactions and in government contracts during World War II. Maguire, who was even more illiberal than Ryan, introduced anti-Semitic policies, leading most of the older *Mercury* associates to resign—even Huie.[120] Until recently the digest continued under Maguire's direction, though William La Varre was listed as editor. Maguire's *Mercury,* considered "an organ of reaction,"[121] had by 1959 gathered together 60,940 readers capable of being constantly alarmed by frantic exposés of vague "international conspiracies" being hatched by New York Jews.[122] At present the review's control has passed to an organization known as the Defenders of the Christian Faith and the publisher is Gwynne W. Davidson, D.D. The editorial offices have shifted from New York City to Oklahoma City, Oklahoma. Nevertheless, most of the Maguire editorial staff has been retained, and the editorial policies remain unchanged. Such is the paranoiac descendant of Mencken's and Nathan's bright dream of 1923.

[120] "Blowup at the *Mercury," Time,* LXVI (Oct. 3, 1955), 69.
[121] Peterson, *Magazines in the Twentieth Century,* p. 381.
[122] The most important study of the anti-Semitism in the present-day *Mercury* is Angoff, "From Mencken . . . to Maguire: The Tragedy of the American Mercury," *ADL Bulletin,* XIV (May, 1957), 4-6.

10

CONCLUSIONS

THE *MERCURY* ACCOMPLISHMENT

WHEN, in the fall of 1910, H. G. Wells presented his dream of a critical tory magazine (". . . we would use the *Blue Weekly* to maintain a stream of suggestion against crude thinking, and at last scarcely a week passed but some popular distinction, some large imposing generalisation, was touched to flaccidity . . ."),[1] he could not have suspected how influential his idea might become. In 1923 Mencken and Nathan, ending their long and successful guerrilla warfare in the *Smart Set* against the American booboisie, finally were able to establish their green version of Well's "Blue Weekly" and W. H. Wright's abortive *Blue Review*. The *Mercury* quickly drew enough support to insure continuance. With essentially a skeptical, anti-Puritan, urban, and sophisticated editorial viewpoint, the early *Mercury* printed a variety of material dealing with the American scene. Although Mencken exercised strict control over the journal, especially after 1925, and although he soon created a reservoir of contributors willing to tailor their language and attitudes so as to share his swelling personal popularity, he also drew into his magazine work by authors whose independence he did not compromise.

The result was a handsome, unillustrated magazine which, from 1924 until about 1927 was one of the best American quality periodicals; in addition, it was very likely

[1] "The New Machiavelli," *English Review*, V (Sept., 1910), 299.

the most influential. His monthly lent support to the realist faction in American letters, performing notable services to writers like Sinclair Lewis. The *Mercury* drew manuscripts from far corners of the country, writings whose realism, however homely, at times, helped preserve the contents of the magazine from becoming extensively dated.

It was as an organ of satire and humor, however, that the *Mercury* made its greatest impact on American thought. Its audacious editor, by his early editorials and book reviews, made himself the most remarkable contributor of satire. Second in worth as a satirist was George Jean Nathan, whose "Clinical Notes" and "The Theatre" made the monthly a repository for wit as well as valuable reviews of the contemporary stage. Next in importance is "Americana," a compilation which, viewed over a span of several years, constituted a vast comic epic of Coolidge's America, a satiric panorama nearly as important to America as Pope's *Dunciad* was to the England of his day. In both instances, minor fools and their chicaneries were preserved in an amber that immortalized follies far more cleverly than they deserved; Mencken's boobus americanus was correctly seen as "an ideal monster, exactly like the Yahoo of Swift," having "almost the same dreadful reality."[2] Last, scores of excellent essays and short stories by diverse hands further insured the reputation of the review as the best satirical periodical of the twenties. That a shift in sensibility has led Americans of today to dislike satire should not lead the critic to neglect the review's accomplishment in that genre. And it would be unjust to forget the firm editorial guidance needed to conduct a magazine of outspoken denunciation toward political personages, professors, and powerful religious groups without seeking the consolations of some official ideology or party alliance. Mencken's services against Prohibition, censorship, and other tamperings with

---

[2] Edmund Wilson, "Mencken's Democratic Man," *New Republic*, XLIX (Dec. 15, 1926), 111.

liberty required, during the middle twenties, considerable strength of mind.

The vitality of the *Mercury* during its heyday can best be gauged by the carnival of adverse comment which it stimulated. Most of this criticism, before 1928, was centered upon the magazine's lack of idealism, whether religious, political, or esthetic. If much of the conservative criticism of the twenties today seems feeble, some of the leftist attacks during the early thirties appear equally ineffectual. That Mencken's review was harmfully irresponsible was exaggerated in many of the liberal and radical discussions not only when the periodical was declining, but long afterward.[3]

The twenties saw a new awakening to America on the part of its more intelligent citizens, and in this nationalistic awareness the part of the *Mercury* was healthy: it encouraged self-criticism and lampooned many forms of pussyfooting, yet, for many years, it seemed to avoid didacticism. From the point of view of literary creativity, the monthly helped make a lively cultural background during a decade that responded to vigor and audacity; Mencken's editorial flamboyance was perhaps as catalytic for writers of the twenties as were the sober visions of public works of the thirties. Altogether, it can be seen that the magazine will not come into just respect as an organ of literary importance, first, until satire is better received, and second, until the "Middle Generation"— or indeed, the entire realist and naturalist wing of American writing in the twentieth century—receives more cordial treatment by literary historians.

[3] The most elaborate of these discussions is Harold Laski, *The American Democracy: A Commentary and an Interpretation* (New York, 1938), pp. 665-667. Excellent antidotes to Laski's charges are James T. Farrell, *Reflections at Fifty and Other Essays,* pp. 44-47; William Manchester, "Mencken and the *Mercury*," *Harper's,* CCI (Aug., 1950), 65-73.

THE *MERCURY* DEFEAT

IT is difficult to judge so sprawling a thing as the ten-year output of a magazine, even when it was conceived and guided by one intelligence. Still, the *Mercury* adventure under Mencken ended in defeat. If the editor's rise and fall make a kind of tragedy, a few remarks about the characteristic weaknesses of the enterprise are in order.

The most obvious handicap for the periodical was its close identity with a single man. Inevitably, most of the faults of the magazine, such as mediocre poetry, unimaginative fiction, and stereotyped essays, mirror the limitations of its editor. Many of Mencken's own contributions were designed simply to shock. This dissent from the ideas cherished by the gaping American Everyman by the end of the twenties had largely become a routine aped by less gifted imitators. The gay detachment of these disciples of Mencken, however clever, gave the impression that they were merely playing with surfaces: "The *Mercury* was brilliant," recently reflected Norman Cousins, "but it was cold. It would have been fine for a static civilization. . . ."[4] Yet when the editor did choose to be warmly sympathetic, as he was toward E. W. Howe, Jim Tully, and Joseph Hergesheimer, his genuine admiration was being given to the palpably second-rate. These partialities, combined with his fascination with subliterary and obviously ephemeral writings, threaten to make "The Library" as little significant as his "Check List of New Books." Often one feels of "The Library" that the space could have been put to better use by others.

Had the Depression not occurred, Mencken would have run into difficulties nevertheless. During most of his *Mer-*

[4] "Our Times and the *Mercury*," *Saturday Review*, XXXVII (June 12, 1954), 22. Angoff has countered Cousins' opinions ("The Inside View of Mencken's Mercury," *New Republic*, CXXXI [Sept. 13, 1954], 18-22).

cury career, he was intellectually "coasting" on insights stored up while working on the *Smart Set*. His *Smart Set* ideas were often liberating, and he achieved considerable influence by dressing them out as *Mercury* editorials during the twenties, but his mind ceased to grow and change with the times. Therefore, when the thirties entered with new problems, the *Mercury* was vulnerable to enemies speaking for either rightist or leftist points of view. The New Humanists could persuasively claim that Mencken and his magazine were unable to offer authoritative treatment of the American scene because of a neglect of valuable American and European heritages. The liberals and radicals, on the other hand, could plausibly charge the journalistic venture with a breach of its original pledge to scrutinize, without cant, all areas of contemporary American experience.

Nevertheless, the accomplishment of the *Mercury,* during its first decade, was truly formidable; perhaps no other magazine of comparable circulation has so strongly caught the national imagination; the green-covered review has to some extent entered into the folklore of urban sophisticates. But serious students of American letters should take Mencken and his magazine out of the realm of legend and carefully define his greatness as an editor and stylist.

SELECTED BIBLIOGRAPHY

MENCKEN MANUSCRIPT COLLECTIONS

Duke University Library Manuscript Collection, Duke University Library, Durham, North Carolina.
Enoch Pratt Free Library H. L. Mencken Collection, Enoch Pratt Free Library, Baltimore, Maryland.
New York Public Library H. L. Mencken Collection, New York Public Library, New York City, New York.
Princeton University Collection of H. L. Mencken Correspondence in Transcript, Princeton University Library, Princeton, New Jersey.

PERIODICAL FILES

American Mercury, I-LXXXVIII (Jan., 1924-June, 1959).
Smart Set, I-LXXII (Jan., 1900-Dec., 1923).

ARTICLES FROM OTHER MAGAZINES

ALLEN, FREDERICK L. "The American Magazine Grows Up," *Atlantic,* CLXXXVI (Nov., 1950), 77-82.
——. "Sedgwick and the Atlantic," *Outlook and Independent,* Dec. 26, 1928, 1406-1417.
ALLEN, HARBOR. "Our Foremost Critic," *New Masses,* II (Jan., 1927), 26.
"Americana," *Saturday Evening Post,* CIC (May 21, 1927), 52.
"Americana," *Saturday Evening Post,* CIC (June 25, 1927), 49-50.
"Americana," *Saturday Evening Post,* CC (Aug. 13, 1927), 35, 148.

"Americana," *Saturday Evening Post,* CC (Sept. 10, 1927), 58, 238.

"Americana," *Saturday Evening Post,* CCI (Nov. 12, 1927), 49.

ANGOFF, CHARLES. "From Mencken . . . to Maguire: The Tragedy of the American Mercury," *ADL Bulletin,* XIV (May, 1957), 4-6.

———. "The Inside View of Mencken's Mercury," *New Republic,* CXXXI (Sept. 13, 1954), 18-22.

ANON. "The American Mercury. . . ," *Nation* CXVIII (Jan. 9, 1924), 23.

ANON. "The American Mercury," *New Republic,* XXXVII (Feb. 6, 1924), 274.

ANON. "The 'American Mercury,'" *Outlook,* CXXXVI (Jan. 16, 1924), 90.

ANON. "'The American Mercury': A New Magazine Announced by Knopf," *Publishers' Weekly,* CIV (Aug. 18, 1923), 553.

ANON. "'American Mercury' Wins Injunction," *Publishers' Weekly,* CIX (May 29, 1926), 1795.

ANON. "The American Spectator," *Bookman,* LXXV (Dec., 1932), 830-833.

ANON. "Are We More Banal than Others?" *Literary Digest,* LXXXVIII (Jan. 23, 1926), 29.

ANON. "Blowup at the *Mercury,*" *Time,* LXVI (Oct. 3, 1955), 69.

ANON. "Book News," *News-Week,* II (Sept. 16, 1933), 38.

ANON. "The Case of the April *Mercury,*" *Publishers' Weekly,* CIX (April 10, 1926), 1334.

ANON. "Chronicle and Comment," *Bookman,* LXX (Oct., 1929), 176-192.

ANON. "Chronicle and Comment," *Bookman,* LXX (Jan., 1930), 529-544.

ANON. "Contest," *Time,* XIV (Oct. 7, 1929), 46.

ANON. "Contributors to This Number of the Journal," *Journal of Social Forces,* III (Nov., 1924), 4.

ANON. "Current Magazines," *New York Times Book Review,* Dec. 30, 1923, p. 10.

ANON. "Editorial," *American Spectator,* I (Nov., 1932), 1.

ANON. "Editorial Paragraphs," *Nation,* CXVII (Aug. 29, 1923), 205-207.

ANON. "The Gossip Shop," *Bookman,* LVIII (Oct., 1923), 223.

ANON. "Hatrack," *Time,* VII (April 19, 1926), 24, 26.

ANON. "Hazlitt for Mencken," *Time,* XXII (Oct. 16, 1933), 43.

ANON. "H. L. Mencken—Farewell and Hail!," *Panorama: A Monthly Survey of People and Ideas,* Oct., 1933, p. 4.

ANON. "Knopf and English Market," *Publishers' Weekly,* CXIX (March 7, 1931), 1164.

ANON. "Knopf Offices Move to Fifty-Seventh Street," *Publishers' Weekly,* CV (Feb. 23, 1924), 601.

ANON. "Magazine Changes," *Time,* X (Sept. 5, 1927), 20-21.

ANON. "Mencken and God," *Time,* XV (March 17, 1930), 80.

ANON. "Mencken Outmoded," *Literary Digest,* XCVI (Feb. 18, 1928), 27.

ANON. "Mencken Retires as *Mercury* Editor," *Publishers' Weekly,* CXXIV (Oct. 14, 1933), 1330.

ANON. "Mercury: Mencken Retires as Editor of Critical Monthly," *News-Week,* II (Oct. 14, 1933), 28.

ANON. "Mr. Mencken Is Acquitted," *Publishers' Weekly,* CIX (April 10, 1926), 1277.

ANON. "Periodical Notes," *Publishers' Weekly,* CXII (Oct. 22, 1927), 1577.

ANON. " 'Progressives' Flayed," *Time,* XIII (April 1, 1929), 14.

ANON. "The Publishers and the New Season," *Bookman,* LXI (April, 1925), 212.

ANON. *Publishers' Weekly,* CXVI (May 18, 1929), 2311.

ANON. "Things in General," *Reviewer,* IV (April, 1924), 232-233.

ANON. "Think Stuff," *Time,* IX (April 4, 1927), 24, 26.

ANON. "The Week," *New Republic,* XLVII (May 26, 1926), 4.

ANON. "The Week," *New Republic,* LXXXI (Feb. 6, 1935), 345-346.

Anon. rev., *Dial,* LXXX (April, 1926), 342.

ARVIN, NEWTON. "The Passing of the Twenties," *New Freeman,* I (March 15, 1930), 18-21.

BABBITT, IRVING. "The Critic and American Life," *Forum,* LXXIX (Feb., 1928), 161-176.

BARNARD, EUNICE. "G. B. S.: The Father of the Flapper," *New Republic,* XLVII (July 28, 1926), 272-273.

BROCKWAY, LOUIS. "Books in Magazines," *Publishers' Weekly,* CXII (Dec. 10, 1927), 2118.

BROMFIELD, LOUIS. "The New Yorker," *Bookman,* LXI (July, 1925), 578-582.

———. "The Point of View," *Bookman,* LXIII (March, 1926), 1-2.

CALVERTON, VERNON. "The American Literary Radicals," *Modern Quarterly,* III (Sept.-Dec., 1926), 251-262.

————. "Revolt Among American Intellectuals," *New Masses,* IV (April, 1929), 3-5.

————. "Sinclair Lewis, The Last of the Literary Liberals," *Modern Monthly,* VIII (March, 1934), 77-86.

"Capitaliana," *New Masses,* III (Aug., 1927), 13-14.

CASEY, RALPH D. "An Annotated Bibliography of Journalism Subjects in American Magazines," *Journalism Quarterly,* XI (June, 1934), 200-217.

COUSINS, NORMAN. "Our Times and the *Mercury,*" *Saturday Review,* XXXVII (June 12, 1954), 22.

COWLEY, MALCOLM. "Former Fugleman," *New Republic,* LXXXI (Nov. 21, 1934), 50-51.

————. "Smart Set Legend," *New Republic,* LXXXI (Jan. 16, 1935), 281.

D[AVIES], H[UGH] S[YKES]. "Foreign Periodicals: American Periodicals," *Criterion,* XI (Jan., 1932), 361-363.

DAVIS, ROBERT H. "The Literati under the Lens," *Bookman,* LXIX (Aug., 1929), 625-640.

[DELL, FLOYD]. "Popularity," *Liberator,* Dec. 1919, p. 42.

D[OBRÉE], B[ONAMY]. "Foreign Periodicals: American Periodicals," *Criterion,* X (April, 1931), 587-592.

————. "Foreign Periodicals: American Periodicals," *Criterion,* X (July, 1931), 779-782.

DOS PASSOS, JOHN. "The New Masses I'd Like," *New Masses,* I (June, 1926), 20.

DOUGHTY, LEONARD. "On Pre-Adamic Hottentots, Mencken, The Nation, and Others," *Nation,* CXVIII (March 19, 1924), 316.

DREWRY, JOHN E. "American Magazines Today," *Sewanee Review,* XXXVI (July, 1928), 342-356.

————. "Mencken and the Mercury: Magazine Still Reflects the Molding Hand and Policies of Its Initial Editor," *Quill,* XXVI (March, 1938), 10-11, 23.

DURHAM, FRANK. "Mencken as Missionary," *American Literature,* XXIX (Jan., 1958), 478-483.

EDMAN, IRWIN. "God Settles God," *New Freeman,* I (May 24, 1930), 260-261.

ELY, CATHERINE B. "The Sorrows of Mencken," *North American Review,* CCXXV (Jan., 1928), 23-26.

FARRAR, JOHN. "College Reading," *Bookman,* LXIII (April, 1926), 130-131.

————. "The Lurking Cap and Bells," *Bookman,* LXII (Jan., 1926), 533.

———. "Mustard Plaster Mencken," *Bookman,* LXIV (Dec., 1926), 389.

FITZGERALD, F. SCOTT. "How to Waste Material: A Note on My Generation," *Bookman,* LXIII (May, 1926), 262-265.

FLURY, HENRY. "More, Babbitt, and Mencken," *Forum,* LXXXIX (April, 1928), 634.

FORD, FORD MADOX. "Communications," *Transatlantic Review,* I (Jan., 1924), 93-94.

———. "Communications," *Transatlantic Review,* II (Aug., 1924), 210-213.

FREEMAN, JOSEPH. "Sherwood Anderson's Confusion," *New Masses,* IV (Feb., 1929), 6.

———. "Social Trends in American Literature," *Communist,* IX (July, 1930), 641-651.

———. "The 'Wilsonian' Liberals," *Communist,* VII (Aug., 1928), 513-520.

FUCHS, JAMES. "Chronicle of Confusion," *New Masses,* III (May, 1927).

GOLD, MICHAEL. "America Needs a Critic," *New Masses,* I (Oct., 1926), 7-9.

———. "Hemingway—White Collar Poet," *New Masses,* III (March, 1928), 20-22.

———. "Mr. Steffens Liked Everybody," *New Masses,* VII (June, 1931), 5-6.

———. "[An Open Letter to] H. L. Mencken, Editor of the American Mercury," *New Masses,* VII (Sept., 1931), 3-4.

———. "3 Schools of U. S. Writing," *New Masses,* IV (Sept., 1928), 13-14.

———. "Shanty Irish," *New Masses,* IV (Feb., 1929), 26.

GREGORY, ALYSE. "Criticism in America," *Dial,* LXXXIII (Sept., 1927), 252.

GREGORY, HORACE. "Our Writers and the Democratic Myth," *Bookman,* LXXV (Aug., 1932), 377-382.

HEDGES, M. H. "The War of Cultures," *New Masses,* I (May, 1926), 20.

HOFFMAN, K. V. "Mencken, Landlubber," *McNaught's Monthly,* III (March, 1925), 89.

JEWETT, KENNETH. "And From the United States," *Transatlantic Review,* I (April, 1924), 207.

JONES, HOWARD MUMFORD. "Professor Babbitt Cross-Examined," *New Republic,* LIV (March 21, 1928), 158-160.

"Journeyman" [pseud.]. "Miscellany," *Freeman*, VIII (Sept. 19, 1923), 31-32.

Knopf, Alfred A. "For Henry With Love," *Atlantic*, CCIII (May, 1959), 50-54.

Kummer, F. A. "Something Must Have Happened to Henry," *Bookman*, LXV (June, 1927), 408-410.

Lippman, Walter. "H. L. Mencken," *Saturday Review of Literature*, III (Dec. 11, 1926), 413-414.

Long, Walter. "Shots for Four," *Modern Quarterly*, III (Oct.-Dec., 1925), 74-76.

Manchester, William. "Mencken and the *Mercury*," *Harper's*, CCI (Aug., 1950), 65-73.

Mencken, Henry L. "From an Editor and a Gentleman," *Nation*, CXVI (Jan. 24, 1923), 151.

———. "H. L. Mencken," *Nation*, CXVII (Dec. 5, 1923), 647-648.

———. "Hoch Iowish," *Nation*, CXVI (Jan. 17, 1923), 72.

———. "Memoirs of an Editor," *Vanity Fair*, XLI (Feb., 1934), 16, 54.

———. "Mr. Mencken Replies," *Bookman*, LV (June, 1922), 367.

———. "Poetry in America," Chicago *Sunday Tribune*, Nov. 30, 1924, Part Five, p. 1, cols. 1-2.

———. "Testament," *American Review of Reviews*, LXXVI (Oct., 1927), 413-416.

Miller, James. "Professors," *New Masses*, IV (July, 1928), 20.

More, Paul Elmer. "The Modern Current in American Literature," *Forum*, LXXIX (Jan., 1928), 127-136.

Nathan, George Jean. "The Editor and His Public," *Bookman*, LXI (May, 1925), 275-276.

———. "O'Neill," *Vanity Fair*, XLI (Oct., 1933), 31, 54.

Newman, Frances. "The American Short Story in the First Twenty-Five Years of the Twentieth Century," *Bookman*, LXIII (April, 1926), 186-193.

North, Joseph. "Communism Comes to College," *New Masses*, VII (Nov., 1931), 16-17.

Oppenheim, James. "A Man Named Mencken," *New Freeman*, I (July 4, 1930), 280-281.

Paterson, Isabel. "Reading with Tears," *Bookman*, LXIV (Oct., 1926), 192-197.

R[ead], H[erbert]. "Foreign Reviews: American Periodicals," *Criterion*, V (Jan., 1927), 165-172.

———. "Foreign Reviews: American Periodicals," *Criterion*, V (June, 1927), 369-374.

———. "Foreign Reviews: American Periodicals," *Criterion*, VI (Dec., 1927), 571-576.

REPPLIER, AGNES. "American Magazines," *Yale Review*, XVI (Jan., 1927), 261-274.

RYAN, DON. "The Movies Join the Union," *New Masses*, III (Oct., 1927), 11-12.

SHAW, ALBERT. "Mencken and His Aims," *American Review of Reviews*, LXXVI (Oct., 1927), 412.

SHERMAN, RICHARD. "Sophisticate, 1933," *Vanity Fair*, XLI (Feb., 1934), 27.

SHERMAN, STUART. "Beautifying American Literature," *Nation*, CV (Nov. 29, 1917), 593-594.

"SIMON PURE" [pseud.]. "The Londoner," *Bookman*, LV (Aug., 1922), 605-611.

SIMPSON, GEORGE. "Mr. Knopf Makes a Sale," *New Masses*, XIV (Feb. 5, 1935), 20.

SINCLAIR, MARY. "Beware My Dog! (Warning from the Wife of a Friend of Mankind)," *New Masses*, IV (Aug., 1928), 23.

SINCLAIR, UPTON. "Mr. Mencken Calls on Me," *Bookman*, LXVI (Oct., 1927), 254-257.

SPENCER, HAZLETON. "Thunder in the Index," *Saturday Review of Literature*, III (May 28, 1927), 858.

SPINGARN, JOEL E. "The Growth of a Literary Myth," *Freeman*, VII (May 2, 1923), 181-183.

STAGG, HUNTER. "Mr. Boyd's Portraits," *Reviewer*, V (Jan., 1925), 90-93.

SWINNERTON, FRANK. "The Great Mencken Fight," *Bookman*, LXIV (Dec., 1926), 463-467.

THOMAS, NORMAN, *et al.*, "Where are the Pre-War Radicals? A Symposium," *Survey*, LV (Feb. 1, 1926), 563.

TROY, WILLIAM. "The Story of the Little Magazines: II. Making No Compromise with the Public Taste," *Bookman*, LXX (Feb., 1930), 657-663.

VILLARD, OSWALD G. "Editorial Paragraphs," *Nation*, CXXII (April 28, 1926), 464-465.

———. "Editorial Paragraphs," *Nation*, CXXII (May 26, 1926), 567-569.

WALPOLE, HUGH. "An Open Letter to H. L. Mencken," *Bookman*, LV (May, 1922), 225-228.

———. "My Dear Mencken," *Bookman,* LXII (Nov., 1925), 246-248.

WHIPPLE, LEON. "The Revolution on Quality Street, Part I," *Survey,* LVII (Nov. 1, 1926), 119-124, 177-179.

———. "The Revolution on Quality Street, Part II," *Survey,* LVII (Jan. 1, 1927), 427-432, 469-472.

WILSON, EDMUND. "The All-Star Literary Vaudeville," *New Republic,* XLVIII (June 30, 1926), 158-163.

———. "Cabell and Colloids," *New Republic,* LIII (Dec. 7, 1927), 75.

———. "Literary Politics," *New Republic,* LIII (Feb. 1, 1928), 289-290.

———. "Mencken's Democratic Man," *New Republic,* XLIX (Dec. 15, 1926), 110-111.

WOODWARD, W. W. "Debunk," *American Speech,* II (May, 1927), 374.

YOUNG, ART. "He makes his nest . . . ," *New Masses,* I (Aug., 1926), 14.

ANONYMOUS ARTICLES FROM NEWSPAPERS

"Canada Acts on Mercury: Premier Orders Scrutiny of Editorial Criticizing the King," *New York Times,* June 12, 1926, p. 2, col. 5.

"Congratulations Are in Order," *New York Times,* Nov. 23, 1928, p. 24, col. 5.

"Declares Narrative Is Full of Untruths," *New York Times,* July 29, 1929, p. 11, col. 2.

"Magazine will Cater to Civilized Minority," *New York Times,* Aug. 18, 1923, p. 2, col. 3.

"Mencken Retires as Mercury Editor," *New York Times,* Oct. 6, 1933, p. 15, col. 3.

"Mr. Mencken on His Own," *New York Times,* Oct. 7, 1933, p. 14, col. 4.

"Nathan and Mencken Part," *New York Times,* March 1, 1930, p. 12, col. 2.

"Plan a Stage 'Hatrack': Musical Comedy Librettist Takes up a Story Barred from the Mails," *New York Times,* April 30, 1926, p. 17, cols. 4-7.

"Predicted Harding's Rise—Kirby Forecast in 1915 and Facetious

Reply are Recalled," *New York Times,* Aug. 18, 1923, p. 2, col. 3.
"Samuel Knopf Estate $240,974," *New York Times,* June 14, 1933, p. 19, col. 1.
"Spoken Very Sarcastic," *New York Times,* Sept. 30, 1929, p. 24, col. 6.
"Will Issue 300,000,000 of Harding Stamps—First Sheet of Memorial Postage to be Presented to his Widow," *New York Times,* Aug. 18, 1923, p. 2, col. 3.

UNPUBLISHED LETTERS TO THE AUTHOR

ANGOFF, CHARLES. January 11, 1959, New York City, New York.
———. May 23, 1959, New York City, New York.
CAIN, JAMES M. February 1, 1959, Hyattsville, Maryland.
KNOPF, ALFRED A. May 22, 1958, New York City, New York.
———. January 7, 1959, New York City, New York.
———. February 18, 1959, New York City, New York.
———. June 2, 1959, New York City, New York.
———. July 28, 1959, New York City, New York.
READ, SIR HERBERT. June 2, 1959, London, England.

UNPUBLISHED THESES

DOLMETSCH, CARL R. "History of the *Smart Set* Magazine, 1914-1923," unpublished Ph.D. thesis, University of Chicago, 1957.
KRAMORIS, IVAN J. "The Principles of Literary Criticism of H. L. Mencken," unpublished Master's thesis, Marquette University, Milwaukee, Wis., 1928.
MANCHESTER, WILLIAM, JR. "A Critical Study of the Work of H. L. Mencken as Literary Critic for the Smart Set Magazine, 1908-1914," unpublished Master's thesis, University of Missouri, 1947.
SHUFORD, CECIL E. "An Evaluation of the Influence of H. L. Mencken and *The American Mercury* Upon American Thought," unpublished Master's thesis, Northwestern University, 1929.
SINGLETON, MARVIN K. "History of the *American Mercury* Under

the Editorship of Henry Mencken, 1924 to 1933," unpublished doctoral dissertation, Duke University, 1960.

BOOKS AND PAMPHLETS

ADAMIC, LOUIS. *Laughing in the Jungle.* New York, 1932.

———. *My America: 1928-1938.* New York, [1938].

ALLEN, FREDERICK L. *Only Yesterday.* New York, [1957].

———. *Since Yesterday:The Nineteen-Thirties in America.* New York, 1940.

ANDERSON, SHERWOOD. *Letters of Sherwood Anderson.* Ed. Howard M. Jones and Walter B. Rideout. Boston, 1953.

ANGOFF, CHARLES. *A Portrait of Mencken from Memory.* New York, 1956.

———, ed. *The World of George Jean Nathan.* New York, 1952.

BACHMAN, EARLE, *et al. Three Years 1924-1927: The Story of a New Idea and Its Successful Adaptation.* New York, [1927].

BARRY, GERALD. *This England.* London, 1933.

BEAL, FRED. *Proletarian Journey.* New York, 1937.

BEARD, CHARLES, AND MARY BEARD. *The Rise of American Civilization.* 2 vols. New York, 1930, Vol. II.

BEER THOMAS. *The Mauve Decade.* Garden City, N. Y., [1926].

BLANKENSHIP, RUSSELL. *American Literature as an Expression of the National Mind.* New York, [1931].

BOYD, ERNEST. *H. L. Mencken.* New York, 1925.

———. *Portraits: Real and Imaginary.* London, [1924].

BOYNTON, PERCY H. *The Challenge of Modern Criticism.* Chicago, 1931.

BRAITHWAITE, W. STANLEY, ed. *Anthology of Magazine Verse for 1928 and Yearbook.* New York, 1928.

BROCK, H. I. *Meddlers.* New York, 1931.

CABELL, JAMES B. *Let Me Lie.* New York, 1947.

CASH, W. J. *The Mind of the South.* Garden City, N. Y., 1951.

CLEATON, ALLEN, AND IRENE CLEATON. *Books & Battles: American Literature, 1920-1930.* Boston, 1937.

COWLEY, MALCOLM. *Exile's Return.* New York, [1934].

DEARMOND, ANNA J. *Andrew Bradford.* Newark, Del., 1949.

DECASSERES, BENJAMIN. *Mencken and Shaw: The Anatomy of America's Voltaire and England's Other John Bull.* New York, 1930.

DOLE, H. S., AND N. H. DOLE, eds. *The Best Humor of 1925*. Boston, 1926.

DRAWBELL, J. W. *Night and Day*. London, 1945.

DREISER, THEODORE. *Letters of Theodore Dreiser: A Selection*. Ed. Robert H. Elias *et al.*, 3 vols. Philadelphia, [1959].

DULLES, FOSTER RHEA. *Twentieth Century America*. Boston, 1945.

ELDER, DONALD. *Ring Lardner: A Biography*. Garden City, N. Y., 1956.

FARRELL, JAMES T., ed. *Prejudices: A Selection*. New York, 1958.

———. *Reflections at Fifty and Other Essays*. New York, [1954].

FORD, FORD MADOX. *Ancient Lights . . . Being the Memories of a Young Man*. London, 1911.

———. *New York Is Not America*. London, [1927].

FRANK, WALDO. *The Re-Discovery of America*. New York, 1929.

GEISMAR, MAXWELL. *The Last of the Provincials: The American Novel, 1915-1925*. Boston, 1947.

GOLDBERG, ISAAC. *The Man Mencken: A Biographical and Critical Survey*. New York, 1925.

———. *The Theatre of George Jean Nathan*. New York, 1926.

HARRISON, JOSEPH B. *A Short View of Menckenism in Menckenese*. Seattle, Wash., 1927.

HAYS, ARTHUR G. *Let Freedom Ring*. New and rev. ed. New York, 1937.

HEMINGWAY, ERNEST. *The Torrents of Spring*. New York, 1926.

HOFFMAN, FREDERICK J. *The Twenties*. New York, [1955].

———., et al. *The Little Magazine: A History and Bibliography*. 2nd ed. Princeton, N. J., 1947.

HICKS, GRANVILLE. *The Great Tradition: An Interpretation of American Literature since the Civil War*. New York, 1933.

HOLT, HENRY. *Garrulities of an Octogenarian Editor*. Boston, 1923.

HOWE, E. W. *Plain People*. New York, 1929.

HOWE, QUINCY. *A World History of Our Times*. New York, 1949.

HUTCHENS, JOHN K., ed. *The American Twenties: A Literary Panorama*. New York, [1952].

JOHNSON, G. W., et al. *The Sunpapers of Baltimore*. New York, 1937.

KAZIN, ALFRED. *On Native Grounds*. Garden City, N. Y., 1956.

KEMLER, EDGAR. *The Irreverent Mr. Mencken*. Boston, 1950.

KNIGHT, GRANT C., ed. *Readings from the American Mercury.* New York, 1926.

KRAMER, DALE. *Ross and the New Yorker.* Garden City, N. Y., 1951.

KRONENBERGER, LOUIS. "H. L. Mencken," *After the Genteel Tradition.* Ed. Malcolm Cowley. New York, 1937. Pp. 100-112.

LASKI, HAROLD. *The American Democracy: A Commentary and an Interpretation.* New York, 1938.

LERNER, MAX. *America as a Civilization.* New York, 1957.

LEWIS, SINCLAIR. *From Main Street to Stockholm: Letters of Sinclair Lewis.* Ed. Harrison Smith. New York, 1952.

LEWISOHN, LUDWIG. *The Story of American Literature.* New York, [1932].

MANCHESTER, WILLIAM. *Disturber of the Peace: The Life of H. L. Mencken.* New York, [1951].

MENCKEN, HENRY L. *Americana 1925.* New York, 1925.

———. *Americana 1926.* New York, 1926.

———. *The Days of H. L. Mencken.* New York, 1947.

———. *H. L. Mencken's Notebooks: Minority Report.* New York, 1956.

———. "Memorandum," *The Borzoi 1925: Being a Sort of Record of Ten Years of Publishing.* New York, 1925. Pp. 139-141.

———. *A Mencken Chrestomathy.* New York, 1956.

———. *Menckeniana: A Schimpflexicon.* New York, 1928.

———. *Prejudices: First Series.* New York, 1929.

———. *Prejudices: Fifth Series.* New York, [1926].

———. *Prejudices: Sixth Series.* New York, 1927.

———. *Supplement I. The American Language.* New York, 1945.

———. "To the Friends of the American Mercury." Pamphlet. New York, April 16, 1926.

MEZZROW, MILTON, AND BERNARD WOLFE. *Really the Blues.* New York, 1946.

MORAND, PAUL. *New York.* New York, 1930.

MORE, PAUL ELMER. *The Demon of the Absolute: New Shelburne Essays.* Vol. I. Princeton, N. J., 1928.

MORRIS, LLOYD. *Postscript to Yesterday.* New York, 1947.

MOTE, CARL H. *The New Deal Goose Step.* New York, 1939.

MOTT, FRANK L. *A History of American Magazines,* volume IV: *1885-1905.* Cambridge, Mass., 1957.

NATHAN, GEORGE J. *The Critic and Drama.* New York, 1922.

————. *The Intimate Notebooks of George Jean Nathan*. New York, 1932.

————. *The World of George Jean Nathan*. Ed. Charles Angoff. New York, 1952.

————. *The World in Falseface*. New York, 1923.

NEVINS, ALLAN. *American Press Opinion: Washington to Coolidge*. Boston, [1928].

PALM, F. C. *The Middle Classes*. New York, 1936.

PATTEE, FRED LEWIS. *The New American Literature, 1890-1930*. New York, [1930].

PETERSON, THEODORE. *Magazines in the Twentieth Century*. Urbana, Ill., 1956.

PORTER, BERN. *H. L. Mencken: A Bibliography*. Pasadena, Calif., 1957.

POUND, EZRA. *The Letters of Ezra Pound: 1907-1941*. Ed. D. D. Paige. New York, [1950].

RASCOE, BURTON. *A Bookman's Daybook*. New York, 1929.

————. "'Smart Set' History," *The Smart Set Anthology of World Famous Authors*. Ed. Burton Rascoe and Groff Conklin. New York, [1934]. Pp. xii-xliv.

————. *We Were Interrupted*. Garden City, N. Y., 1947.

———— et al. *H. L. Mencken*. New York, 1920.

RICHARDS, ROBERT F. *Concise Dictionary of American Literature*. New York, [1955].

RICHARDSON, L. N. *A History of Early American Magazines*. New York, 1931.

ROBINSON, HENRY M. *Fantastic Interim*. New York, 1943.

ROOSBROEK, G. VAN. *The Reincarnation of H. L. Mencken*. N.p., 1925.

SALISBURY, WILLIAM. "Mencken, the Foe of Beauty." Pamphlet. New Rochelle, N. Y., 1925.

SCHLESINGER, ARTHUR M. *The Rise of Modern America*. New York, 1951.

SINCLAIR, UPTON. *Money Writes!* New York, 1927.

————. *My Lifetime in Letters*. Columbia, Mo., [1960].

SPIVAK, LAWRENCE E., AND CHARLES ANGOFF, eds. *The American Mercury Reader: A Selection of Distinguished Articles, Stories, and Poems Published in The American Mercury During the Past 20 Years, 1924-1944*. New York, 1944.

STEARNS, HAROLD E., ed. *America Now: An Inquiry into Civilization in the United States*. New York, 1938.

————. *Civilization in the United States: An Inquiry by Thirty Americans.* New York, [1922].

SULLIVAN, MARK. *Our Times: The United States 1900-1925,* VI: *The Twenties.* New York, 1937.

TEBBEL, JOHN. *George Horace Lorimer and The Saturday Evening Post.* Garden City, N. Y., 1948.

TOWNE, CHARLES H. *Adventures in Editing.* New York, 1926.

————. *So Far So Good,* New York, 1945.

TRILLING, LIONEL. "Eugene O'Neill," *After the Genteel Tradition.* Ed. Malcolm Cowley. New York, 1937. Pp. 127-140.

WECTER, DIXON. *The Saga of American Society: A Record of Social Aspiration 1607-1937.* New York, 1937.

WELLS, H. G. *Experiment in Autobiography.* New York, 1934.

————. *The New Machiavelli.* London, [1911].

WILHELM, JANE. "H. L. Mencken." Pamphlet issued by Enoch Pratt Free Library. [Baltimore, n.d.].

WILSON, EDMUND. *The Shores of Light: A Literary Chronicle of the Twenties and Thirties.* New York, [1952].

WISH, HARVEY. *Contemporary America: The National Scene since 1900.* New York, 1945.

WOLFE, THOMAS. *The Letters of Thomas Wolfe.* Ed. Elizabeth Nowell. New York [1956].

WOOD, JAMES P. *Magazines in the United States: Their Social and Economic Influence.* 2nd ed. New York, [1956].

WRIGHT, WILLARD H. *The Creative Will: Studies in the Philosophy and the Syntax of Aesthetics.* New York, 1916.

INDEX

Academy, 22
Across the Street, 122
Actor's Equity Association, 128
Adamic, Louis, 7, 150, 152
Adams, Grace, 140
Adler, Elmer, 39, 40
"Aesthete: Model 1924," 49-52
Aesthete 1925, 184, 207-208
Aiken, Conrad, 143
Akins, Zoe, 47
Algonquin Hotel (New York City), 7, 49, 56, 118
All God's Chillun Got Wings, 57, 81, 123
Allen, Frances, 149
Allen, Frederick Lewis, 4, 208
Allen, Harbor, 151
All's Well, 26
Alvord, Clarence W., 68, 140
American Academy of Arts and Letters, 4
American Credo, The, 10, 112
American Federation of Labor, 128
American Language, The, 8, 10, 232
American Legion, 69, 97ff., *passim*
American Medical Association, 147
American Review of Reviews, 191
American Spectator, 7, 184, 226-227
American Tragedy, An, 210
American Weekly Mercury, 34
"Americana," 43-45, 48, 96-110, 167, 174, 178, 183, 184, 186, 187-190, 198, 200, 217, 243
Americana 1926, 97, 213
Ancient Mariner, 80
Anderson, Daniel Merrill, 74
Anderson, George A., 176
Anderson, Judith, 125
Anderson, Maxwell, 124
Anderson, Sherwood, 4, 19, 73, 74, 76, 77, 144, 205, 210 211
Andrist Karl, 142
Androcles and the Lion, 83
"Anglicana," 184
Angoff, Charles, 7, 19, 59, 60, 72,
80, 96, 174, 182, 217, 218, 219, 220, 238, 239
Anthology of Magazine Verse for 1928 and Yearbook, 211
Anti-Saloon League, 91, 93, 196
Antony and Cleopatra, 119
Archer, William, 132
Aristotle, 131
Arizona, 44, 107
Arlen, Michael, 196
Arnold, Matthew, 78
Arrowsmith, 83, 85
Arvin, Newton, 224
Asbury, Herbert, 71, 75, 167, 169, 170
Asquith, Herbert, 94
Athenaeum, 22, 23
Atlantic, 5, 7, 22, 37, 54, 63, 155, 159, 162, 166, 181, 182
Ayre, C. E., 87

Babbitt, 83
Babbitt, Irving, 200
Bachman, Earle, 164
Baltimore, Maryland, 10, 37, 56, 175
Baptists, 71, 90, 93
Barnard, Eunice, 209
Barnes, Harry Elmer, 43
Barnum, P. T., 23, 34, 178
Barrett, Lillian, 142
Barrett Wendell and His Letters, 85
Barrie, James, 118, 126
Barton, Bruce, 100
Beach, Joseph Warren, 145
Beal, Fred, 199
Beals, Carleton, 154
Beard, Charles, 26, 43, 140
Beard, Mary, 26
Beardsley, Aubrey, 50
Beer, Thomas, 145, 147
Beethoven, Ludwig van, 57
Belasco, David, 13
Bennett, Arnold, 193
Berlin, Germany, 53
Best Humor of 1925, The, 188
Bible, 71, 115, 195

Bierce, Ambrose, 80, 89, 138-139
Bismarck, Otto von, 61
Black Mask, 21
Blake, Robert, 81, 152
Blanco, Jorge J., 154
Blanco, Tomás, 154
Blast, 22
"Blue Review," 15, 30, 33
"Blue Weekly," 14, 15, 32, 242
Bodenheim, Maxwell, 143, 145
Bonham, Milledge L., Jr., 70
Bookman, 23, 24, 182, 199, 210, 224, 227
Booth, Ernest, 152, 210
Boston, Massachusetts, 167-168, *passim*
"Box Car Molly," 170
Boyd, Ernest, 47, 48-52, 54, 81, 206, 212, 220, 226
Boyle, Kay, 211
Bradford, Andrew, 34
Bradley, Hugh, 155
Braithwaite, W. Stanley, 211
Brandes, Georg, 47
Bridgeport, Connecticut, *Telegram,* 38
Brieux, Eugene, 119
Britton, Nan, 112
Brockway, Louis, 164
Brödel, Max, 31
Bromfield, Louis, 209
Broom, 22, 51
Brossow, Olive, 141
Brousson, Jean-Jacques, 154
Brown, Slater, 207, 208
Bryan, William Jennings, 41, 90-92, 94, 137
Bullock, William, 67
Burgess, John W., 48
Burke, Kenneth, 50, 207

Cabell, James Branch, 4, 10, 13, 47. 76, 114, 144, 145, 146, 147, 226, 227
Cain, James Mallahan, 38, 69, 81, 137, 142, 182, 223
Cajetan, Brother, 231
Caldwell, Erskine, 144
Calhern, Louis, 125
California, 45, 108, 159
Calverton, Vernon F., 202, 203, 213
Cambridge History of American Literature, 47
Canada, 94
Canby, Henry Seidel, 13
Candida, 126
"Capitaliana," 184
Caragianes, Felix, 177

Carb, David, 47
Cather, Willa, 4, 27
Century, 24, 181, 182, 183
Chafee, Zechariah, Jr., 67
Chase, Franklin, 168, 169, *passim*
"Check List of New Books," 164
Chesterton, G. K., 113-114
Chew, Samuel C., 43, 56, 145
Chicago *Sunday Tribune,* 78
Christian Science, 47
Churchill, Winston, 94
Cibber, Colley, 131
Clark, Emily, 144, 153
Clement, Traverse, 151
Clendening, Logan, 147
Cline, Leonard Lanson, 46
Cobb, Margaret, 69, 142
Cocteau, Jean, 201
Colby, Elbridge, 149
Coleridge, Samuel Taylor, 80
Collier, Jeremy, 131
Collier's Weekly, 12
Collins, Seward, 201
Columbia University, 132, 158
Columbus, Ohio, *Citizen,* 38
Communist, 205
Comstock, Anthony, 168
Conklin, Groff, 7
Connecticut, 106
Conrad, Joseph, 16, 24, 28
Conway, Arlington, 149
Cook, James H., 148
Coolidge, Calvin, 4, 65-67, 93, 191, 199, 230, 243
Cornell, Katherine, 125
Cornell University, 10
Cosmopolitan, 24
Cousins, Norman, 7, 245
Coward, Noel, 119
Cowley, Malcolm, 7, 50, 51, 207, 237
Cramp, J. Arthur, 140, 147
Crane, Hart, 207
Craven, Thomas, 140
Crawford, Nelson A., 211
Criterion, The, 83, 190, 226
Critic, 24
Critique of Humanism, The, 225
Croce, Benedetto, 47
Crowe, Eugene F., 17, 18
Crowell, Chester T., 76, 141, 174
Cullen, Countee, 153
Cummings, E. E., 50-51
Curtis, Charles, 68, 213
Custer, George A., 201
Cyrano de Bergerac, 47
"Czecho-Slovakia," 89

Dada, 49, 50
Dana, Marvin, 13
D'Annunzio, Gabriele, 16
Darrow, Clarence, 68, 92, 142, 171
Daughters of the American Revolution, 69
Davidson, Gwynne W., 241
Davis, Elmer, 146
Dayton, Tennessee, 91-92
Dean, Basil, 125
DeCasseres, Benjamin, 62, 216
Delineator, 27, 212
Dell, Floyd, 16, 202
Denver, Colorado, 100
Desire Under the Elms, 123
Deutsch, Babette, 79
DeVoto, Bernard, 140
Dial, 24, 75, 162, 189, 190, 191, **193**
Dobie, J. Frank, 145
Dodd, William E., 140
Dolmetsch, Carl R., 7, 23
Donnelly, Horace J., 175, 177
Dos Passos, John, 50, 184, 202, 227
Double-Dealer, 26, 46
Doughty, Leonard, 44
Drama League, 128
Drawbell, J. W., 190
Dreiser, Theodore, 4, 9, 10, 12, 16,
  17, 19, 20, 22, 27, 30, 31, 32, 34,
  53, 56, 73, 74, 75, 76, 77, 114, 133,
  143, 210, 211, 226, 227
Drinkwater, John, 47
Dryden, John, 114, 131
Dublin, Louis, 153
DuBois, W. E. B., 153
Dubek, Monsignor J. B., 232
Duke University, 142
Duse, Eleonora, 47, 125
Dye, Richard, 142
Dyke, Henry van, 85
Dynamo, 124

Eastman, Max, 139
Easy Street, 122
Eaton, G. D., 145, 183
Eaton, Walter Prichard, 47, 117, **145**
Eckenrode, H. J., 43
Edinburgh Review, 22
Edman, Irwin, 224
Ehrmann, Herbert B., 172
Eliot, Charles, 113
Eliot, T. S., 83, 157, 190
Elks, 163
Elmer Gantry, 83
El Paso, Texas, 70
Ely, Catherine B., 199
England, 94, 189

English Review, 15, 16, 22
Enoch Pratt Free Library, 9
Episcopalians, 89
Epworth League, 92
Essay of Dramatic Poesy, 131
Europe, 10, 23, 29
Exiles, 126

*Fantastica: Being the Smile of the
  Sphinx and Other Tales of Imagination,* 47-48
Fante, John, 144
Farmington, Missouri, 170, 175
Farrar, John, 51, 158, 209
Farrell, James T., 8, 144, 151, 158,
  223
Father, The, 118
Faulkner, William, 3, 144, 223, 227
Fergusson, Harvey, 69
Ficke, Arthur, 71
Fishbein, Morris, 140, 147
Fisher, Randolph, 153
Fitch, Clyde, 13, 125
Fitzgerald, F. Scott, 19, 73, 76, 82,
  144, 193, 209
Flaubert, Gustav, 106, 200
Fletcher, John Gould, 24
Flury, Henry, 201
Fontanne, Lynn, 125
Ford, Ford Madox, 12, 15, 16, 206
Ford, Henry, 215
Fortnightly Review, 22
Forum, 182, 183, 199
Foster, Stephen, 116
Fountain, The, 123
France, 49
France, Anatole, 13, 94
Frank, Waldo, 118
Frankfurter, Felix, 175
Freeman, Joseph, 205
Freeman, The, 22, 24
Frost, Robert, 86, 95
Funk, Casimir, 140

Gale, Zona, 144
Galsworthy, John, 126
Garamond, Claude, 40
Garrison, Fielding H., 173
Gastonia, North Carolina, 199
Geddes, Norman Bel, 125
Geismar, Maxwell, 188
Gentlemen Prefer Blondes, 212
George V, 94
George Bernard Shaw: His Plays, 10
George, W. L., 16, 154
Georgia, 103
Gilfond, Duff, 69, 137

Gish, Lillian, 125
Goethe, Johann Wolfgang von, 78
Gold, Michael, 6, 150, 184, 203, 204, 205, 225
Goldberg, Isaac, 47, 48, 140, 174, 184, 216
Goldman, Emma, 150, 151
Gómez, Juan, 154
Goodman, Philip, 9, 37, 52, 220, 222, 229
Gordon, Eugene, 153
Grant, U. S., 193
Great Gatsby, The, 82
Great God Brown, The, 123
Greenwich Village (New York City), 7, 41, 49, 78, 129, 155, 206
Greenwood, Major, 154
Gregory, Horace, 225
Grey, Zane, 114
Grissom, Arthur, 13
Guam, 45
Guérard, Albert, 145, 154
Guest, Eddie, 78

Haardt, Sara Powell (Mrs. H. L. Mencken), 21, 31, 33, 144, 217, 220
Hacker, Louis M., 140
Hall, H. Nathaniel, 153
Hall, Leonard, 76
Halstead, William, 173
Hamilton, John Church, 43
Hammond, Percy, 117
Hansen, Harry, 114, 181
Happy Days, 8
Harding, Warren G., 35, 66, 112
Harper's, 5, 7, 22, 24, 34, 181, 182, 226
Harris, Clare, 120
Harris, Frank, 154
Harrison, Henry Sydnor, 20
Hartford, Connecticut, 101
Harvard Classics, 113
Harvard University, 48, 69, 158, 175
"Hatrack," 75, 167-181, 208
Hauptmann, Gerhart, 11, 127
Hayes, Helen, 125
Hays, Arthur Garfield, 171, 172, 173, 176, 179
Hazlitt, Henry, 233, 238
Hazlitt, William, 131
Healy, Thomas F., 152
Hearst, William Randolph, 25, 29, 237
Heathen Days, 8
Hecht, Ben, 19, 144
Hemingway, Ernest, 73-74, 207, 227

Henderson, W. J., 140
Hennessey, Daniel, 151
Herbst, Josephine, 144, 174
Hergesheimer, Joseph, 145, 245
Herskovits, Melville, 139
Heyward, DuBose, 143
Hicks, Granville, 151, 228
"History of the American Mercury under the Editorship of Henry Mencken, 1924 to 1933," 11
"History of the Smart Set Magazine, 1914-1923," 7
Hitler, Adolf, 234
Hoffenstein, Samuel, 143
Hoffman, F. A., 206
Hoffman, Frederick J., 150
Hoffman, K. V., 198
Holsey, Albon L., 153
Holt, Henry, 26
Hoover, Herbert, 221
Hopkins, Arthur, 128
Howard, Sidney, 124, 125
Howe, E. W., 26, 45, 245
Howe, M. A. D., 85
Howells, William Dean, 42
Hoyt, Charles, 125
Hoyt, Julia, 125
Huggins, E. L., 148
Hughes, Langston, 153
Huie, William Bradford, 240, 241
Human Nature, 119
Humanism and America, 225
Huneker, James, 16, 27, 43, 131, 132
Hussey, L. M., 46, 153, 174
Hutchins, J. K., 52
Huxley, Aldous, 154

Ibsen, Henrik, 11, 127
Illinois, 103, 104
Indiana, 10
"Intelligentsia," 183
Iowa Legionnaire, 99

James, Henry, 42
James, William, 192
Jazz Symphony of American Life, A, 129
Jeffers, Robinson, 16, 143
Jeffrey, Francis, Lord, 27
Jeremiah, 148
Jersey City, New Jersey, 100
Jesus, 77
Jewett, Kenneth, 206
Johns Hopkins Medical School, 147
Johnson, Gerald W., 62
Johnson, Hiram, 45

Johnson, James Weldon, 31, 80, 153
Jolas, Eugene, 205
Jones, Howard Mumford, 223
Jones, Idwal, 144, 216
Josephson, Matthew, 50, 207
Josey, Charles, 48
Joyce, James, 118, 126
Judge, 27
Jump, Herbert, 196

Kane, Hermine, 147
Kansas, 44
Kaufman, George, 124
Kazin, Alfred, 7
Keller, A. G., 232
Kent, Frank, 65, 69, 70
Khayyam, Omar, 196
Kiely, John J., 175
Kimball, Alice Mary, 143
Kinsley, Kansas, 100
Kiwanis, 97ff., *passim,* 163, 198
Knight, Grant C., 160
Knopf, Alfred A., 3, 28, 29, 30, 32,
    33, 34, 35, 36, 37, 38, 40, 48, 52,
    55, 56, 57, 58, 59, 81, 156, 157,
    164, 165, 166, 171, 172, 176, 188,
    220, 228, 229, 232, 238, 239
Knopf, Samuel, 30, 166, 229, 232
Krapp, George Philip, 46, 139
Krutch, Joseph Wood, 117
Ku Klux Klan, 41, 69, 92, 97

"Labor Leader, The," 38
Labouchère, 190
Ladies Home Journal, 24, 25
La Farge, C. Grant, 46
Lardner, Ring, 83, 144, 212
Laski, Harold, 6
Last Night of Don Juan, The, 119
La Varre, William, 241
Lawrence, D. H., 16
Lawrence, Gertrude, 125
Lawrence, Vincent, 124
Lawson, John Howard, 129
Lechlitner, Ruth, 143
Lee, Muna, 143, 154
Lengyel, Melchior, 47
Lenormand, H. R., 127
Lessing, Gotthold, 131
Lewis, Sinclair, 3, 4, 10, 67, 73, 74,
    76, 77, 83, 85, 97, 114, 144, 145,
    186, 210, 293
Lewis, Wyndham, 22
Liberator, 128
Life, 27, 181
Lillie, Beatrice, 125
Lincoln, Abraham, 32, 42

Lindsay, Vachel, 3, 79
Lions, 163
Lippman, Walter, 8, 189
Literary Digest, 200
Little Review, 24, 49
Livingston, Edward, 70
Logan, George B., 188
Logan, J. D., 189
Logan, Stanley, 119-120
London, Jack, 13, 25, 126, 127
London Mercury, 32, 33, 35, 184, 207
Long, Walter, 188
Look Homeward, Angel, 75
Loos, Anita, 212
Lorimer, George Horace, 54, 185-187,
    197
Lowell, Amy, 114
Lowell, James Russell, 139
Lowie, Robert H., 140
Lunt, Alfred, 125
Lustgarten, Edith, 55
Luther, Mark Lee, 16
Lutherans, 71
Lyons, Eugene, 240

McAllister, Ward, 70
McClure, John, 46, 80, 145, 174
McClure's, 27
McFee, William, 154
MacGrath, Howard, 173
McIntosh, K. C., 148
Mack, Julian W., 177, 180
McNaught's Monthly, 7, 183
McNitt, V. V., 183
Maeterlinck, Maurice, 127
Maguire, J. Russell, 241
*Main Currents in Nineteenth Century
    Literature,* 47
Malan, Jacques, 140
"Man Who Knew Coolidge, The," 67,
    76
Mann, Colonel William D'Alton, 12,
    13, 20
Mansfield, Katherine, 84
Marco Millions, 123
Marin, Luis Muñoz, 154
Markham, Edwin, 80
Maryland, 105, 175
Mason, Gregory, 146
Massachusetts, 104, 107, 108
Masse-Mensch, 127
Masses, 49, 162, 188
Masters, Edgar Lee, 79, 80, 86, 95,
    145
Matthews, Brander, 13, 132
Maugham, Somerset, 126
Maynard, Lawrence, 152

Maynard, Theodore, 154
Mead, Margaret, 155
Melville, Herman, 138
"Memoirs of an Editor," 9
Mercure de France, 32, 33, 35
Mercurio Peruano, 33
Methodists, 4, 41, 57, 71, 89, 90, 93, 130, 167, 174, 195, 196
Metropolitan, 24
Meyer, Carl, 148
Milburn, George, 8, 144
Miller, Kelly, 153
Mims, Edwin, 196
Minority Report: H. L. Mencken's Notebooks, 235-236
Miracle, The, 124
Mississippi, 102, 103, 108, 196
Money Writes!, 204
Monroe, Harriet, 16
Montenegro, Ernesto, 154
Moore, G. A., 149
Moore, George, 16, 43
Morand, Paul, 126, 201
More, Hannah, 25
More, Paul Elmer, 199
Morgan, Pierpont, 237
Morley, Christopher, 25
Mormons, 47, 71, 155
Morris, Lloyd, 193
Morton, James, 176
Moscow, Russia, 6, 199
Münsterberg, Hugo, 47
Münsterberg, Margaret, 47, 139
Mullen, John J., 172
Mumford, Lewis, 140
Munsey's, 24
Munson, Gorham B., 51
Musical Courier, 27
My Musical Life, 48

Nathan, George Jean, 3, 7, 9, 10, 11, 14, 15, 17, 19, 20, 29, 30, 33, 36, 38, 39, 40, 47, 56, 57, 58, 59, 61, 70, 71, 83, 88, 111-133, 156, 173, 174, 188, 189, 197, 206, 211, 212, 216, 217, 226, 227, 241, 242, 243
Nation (American), 24, 27, 53, 67, 178
Nation (English), 22
National Institute of Arts and Letters, 114
Nebuchadnezzer, 148
Nelson, Victor Folke, 152
Neue Merkur, 35
Nevins, Allan, 193
New, Harry S., 175

New Englander, The, 119
New Freeman, 224
New Machiavelli, The, 14
New Masses, 109, 184-185, 189, 204, 211
New Orleans, Louisiana, 46
New Republic, 24, 49, 54, 178, 185, 189, 212
New York, 108
New York City, 11, 12, 29, 37, 55, 57, 73, 101, 106, 107, 116, 141, 169, 207
New York Herald, 11
New York Times, 35, 178-179, 194, 213, 233
New York Times Book Review, 53
New York University, 141, 142
New York World, 181
New Yorker, 5, 6, 7, 8, 9, 68, 182, 211, 235
Newman, Ernest, 140, 148
Newman, Frances, 74
Newspaper Days, 8
Nichols, Robert, 47
Nietzsche, Friedrich W., 14, 15, 230
Norris, Frank, 13
North, Joseph, 225
North American Review, 24, 32, 182
North Carolina, 102
Northcliffe, Lord, 22, 25
Notes and Queries, 26

O'Casey, Sean, 126
Odets, Clifford, 127
Odum, Howard, 153
Ohio, 104
Oneal, James, 46, 151, 203
O'Neill, Eugene, 11, 57, 81, 97, 118, 122-125, 153, 226
Oppenheim, James, 224
Oregon, 104
Orton, William, 154
Osgood, Henry Osborne, 173, 174
Out of Step, 128
Outlook (American), 24, 53
Outlook (English), 184
Owen Hatteras (pseudonym of H. L. Mencken and George Jean Nathan), 13-14, 16
Owens, John W., 45

Page, Thomas Nelson, 26
Palmer, Paul, 239, 240
Panorama, 7, 184
Paris, France, 49
Parisienne, 21
Parker, Dorothy, 144

Parkhurst, Winthrop, 148
Parmenter, James, 172-174
Parrish, Herbert, 72
Parry, Albert, 145
Patria Nova, 48
Pattee, Fred L., 198, 224
Patterson, Captain, 172
Pearl, Raymond, 68, 140, 147
Peets, Elbert, 149
Pennypacker, Isaac R., 41-42
Peterkin, Julia, 144, 153
Peters, Rollo, 119
Peterson, José M., 154
Pharo, Eugene, 155
Phelps, William Lyon, 114
Philosophy of Friedrich Nietzsche, The, 10
Pickering, E. S., 174
Piña, Roberto, 154
Pinero, Arthur, 126
Pirandello, Luigi, 127, 129
Plain-Talk, 7, 183
Plough and the Stars, The, 126
Poe, Edgar Allan, 24, 27, 139
Poesia e non Poesia, 47
Pooley, Robert C., 232
Pope, Alexander, 243
Porter, William Sidney, 13
"Portrait of a Rolling Mill," 141
Pound, Ezra, 12, 16, 20, 21, 30, 97, 206, 213
Pound, Louise, 27, 139, 223, 235
Prejudices, 8, 10, 85, 88, 123
Prince of Wales, 94
Princeton University, 158
Pringle, Henry, 135
Prisonnière, La, 130
Publishers' Weekly, 178
Puck, 27
Purdy, Richard A., 122
Purroy, David, 152
Putnam's, 24

Quarterly Review, 22, 23
Queen Victoria, 47

Rabelais, François, 193
Race and National Solidarity, 48
Raphael, Santi, 116
Rascoe, Burton, 7, 21, 50, 117, 182, 236
Read, Sir Herbert, 83, 190
Readings from the American Mercury, 160
Recent Changes in American Constitutional Theory, 48
Red Book, 24

Reed, Senator James A., 69
Repplier, Agnes, 192
Revere, Paul, 193
Reviewer, The, 26
Richman, Arthur, 117
Rickel, Harry, 35
Riley, Woodbridge, 47, 140
Rime of the Ancient Mariner, The, 123
Rimsky-Korsakoff, Nikolay, 48
Robert E. Lee, 47
Roberts, Elizabeth Madox, 144
Robeson, Paul, 125
Robinson, Edward, 140, 148
Robinson, Edwin Arlington, 95
Rogers, J. A., 153
Roman Catholics, 71-72, 115, 155, 231
Roosevelt, Franklin Delano, 237
Rorke, John W., 172, 173, 174
Rorty, James, 151
Ross, Harold, 182
Rosser, John, 152
Rostand, Edmond, 119, 127
Rotary International, 4, 97ff., passim, 163, 198, 200
Rutra, Theo, 105
Ryan, Clendenin J., 240
Ryder, David, 174

Saint Joan, 83
Saltus, Edgar, 13
Sampson, Charles, 74
Sancho Panza, 47
Sandburg, Carl, 3, 79, 95
Sanford, Winifred, 74, 76, 144
Sanger, Margaret, 151
Santayana, George, 47
Saturday Evening Post, 5, 24, 25, 54, 109, 185-187, 195, 212
Saturday Review (English), 22, 23
Saucy Stories, 21
Sawyer, H. H., 148
Saxton, Eugene F., 232
Schlesinger, Arthur M., 4
Schnitzler, Arthur, 16
Schubert, Franz, 95
Schuyler, George S., 153
Science: The False Messiah, 87
Scribner's, 5, 7, 22, 24, 155, 162, 181, 231
Seagle, William, 148
Sedgwick, Ellery, 21-22, 37, 63, 166, 181, 232
Seibel, George, 231
Seldes, Gilbert, 49, 50, 51
"Sequence of Five Choruses: Texts from the American Mercury," 6

Serva, Mario Pinto, 48
Seymour, Flora, 197
Shakespeare, William, 130
Shaw, George Bernard, 11, 83, 113, 126, 131, 196, 209
Sherman, Stuart, 210
Shipley, Maynard, 72
Sinclair, D. W., 148
Sinclair, Mary, 204-205
Sinclair, Upton, 6, 30, 32, 145, 180, 202, 204, 205
Sister Carrie, 22
Six Days of the Week: A Book of Thoughts About Life and Religion, 85
Smith, Harry, 148
Smith, Mortimer, 155, 226
"Soap Box, The," 218, 219, 223
South Carolina, 108
Spectator, 22, 23
Spengler, Joseph J., 139
Spingarn, Joel Elias, 132
Spivak, John L., 239
Spivak, Lawrence E., 240
Spoon River Anthology, 79
Stallings, Laurence, 124
Stefansson, Vilhjalmur, 139
Steffens, Lincoln, 225
Stein, Gertrude, 206
Sterling, George, 80, 95
Stevens, Doris, 179
Stevens, James, 7, 8, 76, 152, 174, 210
Strange Interlude, 123
Straton, John Roach, 73
Strindberg, August, 11, 16, 118, 127
Suckow, Ruth, 42, 46, 74, 144
Sunpapers, Baltimore, Maryland, 137, 217, 239
Swift, Jonathan, 193, 209, 243
Swinburne, Charles A., 143
Swindler, Captain Henry, 148
Swinnerton, Frank, 210

Tait, S. W., 174
Tales from Town Topics, 13
Talman, Charles F., 140
Tascheraud, Henri, 152
Tasker, Robert Joyce, 76, 152
Teasdale, Sara, 16
Tetlow, Henry, 149
Texas, 44, 102
Thayer, John Adams, 13, 14, 15, 16, 17
Thomas, Augustus, 125
Thomas, Dorothy, 144
Thomas, Norman, 6, 202

Thompson, Randall, 6
Thompson, Warren S., 140
Thomson, Virgil, 148
Three Years: 1924 to 1927: The Story of a New Idea and Its Successful Adaptation, 192-193
Thurber, James, 211
Time, 158, 179, 185, 191, 233
Timrod, Henry, 26
Titcomb, H. B., 44
Toller, Ernst, 127
Torrents of Spring, The, 207
Town Topics, 12, 13, 24
Towne, Charles Hanson, 13
Transatlantic Review, 206
transition, 205
Treatise on the Gods, 224
True Confessions, 76
Truth, 190
Tully, Jim, 144, 152, 172, 205, 210, 245
Turano, Anthony, 148
Turner, F. P., 195
Turner, W. J., 154
Twain, Mark, 42, 138

Union Hill, New Jersey, 114
Unity, 47
Unpopular Review, 26
Untermeyer, Louis, 143, 231
Up From Methodism, 169

Vajda, Ernst, 127
Van Dine, S. S. (pseudonym of Willard H. Wright), 12
Van Doren, Carl, 3, 32, 42, 145
Vanity Fair, 234
Van Loon, Hendrik Willem, 145
Van Vechten, Carl, 145
Vestal, Stanley, 80, 173
Vildrac, Charles, 118

Wagner, Richard, 120
Walker, Stanley, 73
Walkley, Arthur B., 131-132, 154
Wanlass, W. L., 149
Warner, Eltinge F., 17, 30, 35
Warr, O. L., 69
Washington, George, 41
Washington, D. C., 101, 175
Watch and Ward Society, 72, 172, 191
Wecter, Dixon, 163
Wedekind, Frank, 16, 127
Week-end Review, 184, 190
Welded, 118

Wells, H. G., 12, 14, 15, 32, 126, 242
Wembridge, Eleanor, 153
Werner, Carl, 149
What Price Glory?, 104, 124, 128
Wheelwright, John, 207
Whipple, Leon, 161, 166, 181, 191, 192
White, Owen P., 70, 154
White, Walter, 153
Whitman, Edmund A., 176
Whitman, Walt, 104, 139, 160
Wilde, Oscar, 126, 195
William of Orange, 41
Williams, William Carlos, 207

Wilson, Edmund, 32, 50, 111, 157, 189, 208
Winslow, Thyra, 144
Wolfe, Thomas, 75, 212, 224
Wood, James Playsted, 4
Wright, Willard Huntington, 12, 14, 15, 16, 242

Yale Review, 192
Yale University, 158
Yeats, William Butler, 16
Young, Art, 188, 202, 203

Zedekiah, 148